21世纪旅游英语系列教材

英语导游实务教程

（第二版）

Tour Guide
A Practical English Course

朱 华 编著

北京大学出版社
PEKING UNIVERSITY PRESS

图书在版编目(CIP)数据

英语导游实务教程/朱华编著.—2版.—北京:北京大学出版社,2009.4
(21世纪旅游英语系列教材)
ISBN 978-7-301-07664-4

I.英… II.朱… III.导游-英语-高等学校-教材 IV.H319.9

书　　　名:英语导游实务教程(第二版)
著作责任者:朱华　编著
责 任 编 辑:李　颖
标 准 书 号:ISBN 978-7-301-07664-4/H·1081
出 版 发 行:北京大学出版社
地　　　址:北京市海淀区成府路205号　100871
网　　　址:http://www.pup.cn
电　　　话:邮购部 62752015　发行部 62750672　编辑部 62755217　出版部 62754962
电 子 邮 箱:编辑部 pupwaiwen@pup.cn　　总编室 zpup@pup.cn
印 刷 者:北京飞达印刷有限责任公司
经 销 者:新华书店
　　　　　　787毫米×1092毫米　16开本　13.5印张　420千字
　　　　　　2004年8月第1版　2009年4月第2版
　　　　　　2025年1月第13次印刷(总第16次印刷)
定　　　价:39.00元

未经许可,不得以任何方式复制或抄袭本书之部分或全部内容。

版权所有,侵权必究　举报电话:010-62752024
　　　　　　　　　　　电子邮箱:fd@pup.cn

前　言

　　《英语导游实务教程》(第二版)是教育部"普通高等教育'十一五'国家级规划教材",旨在传授英语导游业务知识,熟悉导游服务规范,解决导游带团工作中可能遇到的各种问题,培养导游运用英语带团的实际工作能力,帮助旅游院校学生考取英语导游证,为我国培养一批具有旅游专业知识、通晓一门外语的优秀导游人才。

　　教程体例新颖,内容翔实,"宽""专"结合。"宽"是指重视导游基础知识学习,包括中国历史文化、民族风情、宗教信仰、自然科学等普及性知识的学习;"专"是指学习导游专业知识,强化导游人员专业技能和操作能力的训练,如导游服务规范、导游应变能力、旅游景点讲解、导游情景对话等。

　　根据我国英语导游培养标准和旅行社对导游带团基本能力的要求,教材主要编写内容如下:

　　● 导游实务。熟悉导游服务规范,培养导游应变能力。全书有40多个导游应变能力训练题,着重拓展和训练导游带团的实际工作能力。

　　● 导游文化。介绍我国多个民族的历史文化,熟悉他们的宗教信仰、民族风情、生活习性等,学习藏文化、彝文化、羌文化、苗文化等少数民族文化。

　　● 景点讲解。掌握我国主要旅游省、市、自治区的旅游景点知识,要求学生通过导游模拟训练进行情景对话和景点讲解。

　　● 讲解方法。学习导游基本讲解方法,提高学生景点讲解的能力,包括突出重点法、虚实结合法、制造悬念法、画龙点睛法等十余种景点讲解方法。

　　● 旅游写作。旨在培养导游"动口"能力的同时,培养导游的"动手"能力,主要有旅游信函、旅游合同协议、导游线路设计、各种旅行表格等。

　　《英语导游实务教程》适用于高等旅游院校旅游英语、导游英语、旅游英语口语等课程的教学,也适用于高等职业技术学院和旅游职中导游专业的英语教学。根据教学单位反馈意见,借修订之际,笔者对本书教学内容和体例做了修改,以便进一步提高教学质量,为我国培养具有国际视野的高素质英语导游人才,尽快实现我国从旅游大国到旅游强国的战略目标。

Contents

目　录

1

Listening

1. How should a guide prepare himself in appearance and attitude before taking a tour group?
   导游人员带团前在形象上和心理上应该做好哪些准备?

2. What are the two certificates and one schedule that a guide must bring with him? If the guide is temporarily transferred from another travel agency or take a group with over 10 members, what else should he bring with him?
   导游员带团时必须携带的"两证一表"是什么? 借用性质的导游和10人以上团队,还应带什么证件物品?

Readings

1. List the basic preparations made by a local guide before he/she takes a tour group.
   列举地陪接团准备工作的主要内容。

2. What details of the reception program should a local guide get to know?
   地陪应当如何熟悉接待计划的细节?

3. What preparations should a guide make for meeting the tour group at the airport or railway station?
   导游员应该如何接站?

Listening

1. What should a guide do on the way from the airport to the hotel?
   地陪率团从机场赴饭店途中应该做哪些工作?

2. What should a guide do when the tour group checks in the hotel?
   团队入住饭店,地陪应做好哪些工作?

Readings

1. What should a guide do when the hotel has sold the reserved rooms to other individual tourists?
   饭店将旅游团队已经预定的住房出售给了其他散客,导游员该怎么办?

2. What should a guide do if the reserved rooms are below the contract standard and no better rooms are available?

某饭店为旅游团队提供的住房不符合合同标准,但饭店确实无房调换,导游员如何处理?

3. What should a guide do if tourists want to exchange for better rooms because of the inadequate facilities of the hotel?

客人进入房间后发现设施陈旧损坏,要求更换好的房间,导游怎么办?

Listening

1. What service should a guide provide to tourists during the mealtime?

当客人用餐时,地陪应该怎样服务?

2. Should a guide agree to tourists' requests for changing food?

游客要求换餐,导游员能否同意?

3. What does a guide do when a tourist has special dietary requirements because of the religious or health reasons?

游客由于宗教或生理上的原因,提出特殊的饮食要求,导游员如何处理?

Readings

1. What does a guide do when a tourist is unwilling to have meals with other tourists?

某游客不愿随团用餐,导游员如何处理?

2. What does a guide do when tourists try to buy and eat Liangfen, a local snack sold by peddlers at the tourist site?

当游客购买品尝某一景点里的小贩出售的凉粉时,导游如何处理?

3. The travel agency has a hotpot party for tourists before they leave the country, but two tourists refuse to eat hotpot. In such a case, what is the guide supposed to do?

离境前旅行社特意安排游客品尝火锅,但有两位客人坚持不吃火锅,导游员如何处理?

3

Unit 8   Tourists' Mind-Sets 游客心理 ·············· 63

Listening

1. What changes of mood might tourists experience at the first stage of travel? What kind of specific service can a guide provide?

在旅游活动的初期，游客会有什么样的心理变化？导游员应该提供哪些针对性服务？

2. How may the tourists' mentality change in the later stages of traveling? What services can a guide provide?

在旅游活动中后期，游客会有什么样的心理变化？导游员应该提供哪些服务？

Readings

What factors affect the tourists' mind-set and how can a guide understand these in order to provide a specific service?

导游员应学会从哪些方面了解游客的心态以提供针对性服务？

Unit 9   Recreation 娱乐活动 ····················· 72

Listening

1. What should a guide do if a tourist is unwilling to attend the entertainment program in the travel schedule?

游客不愿观看计划内的文娱节目，导游员如何处理？

2. The tour group is scheduled to watch the Beijing Opera in the evening, but some tourists would rather attend an international football game. What is the guide expected to do?

团队愿定晚上看京剧，但部分年轻游客想看国际足球比赛，导游员如何处理？

Readings

Under what circumstance should a guide agree or disagree when they request to have the entertainments themselves?

游客要求单独外出娱乐，导游员在什么情况下可以同意，什么情况下不能同意？

5

Unit 12   Incidents while Escorting Tour Group (II) 带团事故(2) ············ 97

Listening

1. What is the incident that a guide fails to meet tourists at the airport or station? How should a guide handle it?
   什么叫"空接事故"？如何处理？
2. What is "an incident of missing the airplane"? What might be the consequences?
   什么叫"误机事故"？其后果如何？

Readings

How should a guide handle "the incident of missing the airplane"?
发生"误机事故"后导游员应如何处理？

Unit 13   Documents and Luggage Lost 遗失证件、行李 ······················ 104

Listening

1. If a tourist loses his documents and belongings, how should a guide handle the case?
   游客遗失证件物品，导游员如何处理？
2. How does a foreign tourist apply for a new passport and visa if he loses them in China?
   外国游客在华丢失护照和签证，应如何申请补办？

Readings

1. What should a citizen of Hong Kong, Macao or a compatriot of Taiwan do if he loses his travel certificate?
   港澳居民和台湾同胞丢失旅行证明，应该如何处理？
2. What should a guide do when a tourist finds his luggage missing when he arrives at the airport?
   游客到达机场后发现行李丢失，导游员如何处理？

Listening

1. If a tourist suddenly becomes seriously ill on journey, how should a guide handle the case?

旅游途中游客突发重病,导游员该如何处理?

2. What a preliminary treatment can the guide provide for the wounded tourist? What should he do if the tourist has suffered a fractured limb?

游客受伤或发生骨折,导游员应做哪些初步处理?

Readings

1. How should a guide treat the tourist who has been stung by a bee or a scorpion?

游客被蜂、蝎蜇伤后应如何处理?

2. How should a guide treat the tourist who has been bitten by a poisonous snake?

游客被毒蛇咬伤,导游员应如何抢救?

Unit 17　Traffic Accidents 交通事故 ·············· 141

Listening

1. What are the possible consequences of a traffic accident on journey? What precautions can be done to minimize its occurrence?

旅游交通事故会造成什么后果?如何预防?

2. How should a guide handle a fatal traffic accident?

发生恶性交通事故后导游员应如何处理?

Readings

On the way to a tourist site, the guide is informed that the site is closed because of a traffic accident. What is the guide expected to do in such a case?

导游率团前往某景点途中,突然得知该景点因交通事故而封闭,导游该怎么办?

Unit 18　Breach of Security and Fire Disaster 治安事故与火灾 ·············· 152

9

2. If a foreign tourist must quit the tour midway due to an urgent business at home, how does a guide handle the related fares?

外国游客因家中急事要求中途退团,有关费用怎么处理?

Readings

Can a guide agree when a tourist requests to extend his travel time?

游客要求延长旅游期,导游员能否同意?

Listening

1. How can a guide avoid the complaints?

导游人员应怎样避免旅游投诉的发生?

2. How does a guide handle the tourist's complaints?

导游员应如何处理游客的投诉?

Readings

How does a guide make an apology to tourists?

导游如何向游客道谦?

Listening

1. What preparations does a guide make before the departure of the group?

在送行前,导游员应提前落实哪些事宜?

2. What is the difference between an OK ticket and an OPEN ticket? If a tourist who has an OK ticket does not depart within 72 hours, what procedures does he need to follow?

OK 票和 OPEN 票有何区别? 持 OK 票的游客如果停留超过 72 小时,应该办理什么手续?

Unit 1 Tour Guide

导游员

PART I ABC for Tour Guides

New Words and Expressions

itinerary	/ai'tinərəri, i't-/	n.	线路
sightseeing	/'saitsiːiŋ/	n.	观光
collaboration	/kə,læbə'reiʃən/	n.	协作,与……合作
feedback	/'fiːdbæk/	n.	反馈,反应
outbound	/'autbaund/	adj.	开往外地的,开往外国的
assign	/ə'sain/	v.	分配,指派
liaison	/li(ː)'eizɑːn, -zən/	n.	联络
implementation	/,implimen'teiʃən/	n.	执行

Proper Nouns

local guide	地陪	national guide	全陪
tour leader	领队	origin country	客源国家
destination country	目的地国家	local travel agency	地接社

Listening

Direction: Listen to the passages carefully and fill in the blanks with the missing information you have heard from the tapes.

1. **What are the main obligations of a guide?** 导游员工作的基本内容是什么?

    (1) Arrange the itinerary and (A) _____ according to the contract signed between the travel agency and the tourists.

    (2) Arrange for meals, accommodation, transportation, shopping and (B) _____ for tourists, in collaboration with the national guide and tour leader.

    (3) Provide guiding services for the tourists and introduce the local culture and tourism resources.

1

(4) Ensure the security of the tourists' property and their (C) _____.

(5) Cooperate and work with various service departments to solve problems during the journey.

(6) Report tourists' opinions and suggestions to the travel agency and arrange meetings for on-tour (D) _____.

2. **What are the major differences of their obligations for a local guide, a national guide and a tour leader?** 地陪、全陪、领队工作内容的主要区别是什么?

(1) The tour leader, also referred to as the tour escort in Central America, or tour conductor in Japan, is assigned by the travel service to escort the (E) _____ tour group. He escorts the tour group all the way from the origin country to the destination country until they come back safely. He supervises the contract obligations of the local travel agency in the destination country.

(2) The national guide is assigned by the travel service at the tourist origin. He is in charge of the (F) _____ work for the tour group who travels to the destination, supervises the implementation of the contract by the local travel agency, and take tourists back safely to the origin.

(3) The local guide is assigned by the local travel agency. He meets the tourists and provides the local guiding service including sightseeing, transport, accommodation, (G) _____ and so on.

New Words and Expressions

conflict	/'kɔnflikt/	n.	斗争,冲突
persuasion	/pə(ː)'sweiʒən/	n.	说服,说服力
dignified	/'diɡnifaid/	adj.	有威严的,有品格的
humiliate	/hju(ː)'milieit/	v.	羞辱,使丢脸
courtesy	/'kəːtisi, 'kɔː-/	n.	谦恭,礼貌
dignity	/'diɡniti/	n.	尊严,高贵
reputation	/ˌrepju(ː)'teiʃən/	n.	名誉,名声

Readings

Direction: Read the following passage aloud and fill in the blanks with words or phrases you think appropriate.

| sympathy | confuse | conflict | chaos | courtesy |
| concise | reputation | talkative | accommodation | public |

1. **How could a local guide cooperate with the tour leader?** 地陪人员如何与领队合作?

   (1) Always listen to his opinions and suggestions, especially when you disagree with him. Respect the tour leader and always discuss the itinerary, schedules and (A) _____ arrangements with him.

   (2) Support the tour leader's work and always listen to his suggestions. Do not get involved when a conflict occurs among group members or between the tour leader and the tourists. Help the tour leader settle the (B) _____ by the way of patient explanations and persuasion.

   (3) Treat the tour leader with a respectful attitude. Try to persuade the tour leader with a reasonable and dignified manner when you have different opinions. Avoid a (C) _____ conflict with the tour leader; and never humiliate him; always respect and communicate with him even after the conflict; you may need his help in the future.

2. **How should a local guide deal with a troublesome national guide?** 地陪带团过程中遇上个别无理取闹、故意刁难的全陪导游员该怎么办?

   (1) Treat the troublesome national guide with (D) _____ and with as much dignity as possible.

   (2) Try to persuade the national guide with a reasonable and pleasant manner;

   (3) Win the support and (E) _____ from the majority of tourists;

   (4) Avoid a public conflict with the national guide; and never humiliate him;

   (5) Treat him with a dignified manner and communicate with him even after the conflict. Your (F) _____ may depend on it.

Quickies

1. **True or False:**

   (1) _____ The first impression is crucial: dress properly and act and speak sincerely in order to win the tourists' trust.

   (2) _____ For a tour guide, a good command of professional knowledge, hard work, and the ability to solve problems are more important than first impression.

   (3) _____ The commentator who works at a museum or a scenic area may escort tour groups.

   (4) _____ Anyone who acquires his tour guide certificate can take a tour group to travel abroad.

2. **Role-play:** Mr. Wang is taking tourists around the Summer Palace according to the travel schedule, but the tour leader insists on ending up the tour earlier in order to hurry up to the Great Wall. What would you do as a local guide?

PART II *Welcome Speech*

New Words and Expressions

facility	/fə'siliti/	n.	设施,工具
vocational	/vəu'keiʃənəl/	adj.	职业的
colleague	/'kɔliːg/	n.	同事,同僚
rewarding	/ri'wɔːdiŋ/	adj.	有益的,值得的
appreciate	/ə'priːʃieit/	v.	赏识,感激
luxurious	/lʌg'zjuəriəs/	adj.	奢侈的,豪华的
mobile	/'məubail/	adj.	可移动的,机动的
imperia	/im'piəriəl/	adj.	皇帝的
magnificent	/mæg'nifisnt/	adj.	华丽的,宏伟的
delicious	/di'liʃəs/	adj.	美味的
fantastic	/fæn'tæstik/	adj.	幻想的,奇异的
landscape	/'lændskeip/	n.	风景

Proper Nouns

State Council	国务院	Forbidden City	紫禁城
Summer Palace	颐和园	Great Wall	长城
Tiananmen Square	天安门广场	Quanjude Restaurant	全聚德餐厅

To deliver a welcome speech, a tour guide should first express his warm-hearted welcome and extend his greetings to the tourists who have just arrived; second, he should introduce himself, the driver and the travel agency he works for; third, he should express his wish to provide quality service; fourth, he may inform tourists of the hotel in which they are to check in, and its location and facilities; he may also give a brief introduction to the tourist sites that tourists plan to visit. Last but not the least, try to take this chance to wish tourists have a good time during their stay. If a guide has something important to remind tourists, don't forget to repeat it until every tourist learns it by heart.

A Welcome Speech

Good morning, ladies and gentlemen!

Welcome to Beijing!

Please sit back and relax. Your luggage will be sent to the hotel by another coach, so you don't have to worry about it.

Let me introduce my Chinese colleagues. This is Mr. Huang Jun, our driver. He is an experienced driver and has a driving experience of more than 15 years. Miss Ma Juan has just graduated from Beijing Tourism Vocational School, a trainee guide in our travel service. My name is Li Yunfang. My English name is Jane. You can just call me Jane or Xiao Li. We're from the China International Travel Service, Beijing Branch. On behalf of the travel service and my colleagues, I'd like to extend a warm welcome to all of you.

When you travel in Beijing, Miss Ma and I will be your local guides. We'll try our best to make your journey go smoothly. We bet you would have a pleasant and rewarding experience in Beijing. If you have any problems or special requests, please don't hesitate to tell us. As a Chinese old saying goes, "Nothing is more delightful than to meet friends from afar." And we highly appreciate your understanding and cooperation.

Now, we're traveling to Beijing Kunlun Hotel, a luxurious, five-star hotel. As it is the first time for you to come to Beijing, you need to remember the number of our coach. The number is 京 A-786675. Let me repeat it: 京 A-786675. My mobile telephone number is 13096312598. I would have it on for 24 hours. Don't hesitate to contact me whenever you want to.

Beijing is the capital city of China as well as one of the largest metropolises in the world, an ancient city dating back to over 2,000 years. It is among the first group of famous historical and cultural cities ratified by the State Council. The well-known tourist sites in Beijing are the Forbidden City, the Summer Palace, the Great Wall, and the Tiananmen Square, just to name a few. Now I'd like to tell you the itinerary today. I hope you would enjoy it.

At 9:00 this morning, we'll begin to have our cultural tour in Beijing. The first tourist site we shall visit is the Forbidden City, and there you can visit the imperial palace where 24 Chinese emperors used to live. At 4:00 this afternoon, we shall tour the magnificent Tiananmen Square, one of the largest squares in the world. At 6:30 tonight, a welcome party will be specially held for you at the Quanjude Restaurant, where you can enjoy the delicious Beijing Roasted Ducks.

I sincerely wish you a pleasant and comfortable stay and a fantastic holiday in Beijing. I shall do all I can to make everything easy for you. I am sure you are going to enjoy this wonderful trip, and have an unforgettable travel experience in China. It takes us about twenty minutes to get to the hotel. Please have a short rest or enjoy the landscape out of the windows.

Thank you for your attention!

Exercises

1. On behalf of Beijing International Kunghui Travel Service, make a welcome speech to tourists from the United States.
2. Make a welcome speech on behalf of your travel service when you receive a tour group at the welcome party.

PART III *Situational Dialogue*

New Words and Expressions

splendid	/ˈsplendid/	*adj.*	壮丽的,辉煌的
pillar	/ˈpilə/	*n.*	[建]柱子,栋梁
supremacy	/sjuˈpreməsi/	*n.*	至高,无上,霸权
ornament	/ˈɔːnəmənt/	*n.*	装饰物
mausoleum	/ˌmɔːsəˈliəm/	*n.*	陵墓

Proper Nouns

Tian'anmen Gate Tower	天安门城楼	Red Square	红场
Moscow	莫斯科	Arc de Triomphe	凯旋门
Paris	巴黎	Washington Monument	华盛顿纪念碑
Chengtianmen Gate	承天门	Huabiao	华表

Dialogue 1

Tian'anmen Gate Tower (I)

Miss Li Yunfang is taking Mr. Brown around the Tian'anmen Square. Now, they are standing in front of the Tiananmen Gate Tower.

(A=Miss Li Yunfang; B=Mr. Brown)

A: Here we are. This is the Tian'anmen Square, one of the largest squares in the world. Millions of tourists come from all over the world to view its long history and splendid appearance. Now it has become the very image of Beijing's charm.

B: Fantastic! Just like the Red Square for Moscow, the Arc de Triomphe for Paris and the Washington Monument for the United States, I bet it is the symbolic architecture for Beijing.

A: Oh, yeah. The Tian'anmen Square is located on the central axis of Beijing. There are plenty of historical buildings around.

B: Well, what is the building over there? I think it is the grandest architecture in the square.

A: It is the Tiananmen Gate Tower. First it was named Chengtianmen Gate, which means "by the Grace of God." The Chinese emperors

believed they were authorized by God to rule over the country.

B: No wonder it was designed very grand and magnificent. It is the most splendid gate tower I've seen in the world.

A: It was originally a wooden arch with six pillars and five doors, but later it was reconstructed into a nine-room wide and five-room deep gate tower after a fire. The number nine and five embodies the supremacy of the emperor.

B: Very interesting. I see two imposing columns in front of the Tiananmen Gate Tower. What are they?

A: They are called Huabiao. Huabiao is a well-known architectural ornament in China. You may see Huabiaos in other places of China, such as in palaces, imperial gardens or mausoleums.

B: I'd like to have a close look at such a beautiful column.

(to be continued)

Exercises

Do the dialogue again and pay attention to your facial expressions and body language.

New Words and Expressions

emplace	/im'pleis, em-/	v.	陈列,安置
marble	/'mɑːbl/	n.	大理石
dew	/djuː/	n.	露,露水般的东西
spectacular	/spek'tækjulə/	adj.	引人入胜的,壮观的
entwine	/in'twain/	v.	(使)缠住,(使)盘绕
relief	/ri'liːf/	n.	浮雕
squat	/skwɔt/	v.	蹲坐,蹲伏
excursion	/iks'kəːʃən/	n.	远足,游览
supervise	/ˌsjuːpə'waiz/	v.	监督,管理,指导
indulge	/in'dʌldʒ/	v.	纵容
neglect	/ni'glekt/	v.	忽视,疏忽
naïve	/nɑː'iːv/	adj.	天真的

Proper Nouns

Chenlupan	承露盘	kong	犼,古代传说的一种瑞兽。
wangjungui	"望君归"	wangjunchu	"望君出"

Dialogue 2

Tian'anmen Gate Tower (II)

Mr. Brown has a great interest in Huabiao. He looks up at the column and asks why there is a plate emplaced on the top of the Huabiao.

(A=Miss Li Yunfang; B=Mr. Brown)

B: Miss Li, they're really beautiful pillars carved out of marble. Look, there is a plate on the top. What is it used for?

A: It is called Chenlupan for collecting dew. Later, you'll see another pair of such ornamental pillars behind the Tian'anmen.

B: What a spectacular pillar! I see each pillar is entwined by a dragon engraved in relief, and an animal or something like a lion squats on the plate. What is that?

A: You are well-spotted. The animal is called *kong*. This creature is supposed to be son of the dragon. He is good at keeping watch. It is generally referred to as the "stone lion."

B: Stone lions? They look a little bit the same. Then, how many stone lions are there?

A: There are four. The two in front facing south are called wangjungui or "looking out for the emperor's return." Their duty, it is said, was to watch over the emperor's excursions and call him back if he was absent from the palace too long.

B: What about other two? Where are they?

A: You'll see them standing inside the gate facing north. They are called wangjunchu or "looking out for the emperor's progress."

B: What do they expect from the emperors?

A: Their job was to supervise how the emperor behaved in the imperial palace. If he indulged himself and neglect court affairs, the stone lions would remind him of his duties and tell him to go out among the people.

B: Miss Li, I think your explanations reflect the naive wishes of the people for an emperor who would listen to advices and work really for their good.

A: Do you think the emperors would listen to the lions?

B: If the emperors were also the lions they might have listened to them. What a pity! They were not the lions.

(the end)

Cultural Notes

Tian'anmen Gate Tower 天安门城楼：始建于明永乐十五年(公元 1417 年)，是明代皇城的正门，当时叫"承天门"，有承天启运之意。刚开始修建的时候，可不是现在看到的这个模样，而是五座木牌坊，后来改建成九开间门楼。清顺治八年(公元 1651 年)，清世祖福临重新修建这座城楼。建国后，人民政府又重建了城楼上的木建筑、加厚城墙，才成了现在的样子。明、清两朝，这儿是禁地，到公元 1911 年清王朝覆灭为止，除了皇亲贵族，老百姓不准过往。它最大的

用途,是国家有大庆典(如皇帝登基、册立皇后)时在此举行"颁诏"仪式。而如今只要有机会,你随时都能登上这座城楼,去眺望目前世界上最大的广场——天安门广场。

Exercises

Imagine that you are a local guide and your classmates are tourists. Make up a situational dialogue about the Tian'anmen Gate Tower.

PART IV *Practical Writing for Tourism*

Correspondence of Travel Agencies 旅行社信函

Date: May 25th, 2008

Dear Sirs,

Would you please proceed with land arrangements in Beijing for the group, according to the itinerary enclosed and the following items:

1. Members: Sixteen paying members and one free tour leader.
2. Rooms required: Eight double rooms and one single room, each with private bath.
3. Hotels: Holiday Inn
4. Tr./SS: By an air-conditioned coach for transfers and sightseeing
5. Meals: As given in the itinerary.
6. Airport tax: Not included.

We look forward to receiving your confirmation for the group at your earliest convenience.

Yours Sincerely

Wang Xiaoping
General Manager

Exercises

Write a letter of reservation with a hotel for a tour group coming from England according to the sample.

Unit 2 Travel Schedule
旅行计划

PART I ABC for Tour Guides

New Words and Expressions

adjustment	/əˈdʒʌstmənt/	*n.*	调整,调节
sequence	/ˈsiːkwəns/	*n.*	次序,顺序
consult	/kənˈsʌlt/	*v.*	商量,商议
current	/ˈkʌrənt/	*adj.*	当前的,现在的
mutual	/ˈmjuːtjuəl/	*adj.*	相互的,共有的
resolution	/ˌrezəˈljuːʃən/	*n.*	决定,决议

Proper Nouns

sponsor travel agency	组团社	tour code	团号

Listening

Direction: Listen to the passages carefully and fill in the blanks with the missing information you have heard from the tapes.

1. **When the local travel service has made the local travel schedule for the tour group, is it necessary for the local guide to discuss it with the tour leader?** 当地方接待旅行社已经安排好团队在当地的活动计划时,地陪是否还有必要与领队商量日程?

    (1) The local guide should confirm the local tour (A) _____ with the tour leader or the national guide before the group starts the sightseeing.

    (2) He should not change the itinerary at will, but may make reasonable adjustments to the sequence of the travel events, based on the travel schedule or the daily route according to the current (B) _____. He should inform the whole group of the adjustments concerned.

2. **What should a local guide do when there appears to be a great difference between the local guide's travel schedule and that of the tour leader?** 地陪与领队的旅游计划有较大出入时地陪应该怎么办?

   (1) The local guide should consult with his travel agency about the (C) _____ between the schedule provided by the local agency and the schedule offered by the tour leader;

   (2) He should clarify the reasons for the differences and discuss possible resolutions with the tour leader to their mutual (D) _____.

New Words and Expressions

adhere	/əd'hiə/	v.	坚持
feasible	/'fiːzəbl/	adj.	可行的,切实可行的
luxury	/'lʌkʃəri/	n.	奢侈,华贵

Readings

Direction: Read the following passage aloud and fill in the blanks with words or phrases you think appropriate.

rational	expenses	change	adjustments	observe
specified	tackle	transportation	reunification	timetable

1. **How does a guide respond if the tour group requests to change the itinerary and travel schedule upon arrival?** 旅游团队抵达后要求变更旅游计划和日程,地陪应采取什么态度?

   (1) Usually the guide is expected to adhere to the itinerary and travel schedule as (A) _____ _____ in the contract.

   (2) If the change is reasonable and feasible, the guide, after obtaining approval from the sponsor travel agency, may make the appropriate (B) _____.

2. **What should a tour guide take into account when he/she makes up the itinerary?** 导游员在制定旅游线路时应当注意什么?

   (1) An itinerary consists of items such as tour title, tour code, day-to-day events, cities, duration and a descriptive account of the tour.

   (2) An itinerary should include relevant information concerning the level of service; the tour grade (standard group/ luxury group); travel (C) _____; the number of tour members, etc.

   (3) The tour title is an important part of the itinerary, and usually highlights the length and location of the tour, e.g. "Three-Day Tour to Shanghai."

   (4) For day-to-day events, more specific information should be given about the cities, the scenic spots, the hotels and modes of (D) _____.

(5) The descriptive account should give an overall view of the travel route and destinations, in keeping with the contract made between the tourists and the travel agency.

Quickies

Role-play: It is burning hot in the afternoon. Miss Li Ping, a guide from Shanghai Overseas Travel Service puts on a mini skirt and the sunglass. She discusses the travel difference with the tour leader upon his arrival. What would you suggest to her as a senior guide?

PART II *Method of Introduction*

New Words and Expressions

efficacy	/'efikəsi/	*n.*	功效,效验
animate	/'ænimeit/	*v.*	鼓舞,使有生气
participation	/pɑːˌtisi'peiʃən/	*n.*	分享,参与
monologue	/'mɔnəlɔg/	*n.*	独白,独角戏
spoon-feed		*v.*	填鸭式教育
category	/'kætigəri/	*n.*	种类,[逻]范畴
resort	/ri'zɔːt/	*v.*	诉诸,采取
priority	/prai'ɔriti/	*n.*	优先,优先权
interrupt	/ˌintə'rʌpt/	*v.*	打断(正在说话或动作的人),插嘴
consummate	/'kɔnsʌmeit/	*adj.*	圆满的,完美的
decipher	/di'saifə/	*v.*	译解(密码等),解释
layout	/'leiˌaut/	*n.*	规划,设计
riddle	/'ridl/	*n.*	谜,谜语

Proper Nouns

Sanxingdui Ruins	三星堆	Shu State	(古代)蜀国

The Method of Question-and-Answer Introduction
问答法

It is a method of introduction used by a tour guide to ask tourists questions or to encourage them to put forward questions about tourist sites. It targets the efficacy in animating the atmosphere, exercising tourists' imagination, and promoting the communication between the guide and tourists. Eventually, tourists will have the joy of participation and the sense of achievement for better understanding of the tourist sites they are visiting. Meanwhile, a tour guide should attempt to avoid the boring monologue or the method of spoon-feeding.

There are three basic methods of question-and-answer introduction. First, a guide raises questions and answers them by himself. In this case, a guide can control his pace of introduction and avoid some "hard-to-answer questions" put forward by tourists. Second, a tour guide can also use the method of "a guide raises questions and tourists answer them." But this depends on the categories of the tourist sites and kinds of tourists as well as their interests. Third, a guide can also resort to the method of "tourists raise questions and the tour guide answers them." However, a tour guide should give priority to the typical questions related closely to contents of the current introduction, and answers the less important questions later, or after his/her introduction; otherwise his/her introduction may be interrupted by tourists.

Take the Sanxingdui Ruins for example. Before making an introduction, a guide can ask visitors several questions: Where does Sanxingdui civilization originate? Why does Sanxingdui possess such consummate skills of making bronze ware and jade articles? What do the signs on the cultural relics mean? Does Sanxingdui have a written language, and if so, can it be deciphered? What is the layout of the town of Sanxingdui and where is it located? What nationality do the citizens of Sanxingdui belong to? When did the ancient Shu State fall down and why is there no written record about it? After putting forward the questions the guide can answer them or ask the tourists to give replies so that they could feel more interested in the riddles of Sanxingdui Ruins and visit the tourist sites with some questions in their minds.

Questions

1. Why does a guide usually use the method of question-and-answer introduction?
2. What are the three basic methods the guide may use to raise and answer the questions?
3. List the main questions that a guide may raise while he introduces the Sanxingdui Ruins.

Question 1

_____

Question 2

_____

Question 3

_____

Question 4

_____

Question 5

_____

PART III   Tourist Site

New Words and Expressions

artery	/'æːtəri/	n.	动脉,要道
wriggle	/'rigl/	v.	蜿蜒行进,扭动
undulate	/'ʌndjuleit/	v.	波动,起伏
cruise	/kruːz/	v.	巡游,巡航
navigate	/'nævigeit/	v.	航行,航海,航空
meander	/mi'ændə/	v.	蜿蜒而流
Gothic	/'gɔθik/	adj.	哥特式的
Baroque	/bə'rəuk/	adj.	巴洛克式的
Romanesque	/ˌrəumə'nesk/	adj.	罗马式的
renaissance	/rə'neisəns/	n.	文艺复兴,文艺复兴时期
consulate	/'kɔnsjulit/	n.	领事,领事馆

Proper Nouns

Huangpu River	黄浦江	Wusong	吴淞口
East China Sea	东海	Yangpu Bridge	杨浦大桥
Nanpu Bridge	南浦大桥	Bund	外滩

Huangpu River

Huangpu River, the most important shipping artery of Shanghai, wriggles like an undulating muddy dragon from the mouth of the Yangtze River in Wusong to the East China Sea. The yellow and ice-free Huangpu River is 114 kilometers long, 400 meters wide and has an average depth of nine meters.

Huangpu River joins 29 kilometers north of downtown Shanghai and divides Shanghai into two parts: east and west. Cruises are available everyday, including the shorter cruises (navigating the main waterfront area between the Yangpu Bridge and the Nanpu Bridge) and the complete cruises (meandering eastward along the golden waterway, over a distance of 60 kilometers). Whether it is in the daytime or at night, the views along the river are the same beautiful. The great modern skyscrapers and the buildings in different architectural styles are the best records of the development of the city and the

Huangpu River, the birthplace of Shanghai, is the faithful eyewitness.

The most famous and attractive sight which is at the west side of the Bund are the 52 various buildings of different architectural styles including Gothic, Baroque, Romanesque, Classicism and the Renaissance. The Bund was the centre of Shanghai's politics, economy and culture hundreds of years ago, consulates of most countries, many banks, businesses and newspaper offices were settled there, and that's why we have these art-like buildings. Although they were not designed by the same person or built in the same period, the architectural pattern is similar.

Cultural Notes

Huangpu River 黄浦江:黄浦江古名东江,全长 114 公里,流经青浦、松江、奉贤、上海、川沙 5 县及宝山区和上海市区,在市区汇合苏州河,至吴淞口入长江。黄浦江是上海的母亲河,代表着上海的象征和缩影,荟萃了上海城市景观的精华。黄浦江游览是上海旅游中的一个重要的传统旅游节目,可观赏横跨浦江两岸的杨浦大桥、南浦大桥和上海东方明珠广播电视塔等著名景点。西岸一幢幢风格迥异充满浓郁异国色彩的万国建筑与东岸一幢幢拔地而起高耸云间的现代建筑相映生辉,令游客目不暇接。

Quickies

1. **True or False:**

   (1) _____ Huangpu River, the mother river of Shanghai divides the city into two parts: east and west.

   (2) _____ The most famous and attractive sight at the east side of the Bund are the 52 various buildings of different architectural styles.

   (3) _____ The buildings at the Bund were not designed by the same architect, so the architectural pattern is quite different.

2. Read the passage aloud and introduce the Huangpu River using the methods of introduction you have learnt. The method of question-and-answer introduction is one of the choices.

Tips
   - Draft your own commentary before you make your presentation.
   - Speak colloquial English and use simple and short sentences.
   - Animate your introduction with facial expressions and body language.
   - Apply at least one method of introduction. It is highly recommended that you use two or three methods of introduction.

PART IV *Simulated Introduction*

New Words and Expressions

sphere	/sfɪə/	n.	球,球体
unique	/juːˈniːk/	adj.	唯一的,独特的
stanchion	/ˈstæːnʃən/	n.	支柱
module	/ˈmɔdjuːl/	n.	登月舱,指令舱
elevator	/ˈeliveitə/	n.	电梯,升降机
pedestal	/ˈpedistl/	n.	底座,基础
lounge	/laundʒ/	n.	大厅,休闲室
futuristic	/fjuːtʃəˈristik/	adj.	未来派的
rotate	/rəuˈteit/	v.	(使)旋转
complex	/ˈkɔmpleks/	n.	建筑群
circular	/ˈsəːkjulə/	adj.	圆形的,循环的

Proper Nouns

Oriental Pearl TV Tower	东方明珠电视塔
Pudong New District	浦东新区
"twin dragons playing with pearls"	"二龙戏珠"
Toronto	多伦多(加拿大城市)
Shanghai Municipal History Museum	上海历史博物馆
Shanghai & Hong Kong Bank	汇丰银行
Suez Canal	苏伊士运河
the Far East	远东
Shanghai Customs Building	上海海关大楼

The Oriental Pearl TV Tower

Ladies and gentlemen, we're standing in front of the Oriental Pearl TV Tower. It is located in Pudong New District in Shanghai. Look, in the northeast of the tower is the Yangpu Bridge and in the southwest is the Nanpu Bridge. If you had a bird's-eye view of the tower, it would present a picture of "twin dragons playing with pearls." Look up please! Have you seen the pearl-shaped spheres on the tower? Later I'll ask you how many spheres are there. What are they used for?

The Oriental Pearl TV Tower is 468 meters high. It is the third tallest TV and radio tower in the world. Compared with the towers in Toronto and Moscow, it is not the highest one, but surpasses the two because of the unique architectural design. Please look at the base of the tower! It is supported by three nine-meter wide stanchions. The eleven steel spheres are strung vertically through the centre of the tower which are three nine-meter wide columns. Look more carefully! There are three large spheres including the top sphere. They are the space modules. Come on, have a close look! There are also five smaller spheres and three decorative spheres on the tower base. The entire structure just rests on the green grassland and gives you a feeling that small and big pearls falling down on a jade plate. Do you think so?

Ladies and gentlemen, we're going to take the elevator to reach the top. The double-decker elevators can hold up fifty people at the rate of seven meters per second. Once you reach your destination, you will be amazed at the variety of activties available. The different spheres and columns are designed to hold up places of interest, commerce and recreation. The Shanghai Municipal History Museum is located in the tower's pedestal. The five smaller spheres are a hotel that contains twenty-five elegant rooms and lounges. The large lower sphere has a futuristic space city and a sightseeing hall. The "pearl" at the very top of the tower, if you think so, contains shops, restaurants, including a rotating restaurant and a sightseeing floor. From here, you can see all the way to the Yangtze River.

How time flies! We've reached the top of the tower. Look at other side of the river! What a magnificent building complex with the western style! The building complex has architectural features of the Renaissance Period in Europe. Some are in British style, and some are in French style while some are in Greek style. Look at the building with a circular roof in Greek style! It is the famous building of former Shanghai & Hong Kong Bank. The British were proud of it and regarded it as the best building in the area from the Suez Canal to the Far East. Did you see the building next to the former Shanghai & Hong Kong Bank? On the top of it, there is a big clock. It is the Shanghai Customs Building built in 1927. The clock strikes every 15 minutes, and gives out a short piece of music.

Listen, the clock is striking now. You can check your time because it gives you the standard Beijing time. It is half past five in the afternoon. We'll meet at the rotating restaurant after thirty minutes.

Exercises

Make a simulated introduction of the Oriental Pearl TV Tower using the methods of introduction you have learnt. Pay attention to the body language and other tips of introduction.

Unit 3 Preparations for Meeting Tour Group
接团准备

PART I ABC for Tour Guides

New Words and Expressions

decently	/'di:sntli/	adv.	高雅地, 正派地
compatible	/kəm'pætəbl/	adj.	一致的, 兼容的
tatoo	/tə'tu:, tæ'tu:/	n.	文身
dye	/dai/	v.	染
neat	/ni:t/	adj.	整洁的, 灵巧的
sleeveless	/'sli:vlis/	adj.	无袖的
sandal	/'sændl/	n.	凉鞋, 便鞋
excessive	/ik'sesiv/	adj.	过多的, 过分的, 额外
gracious	/'greiʃəs/	adj.	亲切的, 高尚的
mentally	/'mentəli/	adv.	精神上, 在内心
accomplish	/ə'kɔmpliʃ/	v.	完成, 实现

Proper Nouns

tour guide certificate	导游证	operation schedule	运营计划
guide banner	导游旗	insurance policy	保险单

Listening

Direction: Listen to the passages carefully and fill in the blanks with the missing information you have heard from the tapes.

1. How should a guide prepare himself in appearance and attitude before taking a tour group?
   导游人员带团前在形象上和心理上应该做好哪些准备?

   (1) The guide should dress professionally and (A) _____, especially on the occasion of meeting or sending off the group at the airport.

(2) It is generally recommended to dress compatible with the status of a tour guide. For tour guides, (B) _____ and dyed hair are inappropriate for public display. A tour guide should not wear his/her cap backwards or sideways.

(3) During the tour, the guide may dress casually but should look neat and tidy. A male guide should not wear shorts, a (C) _____ shirt or sandals without socks. A female guide should not wear a mini skirt and should not wear excessive makeup.

(4) The guide should be prepared to work with a friendly, gracious and polite manner and be mentally ready to face the (D) _____ from tourists.

2. **What are the two certificates and one schedule that a guide must bring with him? If the guide is temporarily transferred from another travel agency or take a group with over 10 members, what else should he bring with him?** 导游员带团时必须携带的"两证一表"是什么？借用性质的导游和 10 人以上团队，还应带什么证件物品？

(1) While escorting a tour group, the guide should always wear his tour guide (E) _____ and carry with him a copy of the certificate, as well as the operation schedule of the tour group.

(2) If he takes a group of more than 10 members, the guide should bring a guide banner.

(3) If he works for a travel agency other than his own travel agency, the guide should become familiar with the tour group and be prepared to accomplish the required (F) _____.

(4) The guide should bring with him: copies of the insurance policies, various vouchers for settlement of the tickets, the local travel schedule and a (G) _____.

New Words and Expressions

gender	/ˈdʒendə/	n.	性别
banquet	/ˈbæŋkwit/	n.	宴会
confirm	/kənˈfəːm/	v.	确定，确认
parking	/ˈpɑːkiŋ/	adj.	停车的
cardboard	/ˈkɑːdbɔːd/	n.	纸板

Readings

Direction: Read the following passage aloud and fill in the blanks with words or phrases you think appropriate.

| positive | luggage | parking | banner | claim | occupation |
| departure | arrival | telephone | banquets | porter | |

1. **List the basic preparations made by a local guide before he/she takes a tour group.** 列举地陪接团准备工作的主要内容。

(1) Be familiar with the reception program.

(2) Confirm details of transportation, accommodation and (A) _____ delivery before the group arrives.

(3) Bring all necessary items including documentation—tour guide certificate and professional rating card, local travel schedule and the tour guide (B) _____.

(4) Be sure to have and use professional language skills and knowledge.

(5) Be tidy, friendly and use good manners.

(6) Have a (C) _____ attitude and be prepared to face the complaints from tourists.

2. **What details of the reception program should a local guide get to know?** 地陪应当如何熟悉接待计划的细节？

   (1) Basic group information:

   The basic information includes:

   - name of travel agency;
   - name of liaison person in charge of the group and his/her (D) _____ numbers;
   - group code;
   - name of the tour leader or the national guide;
   - number of tourists;
   - names of all tour members including their nationality; gender, (E) _____, age, religion and special requests.

   (2) Confirm itinerary details:

   - transportation, hotels and rooms, restaurant and meals;
   - official reception if any, meetings, (F) _____;
   - special zone entry passes as needed.

   (3) Confirm air tickets, departure and arrival time:

   - check names of tourists again for reservation of air tickets;
   - for international flights—confirm tickets 72 hours prior to (G) _____;
   - for domestic flights—confirm tickets before 12 a.m. two days prior to departure.

3. **What preparations should a guide make for meeting the tour group at the airport or railway station?** 导游员应该如何接站？

   (1) Prior to arrival of the tour group:

   - confirm the expected arrival time of the tour group;
   - arrive at airport or the train station 30 minutes before the expected (H) _____ time;
   - confirm the exact parking place of tour coach in the parking lot;
   - contact the porter and inform him of the luggage (I) _____ area;
   - stand at a highly visible location in the arrival lobby, in full view of arriving tourists with an identifying cardboard sign.

   (2) Upon arrival of the tour group:

   - meet the tour group and check the nationality, group code, number of tourists and name of the tour leader;

- check that all luggage has been claimed and collected by the (J) _____, and delivered to coach;
- take the tour group to the coach and help them get aboard the vehicle. The guide should stand by the door to politely greet tourists and confirm number in group.

(3) En route to hotel:

- inform overseas tourists of the local time;
- inform tourists of first meeting point and (K) _____ place (if applicable).
- Deliver a welcome speech.

Quickies

Role-play: Mr. Wang and the driver are waiting in the airport. They will meet a group of tourists coming from the England. Act as Mr. Wang and the driver, and pick the tourists up at the airport and take them to the hotel.

PART II *Situational Dialogue*

New Words and Expressions

descendant	/di'send(ə)nt/	n.	子孙,后裔,后代
trap	/træp/	v.	诱捕,诱骗
incorporate	/in'kɔːpəreit/	v.	合并,结合
trait	/treit/	n.	显著的特点,特性
tile	/tail/	n.	瓦,瓷砖
capture	/'kæptʃə/	v.	俘获,捕获,夺取

Proper Nouns

the Old Town of Lijiang	丽江古城	Naxi	纳西族
Han	汉族	Bai	白族

Dialogue 1

The Old Town of Lijiang (I)

Mr. Wang Lin, a local guide is taking Mr. Brown around the Old Town of Lijiang, the only town without a city wall in China.

(A=Mr. Wang Lin; B=Mr. Brown)

A: Now we arrive at the Old Town of Lijiang.

B: You said we've arrived at the Old Town, but it looks like that we haven't arrived yet. I haven't seen any city wall as I saw in other ancient towns of China.

A: Don't feel surprised when I tell you the Old Town of Lijiang is the only old town without a city wall in China.

B: Why? There must be something special. Would you please tell me the reason?

A: Well, Lijiang had been ruled over by Mu family for more than 500 years. They believed that the Mu family and their descendants would always be trapped like a rat in a hole if they built a city wall in the town.

B: That's funny, but I still can not understand why there is no city wall in the Old Town of Lijiang.

A: Well, the rolling hills encircle the old town. In ancient times passes were set up on the hills. People believed that the town was quite safe, so no city wall was built in the town.

B: Oh, I got it. I really love the style of the folk houses in the town. It looks like that they are quite different from those I have seen in Beijing.

A: The local people here are Naxi ethnic group. The buildings in the town incorporate the best parts of the architectural traits of Han, Bai, and Tibet into a unique Naxi style.

B: How beautiful the folk houses they are! All of the houses are decorated with figures of people and animals.

A: Naxi people love to engrave vivid figures of people and animals on doors and windows. They also plant beautiful flowers and trees in the garden.

B: I think living in such a beautiful and comfortable environment is a real pleasant thing, isn't it?

A: I couldn't agree with you less. Once you visit the Old Town of Lijiang, I bet the Old Town will capture your heart for the rest of your life.

(to be continued)

Exercises

Do the dialogue again and pay attention to your facial expressions and body language.

New Words and Expressions

pave	/peiv/	v.	铺
bluestone	/'bluː,stəun/	n.	青石,蓝砂岩
antiquity	/æn'tikwiti/	n.	古代,古代的遗物
sluice	/sluːs/	n.	水闸,泄水
flush	/flʌʃ/	v.	冲洗

| distinctive | /dis'tiŋktiv/ | adj. | 截然不同的, 独特的 |
| complicated | /'kɔmplikeitid/ | adj. | 复杂的, 难解的 |

Proper Nouns

| Sifangjie | 四方街 | Black Dragon Pool | 黑龙潭 |
| Venice of the East | "东方威尼斯" | | |

Dialogue 2

The Old Town of Lijiang (II)

Now they arrive at Sifangjie—the Square Street. Mr. Wang Lin explains to tourists the water system of the Old Town.

A: The place where we are standing is the center of the Old Town, Sifangjie—the Square Street. Look around, four main streets extend from here to the four different directions.

B: I see narrow streets winding their ways through the town. I'm afraid we'll get lost if we travel alone.

A: Don't worry! Just follow our tour banner! It is raining now. The road is paved by the local bluestones, so it is neither muddy in the rainy season nor dusty in the dry season.

B: I'd like to walk in the rain if it is not a heavy rain. I think the fine-grained stones add a sense of antiquity and mystery to the Old Town.

A: That's right. The Old Town of Lijiang is also a water town. The sluice at the center of town is opened late in the night. The water flow down along the slope and automatically flushes all the streets to keep the town clean.

B: Wonderful! No wonder the streets are very clean even on a rainy day. Small bridges here and there in the rain are more romantic.

A: Yes, there are almost 350 bridges with distinctive styles in the little town. Quite a few of them were built in the Ming and Qing dynasties.

B: The stream under the bridge is so beautiful. Can I wash my hands in the stream?

A: Why not? You can even drink the water if you want. The water flows into every household from the Black Dragon Pool. There is a complicated water system under your feet!

B: Really?

A: The usage of the water by the Naxi people is very scientific. They build three mouths for every well from the upriver to the downriver. The water in the first mouth is for drinking, the second one is for cleaning the vegetables and fruits, and the last one is used to wash the clothes and streets.

B: Marvelous! I come to know why the Old Town is called 'Venice of the East'.

(the end)

23

Cultural Notes

Old Town of Lijiang 丽江古城:丽江古城又名大研镇,位于丽江坝中部,中国四大古城之一。古城保留了大片明清居民建筑,均为土木结构、瓦屋面楼房。房屋多为三坊一照壁,也有四合院,融合了纳西、白、汉等民族建筑艺术的精华。丽江古城建筑布局灵活,注重装饰,精雕细刻。城中无规矩的道路网,无森严的城墙,布局三山为屏、一川相连;水系利用三河穿城、家家流水;街道布局"经络"设置,呈现"曲、幽、窄、达"的风格;建筑物依山就水、错落有致,这样精巧的古城设计艺术在中国现存古城中极为罕见,有别于世界任何一座古城。1997 年 12 月 3 日,丽江古城被联合国教科文组织列入《世界遗产名录》。

Exercises

Imagine that you are a local guide and your classmates are tourists. Make up a situational dialogue about the Old Town of Lijiang.

PART III *Ethnic Culture*

New Words and Expressions

encounter	/inˈkauntə/	v.	遭遇,遇到
wizard	/ˈwizəd/	n.	男巫,奇才
stockbreeding	/ˈstɔkbriːdiŋ/	n.	畜牧业
botanical	/bəˈtænik(ə)l/	adj.	植物学的
sumptuous	/ˈsʌmptjuəs/	adj.	奢侈的,华丽的
pickle	/ˈpikl/	v.	腌,泡
spouse	/spauz/	n.	配偶(指夫或妻)
monogamous	/mɔˈnɔgəməs/	adj.	一夫一妻制的

Proper Nouns

Dongba religion	东巴教	Jinshajiang River	金沙江
Pipa Pork	"琵琶肉"		

Naxi Culture

The people of the Naxi ethnic minority mostly live in the Naxi Autonomous County in Lijiang, Yunnan Province, while the rest live in Sichuan and Tibet. Before the foundation of modern China in 1949, most of the Naxi held the faiths of Dongba religion, believing that all have spirits and those spirits could never die. When they had significant events such as marriage, death, festivals, or disasters, they would invite a wizard to chant.

The Naxi people live on farming, stockbreeding and handicrafts. The area where they live is abundant in botanical resources such as trees and medicinal herbs. The Lijiang horse has also enjoyed the reputation as one of the "Three Treasures of Lijiang," which were presented to the official courts because of its ability to transport goods in mountainous area.

The Naxi's food presents their distinctive culture. The breakfast is simple and usually consists of steamed bread, but lunch and supper are often more sumptuous. They like pickled pork. The pickled Pipa Pork is one of the most famous foods for the Naxi people.

The Naxi people are warm and kind. After a hunt, they will share a piece of the kill with a casual passerby. When visited, they will prepare six or eight delicious dishes to treat their guests. Most of the young Naxi people insist that they have one spouse and usually they have a very complicated process to protect their monogamous marriage.

Quickies

True or False:

(1) _____ Now, most of the Naxi people believe in Dongba religion. They believe that all have spirits and those spirits could never die.

(2) _____ The Lijiang donkey became famous because of its ability to transport goods in mountainous area.

(3) _____ The pickled Pipa pork is made of pipa, a kind of ancient music instrument in china.

PART IV *Practical Writing for Tourism*

A Letter of Sales Proposal 销售意向书

June 12, 2008
Dar-Handasha Consultants
North Willington Avenue
West Palm Peach, Florida 33040
the United States

Dear Mr. Thompson:

Certainly enjoyed our telephone conversation on Thursday, and needless to say, we are gratified at the prospect of serving your company in August of 2008.

We could very comfortably accommodate you for arrival on Wednesday, August

18 with departure on Sunday, August 22, 2008. We could accept some early arrivals on Tuesday, August 17. However, it would be limited to 30 guest rooms. Therefore, the block of rooms we could make available to you looks something like this:

August, 2008

Day	Tuesday	Wednesday	Thursday	Friday	Saturday	Sunday
Date	17	18	19	20	21	22
Rooms	30	90	90	90	90	0

We have already established our convention rates for the calendar year 2008. Now, our Group Plan No.1 during August is RMB 700 Yuan single and RMB 1000 Yuan double occupancy. Group Plan No.2 includes room, breakfast/lunch/dinner and is currently RMB 1,200 Yuan single and RMB 1,400 Yuan double occupancy. I've enclosed several descriptive brochures together with a most comprehensive fact sheet. As you can see, we do make available this area's most complete convention hotel. Please keep in mind that we are a five-star hotel.

If the arrangements I outlined are agreeable, please drop me a note and I shall reserve some space for you on a tentative basis so that the space does not disappear to another meeting planner.

Thank you again, and please let me know about your travel arrangements and your mobile phone so that I can set aide the necessary time to personally call you.

Cordially yours,
Zhang Xiaoyang
Convention Sales Manager

Encl. Several descriptive brochures

Exercises

Write a letter of sales proposal to promote an exhibition and tourism in your city.

Unit 4 Accommodations

入住酒店

PART I *ABC for Tour Guides*

New Words and Expressions

| overseas | /ˈəuvəˈsiːz/ | adj. | 外国的, 海外的 |
| porter | /ˈpɔːtə/ | n. | 行李员 |

Proper Nouns

| check in | 入住酒店 | hotel facilities | 饭店设施 |
| individual tourists | 散客 | | |

Listening

Direction: Listen to the passages carefully and fill in the blanks with the missing information you have heard from the tapes.

1. **What should a guide do on the way from the airport to the hotel?** 地陪率团从机场赴饭店途中应该做哪些工作?
   (1) He should warmly welcome the tour group.
   (2) He should inform the overseas tourists of the (A) _____ time.
   (3) He should give a brief introduction of the local customs, the location of the hotel and its facilities.
   (4) He should inform the tourists of the first (B) _____ place and parking place if applicable.

2. **What should a guide do when the tour group checks in the hotel?** 团队入住饭店, 地陪应做好哪些工作?
   (1) Help the tour group check in;
   (2) Inform the tour group of the hotel facilities and (C) _____;
   (3) Inform the tour group of itinerary just for day of arrival and the next day;

(4) Ask the porter to deliver the (D) _____ to tourists' rooms;

(5) Confirm arrangements for the first meal for the group;

(6) Arrange morning call for the tourists.

New Words and Expressions

negotiate	/ni'gəuʃieit/	v.	(与某人)商议,谈判
compensation	/ˌkɔmpen'seiʃən/	n.	补偿,赔偿
inadequate	/in'ædikwit/	adj.	不充分的,不适当的

Readings

Direction: Read the following passage aloud and fill in the blanks with words or phrases you think appropriate.

housekeeping	instructions	laundry	terms	tap
requirements	television	reservation	suite	massage

1. **What should a guide do when the hotel has sold the reserved rooms to other individual tourists?** 饭店将旅游团队已经预定的住房出售给了其他散客,导游员该怎么办?

   (1) The guide should lodge a claim against the hotel for compensation.

   (2) He could rent rooms in another hotel for the tourists after having (A) _____ from the travel agency.

2. **What should a guide do if the reserved rooms are below the contract standard and no better rooms are available?** 某饭店为旅游团队提供的住房不符合合同标准,但饭店确实无房调换,导游员如何处理?

   (1) The guide should negotiate with the hotel and demand rooms which are up to the standard contracted.

   (2) If the negotiations are unsuccessful, the guide should lay out the (B) _____ of compensation and discuss them with tourists to gain their support and cooperation.

3. **What should a guide do if tourists want to exchange for better rooms because of the inadequate facilities of the hotel?** 客人进入房间后发现设施陈旧损坏,要求更换好的房间,导游怎么办?

   The tour guide must ask the hotel to meet the (C) _____ stipulated in the contract or compensate the tourists.

Quickies

Role-play: Miss Lin helps the tourists check in and leaves the hotel with the driver because she has to take care of her son in the hospital. After she leaves hotel the tourists complain that the hotel facilities are not up to the standard according to the contract. Please evaluate Lin's guiding service, and what would you do as a local guide in such a case?

PART II *Method of Introduction*

New Words and Expressions

figment	/'figmənt/	n.	臆造的事物,虚构的事
horizon	/hə'raizn/	n.	(知识,思想等的)范围,视野
legend	/'ledʒənd/	n.	传说,伟人传
attraction	/ə'trækʃən/	n.	吸引物,吸引力
render	/'rendə/	v.	致使,实施
precipice	/'presipis/	n.	悬崖
roar	/rɔː/	v.	吼叫,怒号
surge	/səːdʒ/	v.	汹涌,澎湃
grandiose	/'grændiəus/	adj.	宏伟的,宏大的
spectacle	/'spektəkl/	n.	奇观,景象
bumper	/'bʌmpə/	adj.	丰盛的,丰富的

Proper Nouns

Shunan Bamboo Forest	蜀南竹海
Carefree Valley	忘忧谷
Jin'e River (the Golden Goose River)	金鹅江
Huilong Mountain	回龙山
Dadongkan (Big Cave Precipice)	大洞坎
Edong Flying Waterfall (Goose Cave Flying Waterfall)	鹅洞飞泉
Shixi River	石溪河
Jin'e County	金鹅县

The Method of Introduction of Combining Facts and Figments
虚实结合法

This method is to enrich tourists' horizon with historical figures, events and myths, by which they can come to better understand on-the-spot landscape. In the process of introducing the scenic spots or scenery area, a guide can introduce some legends, customs or historical stories in order to add some touches to the scenes. A good guide should avoid introducing the place of interests in a monotonous way. One of the effective introduction methods a guide adopts is to introduce the beauty of the place or the attractions while adding some legendary stories.   For example,   while escorting a group at the Shunan Bamboo Forest the guide may as well tell the beautiful legend of the Carefree Valley,   which will surely render his/her introduction all the more impressive.   We could take the Jin'e River (the Golden Goose River) as one more example:

The legend has it that there once lived a golden goose in the cave at Dadongkan on the Shixi River that flowed by the county.   The golden goose often flew to the deep pool to have a bath under the precipice.   People believed that when the goose came,   there would be a favorable weather and a bumper harvest. Therefore, the county was called Jin'e County and the Shixi River was named Jin'e River.

The Jin'e River runs from east to west,   and breaks into two streams at the foot of the Huilong Mountain.   The water rushes down Dadongkan   (Big Cave Precipice)   to a deep pool, making up a 30-meter high amazing waterfall. The water roars and surges down like a giant goose flying down from the sky. This grandiose spectacle is thus called Edong Flying Waterfall or Goose Cave Flying Waterfall.

Questions

1. What is the legend about the Jin'e River (the Golden Goose River)?
2. What effects can a guide achieve if he introduces the sites using the method of combining facts and figments?
3. List something invented, made up, or fabricated that a guide may apply when he introduces the sites using the method of combining facts and figments.

1. _____
2. _____
3. _____
4. _____

PART III Tourist Site

New Words and Expressions

allies	/'ælaiz/	n.	联盟国,同盟者
invasion	/in'veiʒən/	n.	入侵
detain	/di'tein/	v.	拘留,留住
ally	/ə'lai, æ'lai/	v.	结盟
inaugurate	/i'nɔːgjureit/	v.	创新,举行开幕(落成、成立)典礼
establish	/is'tæbliʃ/	v.	建立,设立
Persian	/'pəːʃən/	n.	波斯人[语]

fanatic	/fəˈnætik/	*adj.*	狂热的,盲信的
prosperous	/ˈprɔspərəs/	*adj.*	繁荣的
comprise	/kəmˈpraiz/	*v.*	包含,由……组成
commentary	/ˈkɔməntəri/	*n.*	解说词

Proper Nouns

Silk Road	丝绸之路	Zhang Qian	张骞
Emperor Wudi	汉武帝	Han Dynasty	汉代
Western Regions	西域	Central Asia	中亚
Parthia	帕提亚(亚洲西部古国,在伊朗东北部)		

The Silk Road

The Silk Road originated in the 2nd century BC from a desire for military and political purpose instead of for trade. In order to seek allies to fight against Hun's repeated invasion, a court official named Zhang Qian was sent by Emperor Wudi of the Han Dynasty to the Western Regions. However, on the way to the Western Regions, the Huns captured Zhang and detained him for ten years. Escaped from the Hun's detention, Zhang Qian continued his journey to the Central Asia. While at that time, the local rulers  were satisfied with their status and refused to ally with Han Empire. Although the mission failed in its original purpose, the information Zhang Qian conveyed to China about Central Asia, and vice versa, made people in each area desire goods produced in the other. Silk that was favored by Persians and Romans, inaugurated the trade along the Silk Road.

When the Silk Road was first established, silk was not the chief commodity. Han Dynasty made very little profit from it until the Romans were fanatic about silk that the large profits came in. The Roams love silk so much that they even exchanged silk for its weight in gold. During the Tang Dynasty, thirty percent of the trade on the Silk Road was comprised of silk. Prosperous as it was, the operation of the Silk Road always be influenced by the political developments. A stable state could ensure the smooth trade on this road, while the troublous one would hurt. When Zhang Qian opened this road, the Han Dynasty and the empire of Parthia in Persia just achieved their golden ages, which give a favorite financial support to the smooth development of this route.

Cultural Notes

Silk Road 丝绸之路:丝绸之路,简称丝路,是指西汉(前 206—公元 25)时,由张骞出使

西域开辟的以长安(今西安)为起点,经甘肃、新疆,到中亚、西亚,并联结地中海各国的陆上通道,总长 7,000 多公里。从公元前 2 世纪到公元 15 世纪,丝绸之路将古老的中国文化、印度文化、希腊文化和波斯文化联结起来。除了将大量的丝绸传到西方外,还有桑蚕技术、火药、指南针、冶铜术、造纸术、印刷术等等通过这条路也先后传到中亚、伊朗、罗马等地。同样的,西方及中亚的物产、佛教、景教(基督教的一派)、伊斯兰教、天文、历法、数学、医学、音乐、美术等也传入中国。丝绸之路是以中国为起点的一条中西交通大动脉,也是中国文化输出、中西文化交流、贸易交流的主要路线。

Quickies

1. **True or False:**

   (1) _____ Zhang Qian was sent by Emperor Wudi of the Han Dynasty to the Western Regions in the 2nd century BC for the purpose of the trade with the countries.

   (2) _____ Han Dynasty made very little profit from the silk and tea until the Romans were fanatic about silk that the large profits came in.

   (3) _____ Both of the Han Dynasty and the empire of Parthia in Persia gave a favorite financial support to the smooth development of this route.

2. Read the passage aloud and introduce the Silk Road using the method of introduction you have learnt. The method of introduction of combining facts and figments is one of the choices.

Tips

- Draft your own commentary before you make your presentation.
- Speak colloquial English and use simple and short sentences.
- Animate your introduction with facial expressions and body language.
- Apply at least one method of introduction. It is highly recommended that you use two or three methods of introduction.

PART IV *Simulated Introduction*

New Words and Expressions

dune	/djuːn/	n.	沙丘
echo	/'ekəu/	v.	发回声,反射
limpid	/'limpid/	adj.	清澈的
breeze	/briːz/	n.	微风
whisper	/'(h)wispə/	v.	耳语;飒飒地响
slide	/slaid/	v.	滑动,滑行
gust	/gʌst/	n.	阵风

friction	/'frikʃən/	n.	摩擦;摩擦力
slip	/slip/	v.	滑倒,失足
collapse	/kə'læps/	n.	倒塌,崩溃
drought	/draut/	n.	干旱
geological	/dʒiɔ'lɔdʒikəl/	adj.	地质的
amorous	/'æmərəs/	adj.	多情的;表示爱情的
seductive	/si'dʌktiv/	adj.	诱人的
cantaloupe	/'kæntəluːp/	n.	香瓜,哈密瓜
gurgle	/'gəːgl/	v.	(流水)汩汩地流
gush	/gʌʃ/	v.	涌出
tranquil	/'træŋkwil/	adj.	安静的

Proper Nouns

| Mingshashan (Singing Dune) | 鸣沙山 | Crescent Spring | 月牙泉 |
| Dunhuang | 敦煌 | Crescent Lake | 月牙湖 |

Mingshashan and Crescent Spring

Ladies and gentlemen, have you ever heard of a dune that echoes to the sound of sand as you slide down its slopes? Can you image a limpid lake in an area of desert sand for thousands of years? Here in Dunhuang, you have the chance to enjoy such a wonderful spectacle—the Mingshashan and the Crescent Spring.

Mingshashan literally means the Singing Dune. It is six kilometers away from the city of Dunhuang. When you look afar, the Dune is just like a golden dragon winding its way over the horizon. As you get close you become aware that the sand has many colors ranging from red to yellow, green, black and white. On days when a strong wind blows, the fast shifting sand roars; but when the wind is little more than a light breeze, the sand produces gentle sounds like music. It is the same when you are sliding down the mountainside. At first, the sand under your feet just whispers; but the further you slide, the louder the sound until it roars like thunder or a drum beat. Some say that the sand is singing, while to others it is like an echo. This is how the mountain gets its name.

You may wonder why the sand makes these different sounds. First of all, I'd like to tell you a legend. A legend has it that, in ancient times, a general led with many soldiers to fight in a war with their enemies here. While they were engaged in a fierce battle, a great gust of

wind buried all the warriors in the sand and the dune was formed.　As the battle was at its height, the soldiers continued to fight beneath the sand. Thus, the sound you hear is said to be the roar of the soldiers. However, the real cause is the friction created as the wind shifts the sand or when you slip down the mountainside.

Just as oil and water don't mix,　so do springs and deserts.　But I'd like to tell you that the Crescent Spring here is an exception. The Crescent Spring has been lying among these sand dunes for thousands of years,　but it has not been buried in the sands.　It is indeed mysterious that the precipitous dunes beside the spring have never collapsed and buried the spring water.　On the contrary, it has surrounded and protected the spring like iron arms and kept the spring water even in long drought. It is a geological wonder, isn't it?

Ladies and gentlemen,　can anybody tell me what the Crescent Spring looks like?　Some say the spring reminds them of the eye of an amorous woman. Some say it looks more like her gentle and seductive lips. What do you think of it? Some of our friends said it looks like a slice of lush, sweet and crystal cantaloupe. I think it looks like a crescent fallen down into this desert. The Crescent Lake is so called because of its crescent shape. Today, the spring still gurgles and gushes clear water; and still remains worthy as the first spring in the desert.

Today, Mingshashan is listed as a key national tourist resort. You may climb it on foot or, if you like, on the back of a camel. You can also take a sand bath treatment if you want. I bet your tour won't be complete in Dunhuang if you don't appreciate the golden sand,　the tranquil lake and the beautiful sunset.

Cultural Notes

1. **Mingshashan (Singing Dune)** 鸣沙山,因沙动有声而得名。古称"沙角山"、"神沙山"。山有流沙积聚而成,东西长约 40 公里,南北宽约 20 公里,最高海拔 1,715 米。其山沙垄相衔,峰如刀刃,远看连绵起伏如虬龙蜿蜒,又似大海中的波涛涌来荡去,甚为壮观。沙粉红、黄、绿、白、黑五色,晶莹闪光不沾一尘。如遇摩擦振动,便会殷殷发声,轻若丝竹,重如雷鸣。故"沙岭晴鸣"为敦煌"八景"之一。游客在这里可以赤足爬山、骑骆驼登沙丘、滑板滑沙、跳牵引伞,还可以进行沙浴、沙疗,情趣盎然。

2. **Crescent Spring** 月牙泉:月牙泉处于鸣沙山环抱之中,因其形酷似一弯新月而得名。古称"沙井",又名"药泉",一度讹传"渥洼池",清代正名"月牙泉"。面积 0.88 公顷,平均水深 3 米左右,水质甘洌,清澈如镜。千百年来沙山环泉而不被掩埋,地处干旱沙漠而泉水不浊不涸,实数罕见。泉内星草含芒、铁鱼鼓浪,山色水光相映成趣,风光十分优美。鸣沙山、月牙泉是大漠戈壁中一对孪生姐妹,"山以灵而故鸣,水以神而益秀"。游人至此,无论从山顶鸟瞰,还是来泉边漫步,都会驰怀神往,遐思万千,确有"鸣沙山怡性,月牙泉洗心"之感。

Exercises

34 *Make a simulated introduction of the Mingshashan and Crescent Spring using the method of introduction you have learnt. Pay attention to the body language and other tips of introduction.*

Unit 5 Dietary Service
饮食服务

PART I *ABC for Tour Guides*

New Words and Expressions

dietary	/'daiətəri/	adj.	饮食的
inspect	/in'spekt/	v.	检查,视察
menu	/'menjuː/	n.	菜单
beverage	/'bevə ridʒ/	n.	饮料
cater	/'keitə/	v.	满足(需要),投合

Listening

Direction: Listen to the passages carefully and fill in the blanks with the missing information you have heard from the tapes.

1. **What service should a guide provide to tourists during the mealtime?** 当客人用餐时,地陪应该怎样服务?
   (1) Inspect the dishes one or two times during the mealtime to make sure the food is up to the (A) _____ specified in the contract.
   (2) Answer questions about the food raised by tourists.
   (3) Urge the restaurant to take measures if the meals are not up to the expected standard.

2. **Should a guide agree to tourists' requests for changing food?** 游客要求换餐,导游员能否同意?
   (1) Generally speaking, restaurants could agree to changing the food if they are informed (B) _____ hours ahead of mealtime. In such a case, the guide may accept the tourist's request.
   (2) If a tourist requests to change the food just before mealtime, the restaurant may refuse to make changes since some of the dishes will have already been (C) _____. In such a case, the guide should graciously decline the request and give explanations.

35

(3) If the tourist insists on changing the menu, adding dishes or a beverage, the guide may agree but should inform the tourist that he/she must bear the (D) _____.

3. **What does a guide do when a tourist has special dietary requirements because of the religious or health reasons?** 游客由于宗教或生理上的原因,提出特殊的饮食要求,导游员如何处理?

   (1) The guide should try his best to meet tourist's requirements if it is related to his/her religious practice or for (E) _____ reasons.

   (2) If the special dietary requirements are specified in the contract, the guide must fulfill them according to the contract.

   (3) If the requirements are not specified in the contract, but put forward upon arrival, the guide should do his best to meet the needs of the tourist. However, the tourist should bear the (F) _____ expenses.

   (4) If the restaurant cannot cater for the special needs of the tourist on this occasion, the tourist has to arrange for the food himself. However, the guide will be responsible for arranging (G) _____ dishes for future meals.

New Words and Expressions

discord	/'diskɔːd/	n.	不一致,意见不合
vendor	/'vendɔː/	n.	商贩
peddler	/'pedlə/	n.	小贩
alternative	/ɔːl'tɜːnətiv/	adj.	选择性的,二选一的
permit	/pə(ː)'mit/	v.	许可,允许,准许

Readings

Direction: Read the following passage aloud and fill in the blanks with words or phrases you think appropriate.

garlic	salt	discord	vinegar	waiter
vendors	restaurant	sanitary	sour	tasteless

1. **What does a guide do when a tourist is unwilling to have meals with other tourists?** 某游客不愿随团用餐,导游员如何处理?

   (1) The guide should encourage the tourist to eat with the group and, if there is a (A) _____ _____, he should make every effort to settle it.

   (2) If the discord cannot be settled, the tourist must make arrangements for the food himself and bear the expense.

2. **What does a guide do when tourists try to buy and eat Liangfen, a local snack sold by peddlers at the tourist site?** 当游客购买品尝某一景点里的小贩出售的凉粉时,导游如何处理?

(1) The guide should discourage the tourists from eating food sold by street (B) _____ .

(2) The guide should encourage them to taste the local snack in clean restaurants.

3. **The travel agency has a hotpot party for tourists before they leave the country, but two tourists refuse to eat hotpot. In such a case, what is the guide supposed to do?** 离境前旅行社特意安排游客品尝火锅,但有两位客人坚持不吃火锅,导游员如何处理?

(1) The guide should try to persuade the tourists to join the tour group for having the hotpot.

(2) If two tourists insist on, the guide may order alternative dishes or permit them to have dinner in another (C) _____ . In the latter case, they must bear the expense for their meal.

Quickies

Role-play: Mr. Zhang Jun, a tourist is having dinner when he feels upset because he eats something forbidden because of the religious practice. Miss Yang Linling, the local guide tries to solve the problem. Who is to blame? Replay the scene.

PART II *Situational Dialogue*

New Words and Expressions

lamasery	/'lɑːməsəri/	n.	喇嘛寺
infinite	/'infinit/	adj.	无穷的,无限的
preserve	/pri'zəːv/	v.	保护,保持
enshrine	/in'ʃrain/	v.	入庙供奉,祭祀
splendid	/'splendid/	adj.	壮丽的,辉煌的
solemn	/'sɔləm/	adj.	庄严的,隆重的
majesty	/'mædʒisti/	n.	雄伟,最高权威
rear	/riə/	n.	后面,背后
mural	/'mjuərəl/	n.	壁画,壁饰
commemorate	/kə'meməreit/	v.	纪念

Proper Nouns

Dazhao Temple	大召寺	Hohhot	呼和浩特
Wuliang Si (Infinite Temple)	无量寺	Inner Mongolia	内蒙古
Silver Buddha Temple	银佛寺	Sakyamuni	释迦牟尼
Fo Tang	佛堂	Jing Tang	经堂

Dialogue 1

Dazhao Temple

Miss Yang Jiaojiao takes tourists to visit the Dazhao Temple, a unique lamasery in Hohhot where they can view three marvelous treasures.

(A=Miss Yang Jiaojiao; B: Abraham)

A: Here is the Dazhao Temple, or "Wuliang Si." It can be interpreted as the Infinite Temple in English. It is the oldest building and the largest temple in Hohhot of Inner Mongolia.

B: But I heard local people call it Yinfo Si or Silver Buddha Temple, why?

A: Because it is here that there is a rare silver statue of Sakyamuni Buddha. The statue is 2.5 meter high, very impressive.

B: I'm very interested in this statue. Where is the statue replaced in the Temple?

A: The perfectly preserved statue of Silver Buddha lies in the Fo Tang. Fo Tang literally means the hall for worshiping Buddha. The Silver Buddha has been enshrined there for some four hundred years.

B: Oh, I see. Miss Yang, the architectural style of the Temple is unique. It looks quite different from other temples I have seen in China.

A: The Temple is a lamasery which combines both Tibetan and Han styles of architecture. That's why it is quite different from other temples in China.

B: Well, what is the building over there? I see a pavilion over there.

A: Now, we're standing in front of the main hall of the Dazhao Temple. The building you see is the main hall of the Temple.

B: It is a very splendid and solemn hall. I see a pair of iron lions squatting in front of the hall. I think their heads held high adds more majesty to the architecture.

A: I couldn't agree with you more. The main hall has three parts. The front part is a two-story hall with a pavilion in the first floor; Jing Tang, the hall for chanting and Fo Tang, the hall for worshiping Buddha are in the middle and rear part.

B: What are the special cultural relics in the Temple? You've told us there is something special here.

A: You'll see the three marvelous treasures: a title given to the Silver Buddha, the carved dragons on the huge golden pillars on either side of the statue of Sakyamuni Buddha and the murals commemorating the Emperor's visit.

B: I'd like to see each of them. Shall we go?

A: That's my pleasure.

B: Thank you very much!

(the end)

Exercises

Do the dialogue again and pay attention to your facial expressions and body language.

New Words and Expressions

wandering	/'wɔndəriŋ/	*adj.*	漫游的,徘徊的
boundless	/'baʊndlis/	*adj.*	无限的,无边无际的
toast	/təust/	*n.*	干杯
mutton	/'mʌtn/	*n.*	羊肉
wrestle	/'resl/	*n.*	摔跤,角力,扭斗
archery	/'ɑːtʃəri/	*n.*	射箭术
bonfire	/'bɔn,faiə/	*n.*	篝火,营火

Proper Nouns

Xilamuren Grassland		希拉穆仁草原	shouba rou 手扒肉
ger	*n.*	(蒙古游牧民族居住的,用毛毡或兽皮搭起的)圆顶帐篷	

Dialogue 2

The Xilamuren Grassland

After they visit the Dazhao Temple the tourists are traveling to the Xilamuren Grassland, one of the four great grasslands in the Inner Mongolia.

(A=Yang Jiaojiao; B: Abraham)

A: After you visited the Dazhao Temple I think you're eager to experience grassland life. Am I right?

B: Certainly. I want to see the blue sky and white clouds, the rolling grass, the wandering sheep on the grassland.

A: You will. On the grassland, you'll see the green of the grassland reaching out as far as your eyes can see. Colorful wild flowers and flocks of sheep look like masses of cloud. All of these make the scene absolutely beautiful.

B: Your description of the grassland is marvelous, but there are lots of grasslands in Inner Mongolia. Which grassland do you suggest we should travel?

A: If you want my opinion I'd like to say the Xilamuren Grassland is a good choice! It is about one hundred kilometers north of Hohhot.

B: Very good! Besides the boundless grassland what else can we see there?

A: A lot. While you listen to the toast songs and appreciate traditional Mongolian dances, you can taste the roasted whole sheep and *shouzhua rou*. *Shouzhua rou* is boiled mutton eaten with hands.

B: I'll certainly taste the whole roasted sheep with my wife. I'll learn how to eat *shouzhua rou* from the Mongolians.

A: You may also put on traditional Mongolian clothes, and take part in horse race, wrestling and archery. These games have been popular in Inner Mongolia for thousands of years.

B: I'll cerfainry take part in some of the competitions. I love wrestling and expect to get a reward.

A: I hope so. A big surprise is probably waiting for you! At night, we'll take part in a bonfire party according to our travel schedule. We'll sit around bonfires, with the mogolians, sing and dance far into night.

B: My wife Marry and I will join them, but where shall we check in after the bonfire party? We want to experience how the Mongolians live.

A: All of us will live in the Mongol ger. Ger means home in Mongolian. I believe living in ger will give you the true feeling of what life is like on the vast Xilamuren Grassland. I bet it won't disappoint you.

B: Thank you very much, Miss Yang!

Cultural Notes

Dazhao Temple 大召寺：大召寺是呼和浩特保存最完好规模最大、年代最久的喇嘛教寺院，蒙语称"依克召"，意为大庙。汉名原为弘慈寺，后改名无量寺，位于呼和浩特市旧城区。明万历八年(1580)寺成，因供奉银佛像，俗称银佛寺。佛殿内有高2.55米的银铸释迦牟尼像。释迦牟尼像前有一对金色木雕巨龙，蟠于木柱之上，作双龙戏珠状。殿前汉白玉方形石座上，有明天启七年(1627)铸造的一对空心铁狮，昂首仰视，形象别致。寺前原有玉泉井一口，泉水清冽，被誉为"九边第一泉"，并将此5字雕成匾额，悬挂在山门上。

Xilamuren Grassland 希拉穆仁草原：希拉穆仁，蒙语意为"黄色的河"，位于呼和浩特以北100公里，是蜚声海内外的草原旅游景点，又因希拉穆仁河畔有座历史久远的席力图召，故又名"召河"。席力图召(希拉穆仁召)建于清朝乾隆三十四年(1769年)，清廷赐名"普会寺"是呼和浩特席力图召六世活佛的避暑行宫，雕梁画栋，颇为壮观。希拉穆仁草原是典型的高原草场，夏秋时节绿草如茵，鲜花遍地，每年都要举行盛大的草原那达慕活动。游客不仅可以观赏草原美景、品味草原游牧民族的豪迈心情，还可以享用草原民族典型的风味餐饮，体会独特浓郁的蒙古民族文化风情。

Exercises

Imagine that you are a local guide and your classmates are tourists. Make up a situational dialogue about the Dazhao Temple or the Xilamuren Grassland.

PART III *Ethnic Culture*

New Words and Expressions

profound	/prə'faund/	*adj.*	深刻的,意义深远的
staple	/'steipl/	*adj.*	主要的,常用的
kumiss	/'ku:mis/	*n.*	(=koumiss) 马奶酒(亚洲牧民用马奶或骆驼奶酿成)
ferment	/'fə:mənt/	*v.*	(使)发酵,(使)激动
threshold	/'θreʃhəuld/	*n.*	门槛
niche	/nitʃ/	*n.*	壁龛
funeral	/'fju:nərəl/	*n.*	葬礼,出殡

Proper Nouns

Mongol	蒙古人;蒙古语
Shamanism	(亚洲北部乌拉尔—阿尔泰山区人信奉的)萨满教
Lamaism	喇嘛教(藏、蒙等地区信奉的佛教)
Nadam Fair	那达慕

Mongolian Culture

The Mongols, also called Mongolian, is brave and unconstrained. Though they called themselves "Mongol," meaning everlasting fire, other people refer to them as "an ethnic minority on the horseback." In the 16th century the Mongolians believe in Shamanism but turned to Lamaism in the Yuan Dynasty.

The Mongolians are living on vast grasslands; therefore, stockbreeding played a major role in their development, together with agriculture, handicrafts, and other processing industries. The Mongolian people take milk and meat as their daily staple food and drink. They enjoy drinking the milk of sheep, horses, deer and camels. Kumiss, fermented out of horse milk, is a kind of distinctive wine with the function of driving out coldness and as well as strengthening the stomach. Tender, boiled mutton, *shouzhua rou* in Chinese, is representative, too, of their traditional food.

When visitors go to a Mongolian's home, they will be treated very well by being given wine. But they must fully respect their hosts' customs such as: they will not step on the threshold, sit beside the niche of Buddha, and touch children's heads, etc. They admire fire and water so guests should not dry their feet or boots on the stove, nor should they wash or bathe in the river, as it is holy and clean in their eyes. In the Mongolian culture, colors are significant. At a Mongolian funeral, red and white should be avoided, whereas during their festivals, black and yellow should not be used.

The grandest festival is the Nadam Fair for five to seven days during late August. Mongolian people, in new clothes, will gather from many areas. Many will participate in the exciting competitions of shooting, wrestling, and horse-riding.

Quickies

True or False:

1. _____ "Mongol" means the everlasting fire, or "an ethnic minority on the horseback."
2. _____ Kumiss, fermented out of sheep milk, is a kind of distinctive wine which can drive out coldness and as well as strengthen the stomach.
3. _____ Tourists should not dry their feet or boots on the stove, nor should sit beside the niche of Buddha, or touch children's heads when they are invited to a Mongolian home.

PART IV *Practical Writing for Tourism*

Hotel Reservation 饭店预订

This agreement is entered into and between Hohhot Ruijing Hotel (hereinafter referred to as Party A), and Hohhot Overseas Travel Service, Ltd,. (hereinafter referred to as Party B). Party A agrees and Party B accepts the following terms on room reservation:

1. Room and meal rates

Room rate for a double room with bath is 250 YUAN (RMB) per night; 20 YUAN for breakfast per person.

2. Reservation

Party B is required to send Party A detailed information of guests (date of arrival/departure, number of rooms needed) ten days before the arrival, and Party B should makc a remittance of the payment at the amount of 82,000 YUAN (RMB) to the bank account Party A, A/C No. 22-807101100166066, China Construction Bank, Changsha Branch.

3. Cancellation

No cancellation fee will be charged if Party A is informed seven days prior to the scheduled arrival of the guests. Room rate of a day will be charged if Party A is informed within seven days.

4. Account settlement

    (1) Party B is responsible for collecting the room rates from the individual guest.

    (2) Excluding room rate and breakfast rate, all other expenses in the hotel should be paid by guests on the spot.

5. Validity

    The term of this contract shall be for the period of 90 days commencing upon May 7th, 2008 and ending on August 7th, 2008.

6. Settlement of Dispute

    Both Parties should act according to this agreement. Should there be any breach by Party B against any of the stipulation in this agreement, Party A has the right to terminate this agreement. Without mutual consent, either Party cannot transfer, to the third party, its right and commitments, as described in this agreement.

    IN WITNESS WHEREOF, the parties hereto affix their names on the date and space specified.

Date: _____   Hohhot Ruijing Hotel

                            (Print Name, Title and Sign)

Date: _____   Hohhot Overseas Travel Service, Ltd.

                            (Print Name, Title and Sign)

Exercises

Write a hotel reservation agreement for a group of 20 tourists who expect to arrive at your city and have a three-day city tour.

Unit 6 Special Requests
特殊要求

PART I ABC for Tour Guides

New Words and Expressions

colleague	/ˈkɔliːg/	n.	同事，同僚
vehicle	/ˈviːikl/	n.	交通工具，车辆
register	/ˈredʒistə/	v.	登记，注册
privilege	/ˈprivilidʒ/	n.	特权，基本公民权利

Listening

Direction: Listen to the passages carefully and fill in the blanks with the missing information you have heard from the tapes.

1. **What does a guide do when tourists want to visit their friends, relatives or Chinese colleagues?** 游客要求探亲访友或会见中国同行，导游员如何处理？

   (1) The guide should do whatever possible to help him if the tourist wants to visit his friends or (A) _____.

   (2) The guide may request the travel agency to contact the departments concerned if the tourist wants to meet his Chinese colleagues.

2. **If a tourist's relative wishes to join the tour group, what are the procedures a guide must accomplish? Who would be discouraged from joining the group?** 办理游客亲友随团的程序有哪些？导游员一般不能同意哪些人随团？

   (1) Provided that there are empty seats of the coach or other vehicles available, the guide should first get (B) _____ from the tour leader and group members. Upon approval from the travel agency, the guide is expected to ask the tourist to register, (C) _____ the appropriate travel expenses, and provide the necessary documentation. The above having been completed, the tourist's relative can travel together with the tour group.

(2) It is recommended that the guide graciously decline tour privileges to a foreign tourist's relative who is a (D) _____.

New Words and Expressions

commission	/kə'miʃən/	n.	委任,委托,代办(权)
recipient	/ri'sipiənt/	n.	接收者,容纳者
consigner	/kən'sainə(r)/		发货人,委托人,交付人
contraband	/'kɔntrə,bænd/	n.	违法交易,违禁品,走私
package	/'pækidʒ/	n.	包裹,包
archival	/ɑː'kaivəl/	adj.	关于档案的
unfamiliar	/'ʌnfə'miljə/	adj.	不熟悉的,没有经验的
objective	/əb'dʒektiv/	adj.	客观的,[语法]宾格的
identify	/ai'dentifai/	v.	识别,鉴别
ambiguous	/,æm'bigjuəs/	adj.	暧昧的,不明确的

Readings

Direction: Read the following passage aloud and fill in the blanks with words or phrases you think appropriate.

lifesaving	emergency	commission	objective	parcel
post	poor	troublesome	contraband	hike

1. **What should a guide do if a tourist asks him to deliver letters or articles to his relative?**
   游客要求导游员帮助转递信件或物品给自己的亲友,导游员如何处理?
   (1) The guide should graciously decline the request and take the tourist to the nearest (A) _____ _____ office. The tourist could post the letters and articles himself.
   (2) If the tourist insists, the guide should request approval from the travel agency. Upon approval, the tourist must complete a formal (B) _____ that specifies the name of the article, the value, the name and address of the recipient, as well as the exact address of the consigner (sender).
   (3) The guide should check the value of the article in the presence of the tourist and determine that there is no (C) _____, drugs or guns in the package.
   (4) Upon receiving the article, the recipient should provide a receipt with his signature that will be sent to the travel agency for archival purposes.

2. **Under what circumstances should a guide decline tourists' requests for individual and unscheduled sightseeing?** 在什么情况下,导游员不宜让游客自由活动?
   The tour guide should graciously decline tourists' requests for individual and unscheduled sightseeing:

(1) near the time of departure;

(2) in a place of (D) _____ public security;

(3) to go bike-riding alone in an unfamiliar place;

(4) to an area not open to the public;

(5) to go boating or swimming in the river or pond without (E) _____ equipment or the presence of a lifeguard.

3. **How could a guide decline an unrealistic request from the tourist?**　导游如何拒绝游客不切实际的要求?

(1) Smile without giving a reply.

(2) Try to make sure what the tourist intends and give (F) _____ reasons for declining the request.

(3) Identify the unreasonable or illogical parts of the request and use them as the reasons for the refusal.

(4) Be ambiguous in language when facing a (G) _____ tourist.

Quickies

1. Fill in the blanks with the proper words or phrases given below:

commission	deliver	stamp	receipt	approval
inspection	presence	refuse	postage	recipient

A Sealed Package Delivery

When a tourist asks the guide to deliver a sealed package he should request the tourist to open the package for (1) _____. Food turns bad easily so the guide should graciously decline the request and ask the tourist to (2) _____ the food himself. When the tourist refuses to open the package for checking, the guide should (3) _____ the request. If the tourist badly needs help the guide should get (4) _____ from the travel agency. Upon approval, the tourist must complete a formal commission that specifies the name of the article, the value, the name and address of the (5) _____, as well as the exact address of the consigner (sender). The tour guide should check the value of the article in the (6) _____ of the tourist. Upon receiving the article, the recipient should provide a (7) _____ with his signature.

2. **Role-play:** Miss Chen Yaling meets her friends in Hangzhou. Her friends propose to join the tour group so that they can help introduce the historical interests in the city. Act as Miss Chen, her colleagues and the local guide and handle the problem according to the guiding procedures.

PART II *Method of Introduction*

New Words and Expressions

vague	/veig/	*adj.*	含糊的,不清楚的
miracle	/'mirəkl/	*n.*	奇迹,奇事
principle	/'prinsəpl/	*n.*	法则,原理
terrain	/'terein/	*n.*	地形
inundate	/'inəndeit/	*v.*	淹没
motto	/'mɔtəu/	*n.*	座右铭,格言
subdue	/sʌb'djuː/	*v.*	制服,控制

Proper Nouns

Yuzui (Fish Mouth)	鱼嘴
Dujiangyan Irrigation Project	都江堰水利工程
Hanjiaba Flatland	韩家坝
"Divide water by 40% and 60%; Subdue flood and drought."	"分四六、平涝旱。"

The Method of Explanatory Introduction
解释法

This method is inclined to help tourists understand some vague points of the tourist sites with plain words. It is applied when a guide introduces acknowledge about the historical interests or scientific principles of the works or some miracle of the tourist sites that tourists may fail to understand. For example, a guide can explain how the Yuzui (Fish Mouth) divides the water flow using the Method of Explanatory Introduction.

The main function of Yuzui (Fish Mouth) of Dujiangyan Irrigation Project is water diversion. Li Bing had the project built here according to the favorable terrain of Hanjiaba Flatland. The outer side of the riverbed is higher than the inner one. To take advantage of the topography, 60% amount of the water, along the lower side of the dike, flows into the inner river in spring when the farmers need water. In the summer, the flow volume increases rapidly and the water level is much higher. Yuzui discharges 60% water to the outer river and leaves only 40% water to the inner river so as to prevent the flood from inundating the Chengdu Plain. The effect of water diversion is summarized as six-character motto, "Divide water by 40% and 60%; Subdue flood and drought."

Questions

1. When does a guide usually apply the method of explanatory introduction?

2. What about the effects of introduction if the guide uses above method together with the question-and-answer introduction?

PART III *Tourist Site*

New Words and Expressions

shallow	/'ʃæləu/	*adj.*	浅的,浅薄的
inlet	/'inlet/	*n.*	入口,水湾
silt	/silt/	*n.*	淤泥,残渣
distinct	/dis'tiŋkt/	*adj.*	不同的
embrace	/im'breis/	*v.*	拥抱,包含
retreat	/ri'triːt/	*n.*	休养所、宁静之处
solitarily	/ˌsɔli'tɛəriə/	*adv.*	独自一人地,寂寞地
blossom	/'blɔsɔm/	*n.*	花,花开的状态
revolutionist	/ˌrevə'ljuːʃənist/	*n.*	革命家
dedicate	/'dedikeit/	*v.*	献(身),致力

Proper Nouns

Gushan	孤山	West Lake	西湖
Solitary Island	孤岛	Plum Blossom Island	梅屿
Zhejiang Museum	浙江博物馆	Zhongshan Park	中山公园
Sun Yat-sen	孙中山	Xinhai Revolution	辛亥革命
Tomb of Qiu Jin	秋瑾墓	Xi Ling Seal Society	西泠印社

Gushan

Originally a shallow sea inlet, due to the laying down of silt this 5.68 square kilometers (about 1,404 acres) of water became the famous West Lake. With an average depth of just five feet the lake comprises five distinct sections. Held in the embrace of hilly peaks on three sides, this water wonderland has been an attraction for centuries and it is small wonder that it was a favourite imperial retreat.

Gushan, just situated at the northwestern corner of West Lake, is 38 meters above sea-level, and covers an area of 300 *mu* (nearly 50 acres). It is the lowest summit, compared to other hills around West Lake, but it is also the biggest island in the lake and the only natural island as well. Gushan got this name because it is surrounded by water, standing solitarily in West Lake. It can also be called Solitary Island, for it is a lonely island rather than a hill. Its other name Plum

Blossom Island, originates from the flourishing plum blossom planted on the hill.

Gushan boasts of beautiful landscapes. In addition, there are a lot of cultural relics in the scenic area. At the south foot lies the Zhejiang Museum and Zhongshan Park in the middle of the hill. The park was rebuilt on the site of an imperial garden of the Qing Dynasty, and was opened in 1927 to commemorate Sun Yat-sen, the great leader of the Xinhai Revolution in 1911. At the west foot is the Tomb of Qiu Jin, a great female revolutionist at the end of the Qing Dynasty. On the top of the hill, there is Xi Ling Seal Society, dedicated to the study of seals. The best time to visit Gushan is in winter or in early spring, for at this time, you can enjoy the plum blossom as well as the usual sights.

Cultural Notes

Gushan 孤山，闻其名便知，乃湖中一孤峙之岛，白居易称之为"蓬莱宫在水中央"。南宋这里兴建四圣延祥观和西太乙宫，作为御花园，清康熙年间又辟为行宫所在地。孤山自然风景绝佳，历史文化积淀深厚。有诗为证："钱塘之胜在西湖，西湖之奇在孤山"。孤山景区的名胜古迹多达30多处，沿湖所能欣赏到的有西泠桥、秋瑾墓、西泠印社、楼外楼、中山公园等。孤山之后是白堤，起自平湖秋月，终于断桥残雪，桥后有著名的宝石流霞等景观。

Quickies

1. True or False:

    (1) _____ Gushan, just situated at the northwestern corner of West Lake, is the highest summit around West Lake.

    (2) _____ Gushan gets other name Plum Blossom Island, which derives from the flourishing plum blossom planted on the hill.

    (3) _____ At the west foot is the Zhongshan Park, which was rebuilt and opened in 1927 to commemorate Sun Yat-sen, the great leader of the Xinhai Revolution in 1911.

2. Read the passage aloud and introduce Gushan using the methods of introduction you have learnt. The method of explanatory introduction is one of the choices.

Tips

- Draft your own commentary before you make your presentation.
- Speak colloquial English and use simple and short sentences.
- Animate your introduction with facial expressions and body language.
- Apply at least one method of introduction. It is highly recommended that you use two or three methods of introduction.

PART IV *Simulated Introduction*

New Words and Expressions

circular	/'səːkjulə/	*adj.*	圆形的;循环的
atmosphere	/'ætməsfiə/	*n.*	气氛
feature	/'fiːtʃə/	*n.*	特征,容貌
float	/fləut/	*v.*	浮动,飘浮
mottled	/'mɔtld/	*adj.*	杂色的,斑驳的
delicate	/'delikit/	*adj.*	精巧的,精致的
extraordinary	/iks'trɔːdnri/	*adj.*	特别的,非凡的
span	/spæn/	*n.*	跨度,跨距
patron	/'peitrən/	*n.*	赞助人,资助人;保护神
poisonous	/'pɔiznəs/	*adj.*	有毒的
rescue	/'reskjuː/	*v.*	援救,营救
prosperous	/'prɔspərəs/	*adj.*	繁荣的
picturesque	/ˌpiktʃə'resk/	*adj.*	独特的
dusk	/dʌsk/	*n.*	薄暮,黄昏
dim	/dim/	*adj.*	暗淡的,模糊的

Proper Nouns

Wuzhen	乌镇	Great Wall	长城
Tongxiang	桐乡	Zhejiang Province	浙江省
Bridge in Bridge	桥里桥	Tongji Bridge	同济桥
Renji Bridge	仁济桥	Fanglu Pavilion (Pavilion of Visits to Lu)	访卢亭
Lu Tong	卢仝	Lu Yu	陆羽

Wuzhen

Ladies and gentlemen, Chinese people say that unless you visit the Great Wall then you haven't been to China. For any travel south of the Yangtze River, one place not to be missed is the town of Wuzhen.

Wuzhen is located in the centre of the six ancient towns south of Yangtze River, 17 kilometers north of the city of Tongxiang, Zhejiang Province. Wuzhen's uniqueness lies in its layout. When you walk along the east-west-east circular route created by the six districts, you will enjoy the atmosphere of the traditional cultures and the original ancient features of the town for hundreds of years. You will also enjoy its two-thousand-year history in its ancient stone bridges floating on mild water, its stone pathways between the mottled walls and its delicate wood carvings.

Look, here is the famous Bridge in Bridge. You may be amazed at the extraordinary scene of Bridge in Bridge created by two ancient bridges. One is the Tongji Bridge which crosses the river from east to west and the other is called Renji Bridge which runs from south to north. Either of two bridges can be seen through the arch of the other, so it is called Bridge in Bridge. Tongji Bridge is a 28.4-meter-long and 3.5-meters-wide arch bridge. It has a span of 11.8 meters.

Renji Bridge has a length of 22.6 meters, a width of 2.8 meters and a span of 8.5 meters. The bridge is a beautiful landscape, isn't it? I'll give you ten minutes to take photos here.

Now, we arrive at the Fanglu Pavilion (Pavilion of Visits to Lu). It is the best teahouse in Wuzhen. The pavilion got its name from a meeting between Lu Tong, the owner, and Lu Yu, the Patron Saint of Tea during the Tang Dynasty. It is said that Lu Yu once mistakenly ate some poisonous leaves and Lu Tong happened to collect tea leaves at that time and rescued him. In return, Lu Yun taught Lu Tong knowledge of tea and tea-making skills. Later Lu Tong's teahouse became prosperous. He became a millionaire in Wuzhen. In order to thank Lu Yu he changed the house's name to Pavilion of Visits to Lu.

Now, we'll have a short rest here. It is the time for free sightseeing. You may drink a cup of tea and overlook the landscape of the water town from the windows of the tea house. You may enjoy the demonstration in the traditional workshops district to watch the famous traditional crafts such as the printing and dyeing of blue printed cloth. You may also walk amongst the picturesque moss-covered streets and the houses decorated with exquisitely-carved wooden and stone doors and windows. At dusk when the street lamps give off their dim lights in the thousand-year-old lanes, I think you will feel your every step echoing with the history of this ancient and attractive town of Wuzhen.

Have fun! We'll meet here at six thirty.

Cultural Notes

Wuzhen 乌镇：乌镇位于浙江省北部，京杭大运河西侧，为国家 4A 级风景名胜区。乌镇是江南水乡六大古镇之一，古风犹存的东、西、南、北四条老街呈"十"字交叉，构成双棋盘式河街平行、水陆相邻的古镇格局。这里的民居宅屋傍河而筑，街道两旁保存有大量明清建筑，辅以河上石桥，体现了小桥、流水、古宅的江南古镇风韵。镇上的西栅老街是我国保存最完好的明清建筑群之一。全镇以河成街，桥街相连，依河筑屋，深宅大院，重脊高檐，河埠廊坊，过街骑楼，穿竹石栏，临河水阁，古色古香，水镇一体，呈现一派古朴、明净的幽静。

Exercises

Make a simulated introduction of Wuzhen using the methods of introduction you have learnt. Pay attention to the body language and other tips of introduction.

Unit 7 Techniques of Tour Guiding
带团技巧

PART I ABC for Tour Guides

New Words and Expressions

feature	/'fiːtʃə/	n.	特征,特点
tempo	/'tempəu/	n.	(音乐)速度、拍子
particular	/pə'tikjulə/	adj.	特别的,独特的
aesthetic	/iːs'θetik/	adj.	美学的,审美的
integrate	/'intigreit/	v.	使成整体,使一体化
dynamic	/dai'næmik/	adj.	动力的,动态的
versus	/'vəːsəs/	prep.	对(指诉讼、比赛等中),与……相对
static	/'stætik/	adj.	静态的,静力的
striking	/'straikiŋ/	adj.	显著的,惊人的

Proper Nouns

sightseeing tempo	观赏节奏	dynamic sightseeing	动态游览
static sightseeing	静态游览		

Listening

Direction: Listen to the passages carefully and fill in the blanks with the missing information you have heard from the tapes.

1. **What is a sightseeing tempo? How does a guide command the tempo?** 何为观赏节奏?怎样掌握观赏节奏?

    (1) The tempo should vary according to the contents of sightseeing, the particular (A) _____ _____ of the group members such as their age, physical condition, and aesthetic standard and the specific time and place.

    (2) The guide should arrange for tourists to rest occasionally and slow down or quicken the (B) _____ according to the specific situation, integrating the tour guiding with their sightseeing needs.

2. **What are some common guiding techniques that a guide may adopt while taking tourists around to appreciate natural beauty?** 导游员引导客人观赏美景的常用方法有哪些？

(1) Dynamic sightseeing versus static sightseeing:

- Dynamic sightseeing: enjoying scenery en route while traveling, so that tourists experience the (C) _____ sightseeing.
- Static sightseeing: stopping at the site for a while to view the scenes attentively so as to create a striking and long lasting impression.

(2) The guide should take tourists to view the scenes from the best (D) _____ and distance, and at the best location.

(3) The guide should advise tourists of the best time to appreciate the scenes.

New Words and Expressions

initiate	/iˈniʃieit/	v.	开始,发动
entertainment	/entəˈteinmənt/	n.	款待,娱乐
promote	/prəˈməut/	v.	促进,发扬
obscene	/ɔbˈsiːn/	adj.	淫秽的,猥亵的
superstitious	/ˌsjuːpəˈstiʃəs/	adj.	迷信的
discrimination	/disˌkrimiˈneiʃən/	n.	歧视
insight	/ˈinsait/	n.	洞察力,见识

Readings

Direction: Read the following passage aloud and fill in the blanks with words or phrases you think appropriate.

jokes	destination	chatting	sightseeing	itinerary
travelogue	delay	insight	superstitious	guidebook

1. **What contents should be included in the on-the-way introduction? What should a guide refrain from doing?** 途中导游包括哪些主要内容？应该注意什么禁忌？

The guiding en route should include the following:

(1) Inform tourists of the (A) _____ of the day;

(2) Introduce the local customs and scenery along the way;

(3) Give the group a brief introduction of the tourist (B) _____;

(4) Initiate entertainment activities to promote friendship among the tourists.

(5) Do not talk about something obscene or (C) _____;

(6) Do not talk about something that shows the ethnic discrimination against the religions, customs and living habits of the minorities.

2. Upon arrival at the scenic area, what should a local guide tell tourists? May a local guide request the commentator to introduce the tourist site?　May a guide recommend that tourists go sightseeing themselves?　地陪率团到达景区后,应首先交代哪些注意事项? 导游员可否自己不讲解而请景点讲解员进行讲解? 能否请游客自行游览?

(1) The guide should tell tourists of the immediate itinerary, including the time and place of departure to avoid any (D) _____ .

(2) At the tourist site, the guide or the site commentator may present the commentary.

(3) The local guide must remain with the tour group and may not dismiss the tourists and let them go (E) _____ on their own.

3. On the way back from the scenic area, what additional introductions should a local guide make?　游览返程中,地陪应该增加哪些讲解工作?

(1) The local guide should sum up the sightseeing activities on the way home in order to promote the friendship among the tourists.

(2) He may make an additional introduction of some places of interest and provide an (F) _____ _____ to some of the major historical interests so that impress the tourists more.

Quickies

1. True or False:

A local guide should provide the following service on the way to the scenic area:

(1) _____ Inform tourists of the travel schedule of the day and next day;

(2) _____ Introduce the local customs and landscape along the way;

(3) _____ Make some jokes or talk about something obscene to arouse tourists' interest;

(4) _____ Have some entertainment activities to promote friendship among the tourists.

2. Discussion: The South African tourists have enjoyed the cruise on the Dongting Lake. On the way back to the hotel the tourists are tired and fall asleep. Mr. Ma Dacha, the local guide makes some practical jokes in order to wake them up. What do you think of his guiding service?

PART II Situational Dialogue

New Words and Expressions

phoenix	/'fi:niks/	n.	凤凰,长生鸟
mythical	/'miθikəl/	adj.	神话的,虚构的
omen	/'əumen/	n.	预兆,征兆
longevity	/lɔn'dʒevəti/	n.	长命,寿命

hover	/'hɔvə/	v.	盘旋
elegance	/'eligəns/	n.	高雅,典雅
primitive	/'primitiv/	adj.	原始的,远古的
dominate	/'dɔmineit/	v.	支配,占优势
stilt	/stilt/	n.	高跷,支柱,脚柱
harmony	/'hɑːməni/	n.	协调,融洽
pastoral	/'pɑːstərəl/	adj.	牧人的,田园生活的

Proper Nouns

Phoenix Town	凤凰镇	Tuojiang River	沱江

Dialogue 1

Phoenix Town (I)

Mr. Tian Li is taking tourists around the Phoenix Town, a small ancient town in Hunan Province. All of the tourists are fascinated by the beautiful landscape.

(A=Mr. Tian Li; B=Mary)

A: Now, we've arrived at Feng Huang Cheng. "Feng Huang" is Chinese for "Phoenix," and "Cheng" is Chinese for "Town."

B: I know Phoenix is the mythical bird of good omen and longevity. She died in the fire and was re-born again from the flames. But why is the town called Phoenix Town?

A: Phoenix Town is so called because legend has it that two phoenixes found the town so beautiful that they hovered there, and didn't leave.

B: I don't think a legend can attract so many tourists to travel here. There must be something special.

A: You're right. When you enter the town you will be impressed by its air of mystery, elegance and primitive simplicity. At the first glance, you will see a world that is dominated by the green colour.

B: What you said is no exaggeration. I see the mountain slopes are covered with green vegetation, the fields are green and even the river reflects the greenery.

A: Look over there, the bridges over the water and the houses built on stilts display a harmony that you could find only in traditional Chinese paintings.

B: What a marvelous landscape! I think the

landscape itself is a classic Chinese painting.

A: This is particularly true when mist rolls in the scene early in the morning or after rain.

B: Look, what are the people doing there?

A: Women are washing their clothes and men are fishing with their nets. It is a common scene you would see in the phoenix Town.

B: But it smells wonderful! Is somebody cooking over there?

A: Yeah, the local people are cooking their food on the bank in much the same way as they have had for hundreds years. Meanwhile, they are watching the splendid waterscape of the Tuojiang River.

B: They live such a pastoral life. I wish I could live here for several days.

A: Sure.

(to be continued)

Exercises

Do the dialogue again and pay attention to your facial expressions and body language.

New Words and Expressions

alley	/ˈæli/	*n.*	小路,巷
gabled	/ˈgeibld/	*adj.*	有山形墙的,有人形墙的
hustle	/ˈhʌsl/	*n.*	挤,推,拥挤喧嚷
bustle	/ˈbʌsl/	*n.*	喧闹,嘈杂的活动
pleat	/pliːt/	*v.*	使……打褶
tie-dye		*n.*	扎染
batik	/ˈbætik/	*n.*	蜡染

Proper Nouns

Huangsiqiao Castle	黄丝桥古城	Qiliang Cave	奇梁洞
Southern Great Wall	南方长城	Shen Congwen	沈从文

Dialogue 2

Phoenix Town (II)

Tourists are walking along the alleys of the Phoenix Town. They are carried away by the unique high gabled wooden houses built on stilts.

(A=Mr. Tian Li; B=Mary)

A: Phoenix Town is a wonderful example of what villages were like hundreds of years ago. When you walk along the alleys you will feel as if you were far away from hustle and bustle of the world.

B: Oh, yeah, I see the typical high gabled wooden houses built on stilts along the banks of the Tuojiang River. I think the wooden folk houses are typical of the phonenix Town.

A: But Phoenix Town is not only famous for its natural beauty, but also for its historical interests. The ancient town has a history of more than 1300 years.

B: Are there any some places of historical interests? I'd like to visit some historical places in the town.

A: Well, according to the travel schedule, we'll visit the Huangsiqiao Castle, Qiliang Cave, the Southern Great Wall, and the tomb of Shen Congwen.

B: Wonderful! Look over there, I see some of the women wear elegant clothes with white scarves. Who are they?

A: They are Miao girls. Most of the residents here are the Miao ethnic minority. A visit to Miao village is a must when you come to the Phoenix Town.

B: How pretty the Miao girls are! I love their pleated skirts very much.

A: The home made tie-dyes, printed and batik cloths are their local specialities. If you love them you may buy some.

B: I'd like to, but I love their silver jewellery more. The hand-made items of silver ornaments are very good souvenirs.

A: I couldn't agree with you less. Now, it is the time for our lunch. Shall we have our lunch in the Miao restaurant?

B: Of course. I am terribly hungry. I'd like to take some local food. You know, eating food is just like eating culture.

A: That's right. Just now, you smell some wonderful food. In fact, they are pickled red peppers. Wonderful! Their smell flows from many small family-run restaurants here.

B: My mouth is watering. I think travel in such a picturesque region will be remembered as an experience of a lifetime.

A: Certainly.

(the end)

Cultural Notes

Phoenix Town 凤凰镇:凤凰镇位于湖南西部,风景秀丽,历史悠久,名胜古迹甚多。这里是"黔楚咽喉",战略地位重要,一直是边陲重镇。凤凰古镇庙宇祠堂众多,大部分集中于古城内。所以古城又有"辉煌的殿堂"之称。古镇建筑设计精美,斗拱飞檐、塑龙雕凤、金漆彩绘。古城一带妩媚青山,半座雅典城池,人文自然风光欣赏不尽。凤凰古镇分为古城景区、南华山景区、奇梁洞景区和黄丝桥古城景区。香炉山古苗寨是凤凰周边最具代表的生苗苗寨之一,圣山、仙池、古树、怪石、奇洞、苗族风情筑了一幅世外桃源般的画卷,可谓山清水秀,人杰地灵,让人流连忘返。

Exercises

Imagine that you are a local guide and your classmates are tourists. Make up a situational dialogue about the Phoenix Town.

PART III *Ethnic Culture*

New Words and Expressions

disaster	/dɪˈzɑːstə/	*n.*	灾难,灾祸
devil	/ˈdevl/	*n.*	魔鬼,恶棍
ancestor	/ˈænsɪstə/	*n.*	祖先,祖宗
sacrifice	/ˈsækrɪfaɪs/	*n.*	祭品,供奉
glutinous	/ˈgluːtɪnəs/	*adj.*	黏性的
rapeseed	/ˈreɪpsiːd/	*n.*	油菜子
edible	/ˈedɪbl/	*adj.*	可食用的
spin	/spɪn/	*v.*	纺,纺纱
bleach	/bliːtʃ/	*v.*	漂白,变白
apron	/ˈeɪprən/	*n.*	围裙
necklace	/ˈneklɪs/	*n.*	项链
bracelet	/ˈbreɪslɪt/	*n.*	手镯
adornment	/əˈdɔːnmənt/	*n.*	装饰,装饰品

Proper Nouns

Youcha (Oiled Tea)　　　油茶　　　　Baizhequn　　　百褶裙

Miao Culture

The Miao ethnic minority has a history of about 5,000 years according to the historical record. They believe that everything in nature has a spirit. Every time there are disasters, they will invite a wizard to perform ceremonies designed to drive out the devil ghost. They worship their ancestors so much that memorial ceremonies are very grand. Sacrifices such as wine, meat, and glutinous rice are costly.

For the three meals of the Miao people, they prefer cooked rice and pickled vegetables. They raise domestic animals and fowl, and are fond of eating dog meat, a saying for it that "A dog for the Miao people is just like the wine for the Yi people." Tea seed oil and rapeseed oil are the main edible oil for them as well as the animal oil. The hot pepper is a most important favorite for the Miao people. There is another saying that "without pepper there would be no dishes." Besides pickled vegetables, the soured soup—one favorite drink of the Miao people—is prepared for in every household. The Youcha (Oiled Tea) is also the common daily drink.

The skirt of the Miao girl is called Baizhequn—a pleated skirt. In fact, there may be 500-odd pleats on only one skirt. The skirt of the Miao girl has many layers, some with even up to 30 or 40 layers on one skirt. The skirts, from spinning and weaving, dying and bleaching, sewing and making, to the last procedure of pattern drawing and embroidering, would be all completed independently by the Miao girls themselves. In addition, they also embroider their flower waist-belts and their flower aprons, etc.

The Miao girls are born beauties, fond of wearing the silver ornaments. In their best holiday the Miao girls wear several necklaces with different sizes around their necks, mostly interlinked up with pretty silver pieces (on which flower patterns made). The Miao girls also wear the silver lock and the silver collar weight in front of the chest, while the silver cloak with many pretty silver-bell weights hangs on the back. The earrings and bracelets are all made of silver. The splendid dress and adornments of the Miao girls may weigh up to several kilograms; some may be handed down from generation to generation.

Quickies

True or False:

1. _____ The Miao people love the hot pepper, pickled vegetables and soured soup, but dislike the dog meat.

2. _____ The skirt of the Miao girl has many layers, some with even up to 30 or 40 layers on one skirt with embroidered flower waist-belts and flower aprons.

3. _____ The Miao girls wear several necklaces and locks around their necks, mostly interlinked up with pretty silver pieces on which flower patterns made.

PART IV *Practical Writing for Tourism*

Travel Contract 旅游合同

A Travel Contract

Contract No._____

China Pearl Travel Agency (hereinafter called Travel Agency) and David Smith (hereinafter called Tourist) have on this 10th day of September 2008 entered into a tour contract under the terms and conditions stated below:

1. Name of tour group

Tourist will join in the 18-day China Discovery Tour (Tour Code _____) organized by Travel Agency. Cities to visit include Beijing, Xi'an, Chengdu, Kunming, Guilin, Guangzhou, Hong Kong. Travel Agency shall provide luxury tour group services to Tourist.

2. Time of departure: October 10, 2008

3. Price: US $2500/p.p

4. The tour fare includes

(1) Accommodations

Travel Agency shall provide Tourist with four-star hotels in the capital cities of provinces in China. Rooms have an attached private bath and air conditioning, as well as a telephone capable of international direct dialing and a television. In smaller towns or rural areas, Travel Agency shall provide simple guesthouses. When the hotel listed in the brochure is not available, the same category hotel will be substituted. Accommodations will be based on double occupancy. If Tourist requests a single room, Tourist shall pay the additional expense.

(2) Meals

Travel Agency shall provide daily meals (breakfast, lunch and dinner) in hotels, local restaurants, except for the one specified differently in itinerary and on plane/train. There will be a mix of Western and Chinese meals. Vegetarian food is available upon request.

(3) Admissions / Entrance Fee

Travel Agency shall proceed with all necessary main entrance fees for the programs or places mentioned in the itinerary.

(4) Transportation

Travel Agency shall proceed with domestic air/train tickets specified in the itinerary and domestic airport taxes (local construction fee). Travel Agency shall provide Tourist with transfer service and coach for overland transportation.

(5) Guide Service

Travel Agency shall provide Tourist with the service of a bilingual national guide as well as local guides.

(6) Travel Protection Insurance

Full coverage of your vacation travel with our protection insurance plan will be provided at no additional cost.

(7) Others

Music and dance performances and other cultural events described in the itineraries will be included in the tour price.

5. The tour fare excludes:

(1) Airfare from Tourist's hometown to the gateway city.

(2) Personal expenses.

Tourist shall pay for the single supplement cost for a single room, meals not mentioned in the brochure, extra beverages at meals, food or snacks at times other than regular meal times, excess luggage fees, laundry, postage, telephone, fax or Internet/E-mail access charges as well as shopping.

(3) Visa costs.

Tourist shall pay US $50 for obtaining an individual entry visa to China.

(4) Supplementary trips and services not mentioned;

(5) The extra cost due to the unforeseen events.

6. Terms of Payment

Tourist shall make the full payment upon confirmation of the reservation, 30 days prior to the departure date. The payment shall be remitted to Travel Agency in US Dollars. Travel Agency may cancel the reservation and not return the deposit.

7. Health

(1) Travel Agency shall ensure that Tourist is provided with hygiene food and accommodation.

(2) Tourist shall determine whether his physical condition is suited for the tour. Tourist shall be responsible for the cost of any medicines or medical care he may require during the trip for any reason.

(3) Travel Agency reserves the right to decline to accept or retain Tourist as a member of the tour, if Tourist's physical condition, mental well-being or behavior interferes with the operation of the tour. There will be no refund in such cases.

8. Baggage

Baggage is at Tourist's risk throughout. Baggage allowance for transpacific flight is two pieces per person for checked baggage with combined total dimension not exceeding 106 inches provided neither one exceeds 62 inches nor 70 lbs. Baggage allowance in China is restricted to one piece only and not to exceed 44 lb. Carry-on baggage is limited to one piece with combined total dimension not exceeding 45 inches. Tourist will pay the excess baggage charge and insurance.

9. Responsibility

(1) Travel Agency acts only in the capacity of an agent for purveyors of transportation, sightseeing and hotel accommodation. All coupons, receipts and tickets issued by Travel Agency are subject to the terms and conditions stipulated by the suppliers. Travel Agency shall be exempt from any liability for loss or damage to property, injury of persons, accidents, delays, irregularities or other occurrences beyond its control.

(2) Should weather or other unforeseen circumstances cause a delay in transportation before the tour departure, Travel Agency may reserve the right to postpone or cancel the tour, and any loss or additional expenses incurred shall be borne by Tourist. Travel Agency reserves the right to rearrange the itinerary and to substitute or delete activities from the schedule if this becomes necessary due to local conditions. If this happens, the tour prices are subject to change. Any additional expenses incurred shall be charged to Tourist.

(3) Tourist shall strictly abide by the laws and regulations promulgated by the governments of the countries visited. Tourist shall be responsible for any and all penalties due to any regulations of the governments of the countries visited.

10. Cancellation & Refund Policy

In the event of cancellation by consumer after confirmation of the booking, the deposit is non-refundable and non-transferable.

After payment is made, refunds will be made as follows:

Cancellation Refund

More than 30 days prior to departure	100% of tour cost
30—10 days prior to departure	90% of tour cost
10—2 days prior to departure	50% of tour cost
Less than two days before departure	No refund

(1) Written notice of cancellation must be received by the Travel Agency either by mail or fax. Oral cancellation by phone will not be acceptable.

(2) In addition to the above stated cancellation charges, if airline tickets have already been issued at the time of cancellation (regardless of number of days prior to departure), the consumer will be assessed an additional airline cancellation penalty and service charge pursuant to the airlines rules and regulations.

(3) When a participant cannot complete the tour for any reason, the unused portion of the tour is nonrefundable.   No refund will be made to those participants who have failed to secure valid travel documents such as passport or visas.

11. Complaints and Arbitration

(1) If Tourist has any complaints during the tour, Tourist may inform the local guide or the local representative specified by Travel Agency. Failure to promptly notify Travel Agency of the complaint may reduce or eliminate any compensation that may be payable. In case that a satisfactory remedy is not achieved, Tourist may submit a written complaint to Travel Agency within thirty days from the end of the tour. Complaints received by Travel Agency will be acted upon promptly and fairly within the terms of these conditions.

(2) All disputes arising in connection with this contract or any modification or extension thereof, should be settled amicably through negotiations. In case no settlement can be reached, the case in dispute shall then be submitted for arbitration in Chinese Arbitration Association in Beijing, China.

12. Validity

This agreement is valid from October 10, 2008 to October 28, 2008 and effective upon signed by the two parties.

13. Original Text

This contract is written in English, in two originals, one for each party.

China Pearl Travel Agency   Tourist

Zhang Ming   David Smith
Manager of Overseas Department

Unit 8 Tourists' Mind-Sets

游客心理

PART I *ABC for Tour Guides*

New Words and Expressions

trivial	/'triviəl/	*adj.*	琐细的,微不足道的
undisciplined	/ʌn'disiplind/	*adj.*	无修养的,任性的
curiosity	/ˌkjuəri'ɔsiti/	*n.*	好奇心
diminish	/di'miniʃ/	*v.*	(使)减少,(使)变小
reiterate	/riː'itəreit/	*v.*	反复地说,重做
assembly	/ə'sembli/	*n.*	集合,集会
punctual	/'pʌŋktjuəl/	*adj.*	准时的

Listening

Direction: Listen to the passages carefully and fill in the blanks with the missing information you have heard from the tapes.

1. **What changes of mood might tourists experience at the first stage of travel? What kind of specific service can a guide provide?** 在旅游活动的初期,游客会有什么样的心理变化？导游员应该提供哪些针对性服务？

(1) Being unfamiliar with the surroundings in which they are traveling, tourists acquire travel (A) _____ . At this time, the guide should try to win their trust through answering their questions and handling any problem, however trivial.

(2) At this stage tourists are always (B) _____ and excited about new things. Therefore, the local guide should provide as much information as possible and answer all the questions patiently, even though some questions may seem silly.

2. How may the tourists' mentality change in the later stages of traveling? What services can a guide provide? 在旅游活动中后期，游客会有什么样的心理变化？导游员应该提供哪些服务？

(1) As time goes by, tourists become quite familiar with each other and with the guide. At such a time, they may become (C) _____ and unruly.

(2) As their curiosity diminishes, tourists may become bored and critical of the guide's service.

(3) At this stage, the guide should arrange the travel activities more carefully and make the introduction of the sites more (D) _____ and wonderful.

(4) The guide should always reiterate the departure time, the sites en route and the place and time for assembly, and remind tourists to be punctual.

New Words and Expressions

introvert	/ˌintrəu'vəːt/	n.	性格内向的人
roundabout	/'raundəbaut/	adj.	迂回的,转弯抹角的
cautious	/'kɔːʃəs/	adj.	谨慎的,小心的
socialize	/'səuʃəlaiz/	v.	合群,社交

Readings

*Direction: **Read the following passage aloud and fill in the blanks with words or phrases you think appropriate.***

shopping	mental	roundabout	talkative
expectations	upset	explore	quite
entertainments	changeable		

What factors affect the tourists' mind-set and how can a guide understand these in order to provide a specific service? 导游员应学会从哪些方面了解游客的心态以提供针对性服务？

(1) Determine their (A) _____ and needs according to their nationality, occupation, age, gender and social status.

(2) Easterners are usually introverts and express their opinions in a (B) _____ manner while westerners are usually straightforward and express their opinions directly, expecting a direct reply.

(3) Tourists who receive good education are usually cautious and expect guiding services delivered tastefully. Ordinary tourists would like to have more (C) _____.

(4) Elderly tourists prefer socializing and chattering with the guide while younger tourists are curious about new things and prefer to (D) _____ what is around them.

(5) Female tourists, especially married, middle-aged women, prefer story-like introductions and are interested in (E) _____, while male tourists are interested in sports and current affairs.

Quickies

1. True or False:

(1) _____ All the tourists are straightforward and express their opinions directly, expecting a direct reply.

(2) _____ At the very beginning tourists want to acquire a sense of security. At this time, a local guide should try to answer their questions, however trival they are.

(3) _____ As time goes by, tourists know each other well. At such a time, the guide should let them travel freely because they will not get lost.

(4) _____ Westerners are usually straightforward and express their opinions directly but they like the introduction in a roundabout way.

2. Role-play: Mary is an old woman and Jack is a college student. They have visited several places of interests in Suzhou and become critical of your introduction. How can you provide the individualized service for them?

PART II *Method of Introduction*

New Words and Expressions

quotation	/kwəu'teiʃən/	n.	引用语
proverb	/'prɔvə(ː)b/	n.	谚语
motto	/'mɔtəu/	n.	座右铭,格言
slang	/slæŋ/	n.	俚语,行话
anecdote	/'ænikdəut/	n.	轶事,奇闻
celebrity	/si'lebriti/	n.	名声,名人
conciseness	/kən'saisnis/	n.	简明;切除
comprehensive	/ˌkɔmpri'hensiv/	adj.	全面的,广泛的
couplet	/kʌplit/	n.	对句,对联
diplomatic	/ˌdiplə'mætik/	adj.	外交的;老练的
compose	/kəm'pəuz/	v.	写作
oriole	/'ɔːriəul/	n.	金黄鹂,白头翁科的小鸟
chirp	/tʃəːp/	v.	叽喳而鸣,尖声地说
willow	/'wiləu/	n.	柳树,柳木制品
heron	/'herən/	n.	苍鹭

flutter	/'flʌtə/	v.	鼓翼,拍(翅)
anchor	/'æŋkə/	v.	抛锚,锚定
abode	/ə'bəud/	n.	住所,住处

Proper Nouns

Du Fu's Thatched Cottage	杜甫草堂	Wanli Bridge	万里桥
Nanmen Bridge (Southern Gate Bridge)	南门大桥	Zhuge Liang	诸葛亮
		Prime Minister	丞相
Shu Kingdom	蜀国	Fei Yi	费祎
Wu Kingdom	吴国	Baihua Pond	百花潭
Longzhua Weir	龙爪堰	Huanhua Brook	浣花溪
Snow-capped Xiling Mountain	西岭雪山	Dongwu	东吴

The Method of Introduction with Quotations
引用法

This method is used to give an account of a tourist site by quoting proverbs, mottos, slangs, anecdotes, legends, folk tales or remarks of celebrities, so as to acquire the effect of vividness, conciseness and comprehensiveness in his introduction. For example, to indicate the location of Du Fu's Thatched Cottage, the tour guide could quote a well-known couplet:

To the west of Wanli Bridge and to the north of Baihua Pond.

It indicates the location of the Du Fu's Thatched Cottage. Wanli Bridge, the present Nanmen Bridge (Southern Gate Bridge) is where Zhuge Liang, the Prime Minister of the Shu Kingdom, sent Fei Yi off to the Wu Kingdom on a diplomatic mission. At thought of the long journey that Fei Yi would take, Zhuge Liang said with a sigh, "A thousand miles' journey begins with the first step." That is the origin of the name of the bridge. Baihua Pond refers to the place now named Longzhua Weir on the upper level of Huanhua Brook.

The guide may also introduce the surroundings of the Du Fu's Thatched Cottage by quoting the poem composed by Du Fu himself so as to arouse tourists' interest, for an example:

Two yellow orioles chirp amid the green willows,

White herons flutter in the blue sky in a row.

The eternal snow of Mount Xiling shines through my window,

And the boats from Dongwu anchor outside my abode.

Questions

1. What can a guide quote when he introduces the site using the method of introduction with quotations?

2. What effects can a guide achieve when he introduces the sites using above method?

3. Write down or point out the quotations in the commentary of Du Fu's Thatched Cottage.

(1) _____

(2) _____

(3) _____

PART III *Tourist Site*

New Words and Expressions

humble	/'hʌmbl/	*adj.*	卑下的,微贱的
horizontal	/ˌhɔri'zɔntl/	*adj.*	水平的
appoint	/ə'pɔint/	*v.*	任命,委任
setback	/'setbæk/	*n.*	顿挫,挫折
abbreviation	/əˌbriːvi'eiʃən/	*n.*	缩写,缩写词
candidate	/'kændidit/	*n.*	候选人,投考者
custody	/'kʌstədi/	*n.*	关押,保管
deride	/di'raid/	*v.*	嘲弄,嘲笑
cord	/kɔːd/	*n.*	缨,绳,索
turbid	/'təːbid/	*adj.*	混浊的,脏的
imply	/im'plai/	*v.*	暗示,意味
corruption	/kə'rʌpʃən/	*n.*	腐败,堕落
fatuous	/'fætjuəs/	*adj.*	愚昧的,昏庸的
seclusion	/si'kluːʒən/	*n.*	隐居,隔离
spacious	/'speiʃəs/	*adj.*	广大的,大规模的

Proper Nouns

Zhuozhengyuan Garden (Humble Administrator's Garden)	拙政园
Wang Xianchen	王献臣
Ming Dynasty	明代
Pan Yue	潘岳
West Jin Dynasty	西晋
Dong Chang	东厂(明官署名,负责侦缉、抓捕嫌疑人。)
Wen Zhengming	文征明
Lesser Canglang	小沧浪

Zhuozhengyuan Garden (Humble Administrator's Garden)

Now, we can see on the horizontal board in the upper part of the brick wall the three gilded characters "Zhuo Zheng Yuan," which means "Humble Administrator's Garden." The Garden was built in 1509, the fourth year of the reign of Zhengde of the Ming Dynasty by a retired official Wang Xianchen. He had once been appointed as minister-level official, and went back to his hometown Suzhou because of the setback in his official career. And the name was an abbreviation from a sentence written by Pan Yue in the West Jin Dynasty.

Wang Xianchen was one of the successful candidates in the highest imperial exams in 1493 and promoted to a higher position later, but his career was not satisfying all the time. He had been taken into custody by Dong Chang (an investigation department for the emperor in Ming Dynasty), and put in jail. He said to Wen Zhengming, "In the past Pan Yue was not successful in his official career, so he put up a cottage and planted many trees and vegetables, taking watering them as his daily work. He derided himself and said, "That is the office work of a humble administrator. I, a retired old man, couldn't do things in politics even as well as Pan Yue, so I decide to go back home to build a garden." That is the reason for his giving the garden such a name. The name of the garden reflected his feelings exactly at that time.

As we walk southward along the corridor, we come to the Lesser Canglang. The name Lesser Canglang comes from the poem "The Fisherman" in *The Verse of Chu*. It said, "When the water of Canglang is limpid, I could wash my hat cords with it; When the water of Canglang is turbid, I could wash my twain feet with it." This implies that "If the government is free from corruption, I would be going to assist the ruler; if the government is fatuous, I would live in seclusion." It is a three-room spacious hall, surrounded by water on two sides. When you stand in the front and look northward, we can see the reflection of Xiao Feihong in the water like a rainbow. This is the best place to see the waterside scenery.

Cultural Notes

Zhuozhengyuan Garden 拙政园：拙政园与北京颐和园、承德避暑山庄、苏州留园并称为我国四大古典名园。拙政园初为唐代诗人陆龟蒙的住宅，后为明代监察御史王献臣归隐之地，取"拙者之为政"的语意而名，曾为太平天国忠王府的一部分，现为全国重点文物保护单位。拙政园全园分东、中、西、住宅四部分，是我国江南园林的代表。古代园艺家通过各种艺术手法，独具匠心地创造出丰富多样的景致。在园中行游，或见"庭院深深深几许"，或见"柳暗花明又一村"，或见小桥流水、粉墙黛瓦，或见曲径通幽、峰回路转，或是步移景易、变幻无穷。

Questions

1. True or False:

(1) _____ Humble Administrator's Garden was built by and for a humble official because he retired and lived in seclusion.

(2) _____ Wang Xianchen was a dignified and upright official who disliked politics and watered the trees and plants in the garden as his daily work.

(3) _____ "When the water of Canglang is turbid, I could wash my twain feet with it." This implies that the writer would assist the government.

2. Read the passage aloud and introduce the Zhuozhengyuan Garden using the method of introduction you have learnt. The method of introduction with quotations is one of the choices.

Tips

- Draft your own commentary before you make your presentation.
- Speak colloquial English and use simple and short sentences.
- Animate your introduction with facial expressions and body language.
- Apply at least one method of introduction. It is highly recommended that you use two or three methods of introduction.

PART IV *Simulated Introduction*

New Words and Expressions

demote	/di'məut/	v.	使降级,使降职
bureaucratic	/ˌbjuərəu'krætik/	adj.	官僚政治的
emphasize	/'emfəsaiz/	v.	强调,着重
weeping	/'wiːpiŋ/	adj.	垂枝的
incredible	/in'kredəbl/	adj.	难以置信的
exquisite	/'ekskwizit/	adj.	优美的,高雅的,精致的
virgin	/'vəːdʒin/	adj.	原始的,未采伐过的
lattice	/'lætis/	n.	格子
intricate	/'intrikit/	adj.	复杂的,错综的
enhance	/in'hɑːns/	v.	提高,增强
rockery	/'rɔkəri/	n.	假山,假山庭园
rubbing	/'rʌbiŋ/	n.	拓片
majestic	/mə'dʒestik/	adj.	宏伟的,庄严的
eaves	/'iːvz/	n.	屋檐

69

Proper Nouns

Canglang Pavilion	沧浪亭
Northern Song Dynasty	北宋
Su Shunqing	苏舜钦
Canglang Weng	沧浪翁
Facing Water Veranda	面水轩
Fishing Terrace	观鱼处(钓鱼台)
Mingdao Hall	明道堂
Astronomic Picture	天文图
Geographic Picture	宋舆图
Pingjiang Prefecture Picture	宋平江图(苏州城市图)
Mountain-Watching Building	看山楼

Canglang Pavilion

Ladies and gentlemen, Canglang Pavilion is located in the southern part of Suzhou. It is one of the four most famous gardens of the city. Canglang Pavilion is the oldest of the Suzhou gardens that can be traced back to the Northern Song Dynasty. During that time, a scholar Su Shunqing was demoted and sent to Suzhou. He bought the garden, built the pavilion near the water and then lived there far away from the bureaucratic life. The Garden was then named Canglang Pavilion in honor of his namesake, Canglang Weng.

Unlike other gardens, Canglang Pavilion emphasizes the harmony between man made buildings and the natural environment. Before you enter the garden, you can see a green water pool that is surrounded by weeping willows. In the garden you will see incredible man-made rock formations that are divided into two parts. On the eastern side, the earth has been mixed with natural yellow stones in such a manner that it looks like a natural hill. On the western side, exquisite stones from the lake have been used to create another naturally appearing hill.

Everybody, we're walking along the winding corridor. The corridor was built with pavilions that link the hills and pools together. As you walk along the corridor you are walking through the unique stone formations with planted ancient trees. It looks as if you were walking in a virgin forest. On the walls of the corridor, there are 108 lattice windows of various designs. You can enjoy the beauty of the pool outside, and watch the hill in the center of the garden through the windows. The intricate patterns of the windows are interesting and, to some extent, enhance the beauty of the corridor.

Here we come to the Facing Water Veranda. It is a four-sided hall beside the water. After a long walk I think you probably are very tired,　so I suggest you sit and drink a cup of tea here while enjoying the quiet and beautiful surroundings of the garden. Now, we come to the eastern end of the corridor. In front of us is a square pavilion which sits on a stone beside the pool. It is called Fishing Terrace. It is a perfect place to sit and watch different kinds of fish swimming in the pool.

Now we leave the corridor and climb up the man made rockery along a gently winding path. Look over there, a square Canglang Pavilion stand among a sea of green trees. The beams of the pavilion are carved with intricate patterns of fairy children,　flowers,　birds and animals.　From inside the pavilion, you can see the beauty of the whole garden.

Here is the Mingdao Hall.　It is the main building in the garden.　In the hall are three rooms that were once used as a place for ancient scholars to study. There are also rubbings of three stone tablets including the Astronomic Picture, Geographic Picture and Pingjiang Prefecture Picture which are the priceless treasures of Suzhou. In a setting of age old trees, the hall looks very solemn and respectful.

Ladies and gentlemen,　a two-storey building called Mountain-Watching Building stands majestically in the southern corner of the garden.　The building has flying eaves and turned up corners. It is one of the most exquisite buildings in the garden. From inside this building, you can see the mountains around the garden as well as the beauty of the entire garden.

Just have a short rest. After fifteen minutes I'll take you to visit this beautiful building.

Have fun!

Cultural Notes

Canglang Pavilion 沧浪亭:沧浪亭位于苏州市城南三元坊附近,是苏州历史最悠久、文化内涵最深,同时也是唯一以"亭"名的园林。北宋庆历五年(1045),苏舜钦蒙冤遭贬,流寓到苏州,见五代孙承佑的废园便以四万钱购得。苏舜钦遭贬后便自号沧浪翁,吟唱着"沧浪之水清兮,可以濯我缨;沧浪之水浊兮,可以浊我足"的渔夫歌,在城市中过起了隐逸山水、逍遥自乐的生活。沧浪亭整个园林以水包围,未入园林先见园景,一弯清流围绕,在城市之中独拥山林之美。廊壁上的漏窗无一雷同,被称作沧浪亭一绝。

Exercises

Make a simulated introduction of the Canglang Pavilion using the method of introduction you have learnt. Pay attention to the body language and other tips of introduction.

Unit 9 Recreation
娱乐活动

PART I ABC for Tour Guides

New Words and Expressions

refund	/riːˈfʌnd/	n.	归还, 退款
implement	/ˈimplimənt/	v.	贯彻, 执行

Proper Nouns

Beijing Opera   京剧

Listening

Direction: Listen to the passages carefully and fill in the blanks with the missing information you have heard from the tapes.

1. **What should a guide do if a tourist is unwilling to attend the entertainment program in the travel schedule?** 游客不愿观看计划内的文娱节目, 导游员如何处理?

   (1) The guide should inform the tourist that it may be impossible to obtain a (A) _____ for the reserved ticket;

   (2) If the tourist wishes to attend any other (B) _____ not specified in the travel schedule he does so at his own expense.

2. **The tour group is scheduled to watch the Beijing Opera in the evening, but some tourists would rather attend an international football game. What is the guide expected to do?** 团队原定晚上看京剧, 但部分年轻游客想看国际足球比赛, 导游员如何处理?

   (1) The guide is expected to implement the reception program.

   (2) The tourists who wish to watch the football game should be informed that it may be impossible to obtain a refund for the opera (C) _____ and that they are expected to make their own arrangements and bear the (D) _____ for attending the game.

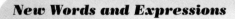

New Words and Expressions

recommend	/ˌrekə'mend/	v.	推荐，介绍
deny	/di'nai/	v.	否认，拒绝

Readings

Direction: Read the following passage aloud and fill in the blanks with words or phrases you think appropriate.

cancel	curiosity	recommend	disco	departure
casino	ski	bar	karaoke	melody

Under what circumstance should a guide agree or disagree when they request to have the entertainments themselves? 游客要求单独外出娱乐，导游员在什么情况下可以同意，什么情况下不能同意？

(1) If there is enough time according to the schedule, the guide may agree to the request, help arrange transportation, and may even (A) _____ good shops.

(2) The guide should graciously deny any request that might delay the scheduled travel or (B) _____.

Quickies

Role-play: The travel service will have a bonfire party according to the travel schedule, but the Smiths would like to go shopping in a bazaar. What would you do as a local guide?

PART II *Situational Dialogue*

New Words and Expressions

fertile	/'fɜːtail/	adj.	肥沃的，富饶的
elevation	/ˌeli'veiʃən/	n.	海拔
extreme	/iks'triːm/	adj.	极端的，极度的
abundant	/ə'bʌndənt/	adj.	丰富的，充裕的
therapy	/'θerəpi/	n.	治疗
shed	/ʃed/	n.	棚，小屋
rheumatism	/'ruːmətizəm/	n.	风湿，风湿病
kebab	/kə'bɑːb/	n.	(=kabob) 烤羊肉串
characteristic	/ˌkæriktə'ristik/	n.	特性，特征

73

Proper Nouns

Turpan	吐鲁番	Xinjiang	新疆
Uigur	维吾尔人	Huo Zhou	火洲
Hometown of Grapes	葡萄之乡	Zhua Fan	抓饭

Dialogue 1

Turpan

Tourists arrive at Turpan, a fire city in Xingjiang, as well as a city with distinctive Uigur culture in China. Miss Yang gives them a general introduction of the city.

(A=Miss Yang Liu; B=Jack)

A: Turpan is an old city with a long history in Xinjiang. Turpan means "the lowest place" in the Uigur language and "the fertile land" in Turki.

B: What is the elevation of Turpan?

A: The elevation of most of the places in the area is below 500 meters. Turpan is the city with the lowest elevation in China.

B: I also heard it was called Huo Zhou, a place as hot as fire. What is the temperature?

A: It is the hottest place in China. There are 152 summer days on average, and 28 really broiling days with the temperature above 40℃.

B: It is really a fire city. I can not imagine how people could survive here.

A: Although they suffer from the extreme heat in summer people can also get some benefits from it. The abundant sunshine gives the melons and grapes ideal conditions to grow. The fruit here is widely known for its high sugar content, especially the grapes.

B: I know Turpan is praised as the Hometown of Grapes. It is a good place to enjoy the grapes of hundreds of varieties.

A: Besides, the local people love the sand therapy very much. They just lie or sit under sheds, bury their bodies in hot sand about 50℃ to 60℃. It is said it is a good way to treat rheumatism and skin disease.

B: I love this sand burying therapy. In fact, I just enjoy myself in the sand instead of curing the diseases. It is a special experience in the desert.

A: After the sand therapy you can enjoy Uygur snacks. I bet the Kebabs, Zhua Fan (Rice Eaten with Hands), Roast Lamb will make your mouth water.

B: I also want to take some souvenirs home for my girlfriend. What do you suggest?

A: The traditional handcrafts are exquisite and are worth collecting. Carpets, clothes, caps and knives are all choices. They all have distinctive folk characteristics in Xinjang.

B: Thank you, Miss Yang.

Exercises

Do the dialogue again and pay attention to the facial expressions and body language.

New Words and Expressions

minaret	/'minəret/	n.	尖塔
Islamic	/iz'læmik/	adj.	伊斯兰的,伊斯兰教的
extant	/eks'tænt/	adj.	现存的,未毁的
Moslem	/'mɔzlem/	n.	穆斯林
stele	/stiːl/	n.	石碑,石柱,匾额
inscription	/in'skripʃən/	n.	题字,碑铭
gratitude	/'grætitjuːd/	n.	感谢
defend	/di'fend/	v.	防护,辩护
unification	/ˌjuːnifi'keiʃən/	n	统一,一致
rebellion	/ri'beljən/	n.	谋反,叛乱
dome	/dəum/	n.	圆屋顶
rhombus	/'rɔmbəs/	n.	菱形,斜方形
spiral	/'spaiərəl/	v.	螺旋形上升(或下降)
ventilation	/ˌventi'leiʃən/	n.	通风,流通空气
attic	/'ætik/	n.	阁楼,顶楼
scarlet	/'skɑːlit/	adj.	鲜红的,深红的
crystal	/'kristl/	adj.	结晶状的

Proper Nouns

Emin Minaret	额敏塔(苏公塔)	Emin Khoja	额敏和卓
Allah	(伊斯兰教的)阿拉,真主	Jungar	准噶尔
Tianshan Mountain	天山	Flaming Mountain	火焰山

Dialogue 2

Emin Minaret

After they have the sand therapy in Turpan they visit the Emin Minaret. It is the largest old tower with Islamic architectural art.

(A=Miss Yang Liu; Jack)

A: This is the famous Emin Minaret. It is the largest extant old tower in Xinjiang, the only Islamic tower among the hundred famous towers in China.

B: The tower is a masterpiece of the Moslem architectural art. It is one of the best towers I have seen in China.

A: Here we are at the entrance to the minaret. Look, two steles were set up at the entrance. One stele was carved with a Uigur inscription to give thanks to Allah. Another stele was carved with a Chinese inscription to explain the purpose of the building minaret.

B: What is the inscription in Chinese?

A: First, show gratitude to the Qing Dynasty; second, commemorate achievements of Emin Khoja.

B: Who is Emin Khoja?

A: Emin Khoja is an outstanding patriot. He and his seven sons defended the unification of China during the war against Jungar rebellions.

B: I come to know why this tower got its name.

A: So much for my introduction of the history of the tower! Now, we'd like to introduce this remarkable tower. The tower is 44 meters high. From the base of the tower the minaret grows smaller up to an Islamic dome.

B: I think it is a unique architecture. The huge columns are marvelous. you see, they are made of grey bricks with 15 different patterns such as waves, flowers or rhombuses. Can we walk up the tower?

A: Of course, in the center of the minaret is a brick-piled pillar with 72 steps which spirals to the top. There are 14 openings for ventilation and lighting in different directions and at various heights.

B: The interior design is very delicate. Can we continue to walk up to the dome?

A: Follow me please! The steps are very steep. Here we come to the top. It is an attic of 10 square meters with large windows on the four sides. Here you can appreciate the marvelous landscape below.

B: Wow, how beautiful! I could look over at the silvery Tianshan Mountain and the scarlet Flaming Mountain!

A: But when you walk down and look up at the minaret again you will find how crystal blue and high the sky of Turpan is!

B: That's true!

Cultural Notes

Turpan 吐鲁番：吐鲁番突厥语意为"富庶丰饶之地"，天山山脉与塔克拉玛干沙漠之间，包含了西域风物的全部经典，是我国丝路遗址最丰富的地区，古城、石窟寺、烽燧、墓葬、岩画等达20余处，其中国家级文物单位5处，占新疆近一半，居全国第九位。吐鲁番地区是中国最低、最热、最干、最甜的地方，是极干旱地区独特自然生态环境与绿洲文明的典型代表，有艾丁湖、葡萄沟、火焰山、坎儿井、魔鬼城、库姆塔格沙漠等众多独有的自然景观。吐鲁番也是维吾尔民族文化的两大中心之一，民居、服饰、音乐、舞蹈、宗教和生活习俗等独具魅力。

Emin Minaret 额敏塔：额敏塔全称为额敏和卓报恩塔，又称苏公塔，当地维吾尔群众称之为吐鲁番塔，高高耸立于吐鲁番市区以东2公里处。额敏塔建于清乾隆四十三年(1778年)，是新疆现存最大古塔，也是全国伊斯兰建筑风格的唯一古塔。整个建筑群由古塔和清真寺两大部分组成的，古塔是灰砖结构，为清代维吾尔建筑大师伊不拉欣所建，除了顶部窗棂外，基本不用木料。塔身浑圆，自下而上，逐渐收缩。塔基直径达10米，通高40米。顶呈盆形，塔身在不同高度和方向开出14个窗口，人们沿梯可直上塔顶瞭望室欣赏四周风光。

Exercises

Imagine that you are a local guide and your classmates are tourists. Make up a situational dialogue about the Turpan or the Emin Minaret.

PART III *Ethnic Culture*

New Words and Expressions

Uigur	/'wiːɡuə/	n.	维吾尔人[语]
alliance	/ə'laiəns/	n.	联盟,联合
talented	/'tæləntid/	adj.	有才能的
gem	/dʒem/	n.	宝石,美玉
decoration	/ˌdekə'reiʃən/	n.	装饰,装饰品
crisp	/krisp/	adj.	脆的,易碎的
pie	/pai/	n.	馅饼
component	/kəm'pəunənt/	n.	成分
demonstrate	/'demənstreit/	v.	示范,证明
distinguished	/dis'tiŋgwiʃt/	adj.	卓著的,著名的

Proper Nouns

Xinjiang Uigur Autonomous Region	新疆维吾尔自治区	Hetian	和田
Nang	馕		

Uigur Culture

The Uigur ethnic minority lives mainly in the Xinjiang Uigur Autonomous Region, especially to the south of Mt. Tianshan. The name Uigur, which they also use to refer to themselves, means alliance or assistance. Historical records indicate that Uigur people had strong trade and communication links with a variety of middle Asian countries and other ethnic groups of China. They work mainly with agriculture though are talented in the handicrafts which are made for commercial purposes. Uigur people are renowned for their abilities in processing gold, gem, silk and leather goods. Hetian is rich and proud of its fine jade, which is regarded as a rare first-class gem.

The Uigur people's staple food is Nang, noodles and Zhuafan. Nang is a kind of crisp baked pie, usually eaten with tea. Popular drinks include tea, milk tea and oil tea. Various fruits, mutton and beef are also typical favorites. They like to wear cotton clothes. Typically men wear gowns while women prefer to wear one-piece dresses. Many decorations such as ear rings, bracelets, and necklace and so on are women's favorite. Colored and embroidered caps are an important component of Uigur people's dress.

The Uigur people particularly enjoy dancing and singing. Festivities such as wedding ceremonies are celebrated with all guests, joining in their traditional folk dance. There are a number of important customs relating to appropriate behaviors of visitors. Eldest people sit in the most distinguished seat and guests are expected not to look around the house. Leaving a small amount of food in your bowl demonstrates impolite to your host. The Uigur culture reflects its wisdom, literary and artistic talents. Poems and oral legends are always popular amongst the Uigur people.

Quickies

True or False:

1. _____ Uigur people are well-known for their abilities in processing gold, gem, silk and leather goods, among which the silk made in Hetian is regarded as a rare first-class silk.

2. _____ The Uigur men wear gowns while women prefer to wear one-piece dresses. Colored and embroidered caps are an important component of Uigur people's dress.

3. _____ Guests are expected not to look around the house. They should leave a small amount of food in their bowl to show polite to their host.

PART IV *Practical Writing for Tourism*

Tour Itineraries 旅游线路

China Discovery

Cities to visit: Beijing, Xi'an, Chengdu

Quotation: US $2500/p.p.

Departure time: March, April, May, June, September, October, November, 2008.

Tour Description: The 10-day tour will present you a panoramic view of China, including the modern capital of Beijing to see the well-known Great Wall & Forbidden City; the ancient capital city of Xi'an known for its Terra-cotta Warriors and Horses; and Sichuan, the "Land of Abundance," known for the Jinsha Ruins and Mount Emei. So the 10-day tour will acquaint you with essence of the Chinese history, culture, nature and its hospitable people.

Day 01

Arrive in Beijing by International airline at 4 o'clock in the afternoon (Beijing Time), meet your guide and transfer to the Beijing Hotel. Welcome dinner in the evening. (LD)

Day 02

American buffet breakfast between 07:00—08:30, and take a bus ride to the Temple of Heaven in the morning. Back to the hotel after lunch for a break. 14:00 to visit the Tian'anmen Square and the Forbidden City. Deluxe Beijing Duck Banquet in the Quanjude Restaurant. (BLD)

Day 03

Leave at 8:30 in the morning after a good sleep and breakfast; take one-hour drive to the Great Wall, one of the seven great wonders in the world. Lunch at the Siwei Restaurant. Then visit the Deling Tomb, one of the well-known Ming Tombs. Back to hotel about 17:00, have the dinner, go to watch acrobatics show. Back to the hotel, pack your luggage, and then enjoy your last night in Beijing. (BLD)

Day 04

Leave your checkout luggage out of your room at 07:30, finish your breakfast and check out of hotel before 08:30, take a bus ride to the Summer Palace, the most beautiful lake park in China. After lunch, visit the Beijing Hutong (Lanes). In the afternoon, take a fight to Xi'an, and transfer to the Dynasty Hotel. (BLD)

Day 05

Breakfast between 07:30—8:30, and then go to see the Terra-cotta Warriors and Horses. After lunch, visit a local village to see the country of northern China and farmers' life. Back to the hotel around 17:00. Take a break for half an hour, and then watch the Tang Dynasty Show after the Imperial Dumpling Banquet. Pack your luggage before going to bed. (BLD)

Day 06

Leave your luggage out of your room before 07:30, finish your breakfast and check out of the hotel before 09:30. Take bus to the Forest of Steles, Big Goose Pagoda and Tang Dynasty Museum. Lunch at airport hotel, then fly to Chengdu, check in the Rongcheng Hotel. Free. (BL)

Day 07

Breakfast between 07:30—8:30. Visit the Chengdu Giant Panda Breeding Center in the morning. After lunch, come back to Chengdu to visit the Wuhou Temple. Enjoy a Sichuan Opera show and watch famous programs like Changing Faces. (BLD)

Day 08

After the breakfast, drive to Leshan (about one hour). After a boat excursion of the Sleeping Buddha, visit the 71m-high Giant Buddha and ancient Mahao Cliff Tombs. Transfer to Emei City by coach; Overnight at the Huasheng Hotel. Free. (BD)

Day 09

Breakfast between 07:00—8:00. Take a chartered bus to Mt. Emei and view the landscape on the way. Tour the Golden Summit, which presents four wonders of the mountain (cable car up and down). Drive back to Chengdu. Have Sichuan hotpot for dinner. Pack your luggage before going to bed. (BD)

Day 10

Get ready with luggage and carry-on before 8:00 in the morning. Take a flight to San Francisco. (BL)

Exercises

1. Arrange a 3-day itinerary for a group in your city, and discuss it with the tour leader.
2. Plan a 7-day itinerary for a group from UK who will travel around northwest China.

Unit 10 *Shopping*

带团购物

PART I *ABC for Tour Guides*

New Words and Expressions

designate	/'dezigneit/	*v.*	指定的,派定的
extra	/'ekstrə/	*adj.*	额外的
antique	/æn'tiːk/	*n.*	古物,古董
authenticity	/ˌɔːθen'tisiti/	*n.*	确实性,真实性
reliable	/ri'laiəbl/	*adj.*	可靠的,可信赖的
musk	/mʌsk/	*n.*	麝香
rhinoceros	/rai'nɔsərəs/	*n.*	犀牛
forbid	/fə'bid/	*v.*	禁止,不许
prohibit	/prə'hibit/	*v.*	禁止,阻止

Proper Nouns

Customs   海关   traditional Chinese medicine   中药

Listening

Direction: Listen to the passages carefully and fill in the blanks with the missing information you have heard from the tapes.

1. **What should a local guide pay attention to when he takes the tour group to go shopping?**
   地陪率团购物,应该注意哪些问题?

   (1) The local guide should take the tour group to go shopping only at shops designated in the contract. The local guide is not permitted to add (A) _____ shops or shopping time.

   (2) If tourists request to go shopping themselves, the local guide may agree if there is enough time.

   (3) If tourists purchase antiques, the local guide should tell them they must get permission from the State Bureau of Cultural Relics first, and present sales (B) _____ at the Customs when they leave China. Antique shops designated by the State Bureau of Cultural

81

Relics will provide such documents; antiques sold by (C) _____ usually do not have signs of authenticity, and tourists are not allowed to take them out of China.

2. **What should a guide advise tourists when they buy traditional Chinese medicine?** 游客购买中药时,导游员应告诉游客哪些注意事项?

   (1) The guide should recommend (D) _____ drugstores to tourists.

   (2) The guide should tell tourists there is a limit to the amount of (E) _____ abroad; RMB 1,500 for tourists going to Hong Kong and Macao.

   (3) Items such as musk, rhinoceros horn and (F) _____ bone are prohibited from being taken out of China.

New Words and Expressions

rake-off	/'reɪkɔf/	n.	<俚>佣金,回扣
kickback	/'kɪkbæk/	n.	<口>回扣;退回赃物
exaggerate	/ɪɡ'zædʒəreit/	v.	夸大,夸张

Readings

Direction: *Read the following passage aloud and fill in the blanks with words or phrases you think appropriate.*

ink	authenticity	brush	antique	fake
quality	rake-off	voice	designated	induce

1. **A Japanese tourist intends to purchase works of the ancient Chinese calligraphy and painting, and what should the guide advise him?** 一位日本游客希望购买中国的古字画,导游员应告诉他哪些注意事项?

   (1) The guide should advise him to go shopping in the (A) _____ shops and keep the sales receipt for the customs check on departure from China.

   (2) The guide should inform him that he must get permission from the State Bureau of Cultural Relics first, and present sales receipts at the Customs when they leave China. Antique shops designated by the State Bureau of Cultural Relics will provide such documents; antiques sold by peddlers usually do not have signs of (B) _____ and peddlers cannot give necessary documents. Tourists are not allowed to take them out of China.

2. **What do you think of the rake-off (kickback) that a guide takes from shopping or entertainment items? How can that be avoided?** 谈谈你对导游人员从购物、文娱表演中拿回扣问题的看法。你认为如何才能真正做到令行禁止?

   (1) According to the relevant regulations, the tour guide is not allowed to ask for a (C) _____.

   (2) The guide should not add extra shopping programs, extend the shopping time or lead the group to shops other than the (D) _____ ones.

(3) The guide should not exaggerate the (E) _____ of tourism products. He must not cheat, or force tourists to buy certain products.

Quickies

1. True or False:

(1) _____ The guide should advise tourists to go shopping in the antique shops and keep the sales receipt for the customs check on departure from China.

(2) _____ The tourists can get a refund for the tickets if they do not attend the entertainment according to the travel schedule.

(3) _____ Traditional Chinese medicine such as musk and tiger bone can be taken out of China if tourists have a receipt.

2. Role-play: Mr. Wang Ning takes some English tourists to buy antiques sold by the peddlers in the street. Imagine you were the guide and try to get the rake-off. Do you think the guide should take the rake-off? How would the tourists feel when they know they buy the fake products in China?

PART II *Method of Introduction*

New Words and Expressions

analogy	/ə'nælədʒi/	n.	类似,类推
logical	/'lɔdʒikəl/	adj.	合乎逻辑的,合理的
inference	/'infərəns/	n.	推论
assumption	/ə'sʌmpʃən/	n.	假定,设想
similarity	/ˌsimi'læriti/	n.	类似,类似处
dissimilar	/di'similə/	adj.	不同的,相异的
diversity	/dai'vəːsiti/	n.	差异,多样性
construe	/kən'struː/	v.	解释,分析
associate	/ə'səuʃieit/	v.	使发生联系
enumerate	/i'njuːməreit/	v.	列举
analogical	/ˌænə'lɔdʒikəl/	adj.	相似的,类推的

Proper Nouns

Baoguang Temple	宝光寺	Xindu	新都
Wenshu Temple	文殊院	Jinshan Temple	金山寺
Gaomin Temple	高旻寺	Yangzhou	扬州
Zen	禅宗	Jiuzhaigou Valley	九寨沟
Lijiang River	漓江		

83

The Method of Tracing Analogy Between Two Events
类比法

Analogy is a form of logical inference or an instance of it, based on the assumption that if two things are known to be alike in some respects, then they must be alike in other respects. This method is applied to help tourists further understand the tourist site and deepen their impression by analogizing the similarity in some respects between things that are otherwise dissimilar. Owing to the diversity in geography, history, nationality, culture and religion, it is none of an easy matter to make everyone construe whatever the guide introduces. Therefore, the method of tracing analogy between two events is surely utilized under such a circumstance. In this way, the guide makes it easier for tourists to appreciate the unfamiliar scenery or understand information that they could hardly understand. For example, when a guide introduces the Baoguang Temple in Xindu, he may associate it with Wenshu Temple in Chengdu, Jinshan Temple in Zhenjiang, and Gaomin Temple in Yangzhou. The guide can enumerate their similarities: The temples mentioned above are all regarded as the greatest Zen Buddhist temples in China. When he introduces the landscape of Jiuzhaigou Valley the guide may have an analogical account of the Lijiang River because both of them are famous for the water landscape in the world.

Questions

1. Why does a guide sometimes use the method of tracing analogy between two events?
2. List similarities and dissimilarities of the Jiuzhaigou Valley and the Lijiang River.

(1) _____

(2) _____

PART III Tourist Site

New Words and Expressions

secluded	/si'kluːdid/	adj.	幽静的,隐蔽的
steepness	/'stiːpnis/	n.	险峻
grandeur	/'grændʒə/	n.	庄严,伟大
acclaim	/ə'kleim/	n.	喝彩,称赞
lush	/lʌʃ/	adj.	青葱的,繁荣的
encircle	/in'səːkl/	v.	环绕,围绕
luxuriant	/lʌg'zjuəriənt/	adj.	丰富的,肥沃的
ratify	/'rætifai/	v.	批准,认可
inscribe	/in'skraib/	v.	记下,列入
synonym	/'sinənim/	n.	同义字

serenity	/si'reniti/	n.	平静,宁静
leisure	/'leʒə; 'liːʒə/	n.	闲暇,悠闲
serene	/si'riːn/	adj.	平静的
fragrance	/'freɪɡrəns/	n.	芬芳,香味
incense	/in'sens/	n.	熏香
ambience	/'æmbiəns/	n.	周围环境,气氛
essential	/i'senʃəl/	n.	本质,实质
sanctuary	/'sæŋktjuəri/	n.	圣所,圣殿

Proper Nouns

Mount Qingcheng	青城山	Jianmen	剑门
Mt. Emei	峨眉	Kuimen	夔门
Tianshi Cave	天师洞	Taoism	道教,道家学说
List of World Cultural Heritage	世界文化遗产名录		
UNESCO	联合国教科文组织		

Mount Qingcheng

Mount Qingcheng is situated 63 kilometers west of Chengdu. Characterized by its secluded and quiet environment, the scenic area is surrounded by ring-shaped peaks. It enjoys equal fame for steepness with Jianmen, for elegance with Mt. Emei and for grandeur with Kuimen. It has been widely acclaimed as "the most secluded mountain under the heaven." In Chinese Qingcheng literally means "green city." Mount Qingcheng gets its name because the main scenic spots such as the Tianshi Cave are all surrounded by 36 mountain peaks with their forests of lush evergreen trees encircling each spot like a city wall.

The ring-shaped hills, cool, tranquil and secluded, covered with luxuriant vegetation, make Mount Qingcheng, in the western part of Sichuan Province, a famous tourist site and a summer resort. As a place where Taoism originated and an important base of Taoism development, it has been a famous Taoist mountain for almost 2000 years. In 1982, it was ratified as one of first group of China National Key Tourist Resorts by the State Council. In 2000, together with the Dujiangyan Irrigation Project, it was inscribed on the List of World Cultural Heritage by UNESCO. Mount Qingcheng is unique for its secluded environment and for its Taoist significance.

Mount Qingcheng is popular all over the world for its "You"(幽). Frankly speaking, it is hard to define this Chinese word "You" because there is no English synonym. In Chinese,

"You" has a host of various meanings such as the serenity, leisure and seclusion. "You" on Mount Qingcheng is vividly reflected in its serene paths, secluded woods, quietly flowing streams, pavilions made of tree barks, the fragrance of burning incenses from temples and Taoist culture. You could feel the elegant ambience of the unique "You" on the way to the mountain. However, it would be helpful if you could understand the essentials of Taoism before you visit the Taoist sanctuary.

Cultural Notes

Mount Qingcheng 青城山：青城山上中国著名的道教名山，中国道教的发源地之一，自东汉以来历经两千多年。青城山位于位于四川省都江堰市西南，古称丈人山。青城山靠岷山雪岭，面向川西平原，主峰老霄顶海拔 1260 米。全山林木青翠，四季常青，诸峰环峙，状若城郭，故名青城山。青城山丹梯千级，曲径通幽，以幽洁取胜，自古就有"青城天下幽"的美誉，与剑门之险、峨眉之秀、夔门之雄齐名。古人记述中，青城山有三十六峰、八大洞、七十二小洞、一百八景之说。

Questions

1. **True or False:**

   (1) _____ Mount Qingcheng enjoys equal fame for steepness with Jianmen, for grandeur with Mt. Emei and for elegance with Kuimen.

   (2) _____ The ring-shaped hills, cool, tranquil and secluded make Mount Qingcheng a famous tourist site and a winter resort.

   (3) _____ The Chinese word "You" refers to serenity, leisure and seclusion. You can feel its ambience only when you travel in the secluded woods, quietly flowing streams and the pavilions made of bark.

2. Read the passage aloud and introduce Mount Qingcheng using the methods of introduction you have learnt. The method of tracing analogy between two events is one of the choices.

Tips
- Draft your own commentary before you make your presentation.
- Speak colloquial English and use simple and short sentences.
- Animate your introduction with facial expressions and body language.
- Apply at least one method of introduction. It is highly recommended that you use two or three methods of introduction.

PART IV *Simulated Introduction*

New Words and Expressions

exploration	/ˌeksplɔːˈreiʃən/	n.	探险,探查
juncture	/ˈdʒʌŋktʃə/	n.	接合点
alpine	/ˈælpain/	adj.	高山的,阿尔卑斯山的
exotic	/igˈzɔtik/	adj.	异国情调的,奇异的
drift	/drift/	v.	漂流
trough	/ˈtrɔːf/	n.	槽,水槽,饲料槽
hollow	/ˈhɔləu/	v.	挖空,弄凹
trunk	/trʌŋk/	n.	树干,躯干
fir	/fəː/	n.	[植]冷杉,杉木
drown	/draun/	v.	溺死,淹死
livestock	/ˈlaivstɔk/	n.	家畜,牲畜
survivor	/səˈvaivə/	n.	生还者,残存物
matrilineal	/ˌmætriˈliniəl/	adj.	母系的
adult	/əˈdʌlt, ˈædʌlt/	adj.	成人的,成熟的
puzzle	/ˈpʌzl/	v.	(使)为难,迷惑不解

Proper Nouns

Lugu Lake	泸沽湖	Mosuo	摩梭族
"Xie Na Mi"	"谢纳米",意为母亲湖。	Ninglang County	宁蒗县
Yanyuan County	盐源县	"walking marriage"	"走婚"
"Zhu Cao Chuan"	"猪槽船"	Noah's ark	诺亚方舟
Bible	《圣经》	Yongning Village	永宁乡
"Azhu marriage"	"阿注婚"		

Lugu Lake

Here we are. This is our destination—Lugu Lake. Everybody! Are you ready? We'll begin our exploration of the mysterious "Girls' Kingdom." Please get off!

Lugu Lake, Mosuo people call it "Xie Na Mi", means the mother lake. It is located in the juncture of Ninglang County of Yunnan Province and Yanyuan County of Sichuan Province. Lugu Lake is a beautiful alpine lake of 2,688 metres above the sea level. It is a unique tourist resort in China and even in the world for its social habits, exotic folk customs and primitive culture, especially for "the walking marriage."

Look ahead! Have you noticed the elegant wooden boat drifting near the lakeside? It is called "Zhu Cao Chuan" or "pig trough boat" by the local people. Sounds strange? Would you please look at it more carefully! Don't you think the boat is like the trough which holds feeds for pigs? In fact, the boat is made of the hollowed trunk of a big fir tree, and it is the main transport for the local people.

According to a legend, a flood occured and the water flooded the land and drowned people and their livestock. When the terrible flood came, a Mosuo woman was feeding her pigs. She jumped into a wooden pig trough and fortunately survived the flood. The flood-stricken area became a lake and she was the only survivor of the disaster. She lived on the lakeside and raised her children there. The legend sounds like Noah's ark in the *Bible*. Do you think so? From that on, the matrilineal folk customs of honoring the mother has been handed down. The tradition of using the pig-trough boat as their main mode of water transport has also been handed down for many centuries.

Well, let's get on the boat. We are going to one of the most primitive village, Yongning Village. How time flies! We've reached the village. Before you enter their house I'd like to say something you have to follow: do not ask something about Azhu or the uncle; do not walk across the fire pit and do not enter the flower room without permission.

Come in please! See? That's it, the flower room is on my left side. Hey, a moment please! Don't open that door. The flower room is only for the adult Mosuo woman and her Azhu. You can not enter that room unless you are accepted as her Azhu. What does Azhu mean? Mike, you look puzzled. Maybe you don't know, and let me tell you about it. Azhu is what a Mosuo woman calls her lover or a man calls his love. The Mosuo man usually visits his love, stays in her room at night and goes back to his own house early next morning. The local people call their love affairs "Azhu marriage" or "walking Marriage."

Now, it's time for free sightseeing. After we take our supper, I'll take you to have a wonderful bonfire party. Didn't I tell you that the fish soup here is very delicious? We'll have fish soup tonight.

Have a good time!

Cultural Notes

Lugu Lake 泸沽湖：泸沽湖素有"高原明珠"之称。湖的水域面积达 58 平方公里,海拔 2690 米,平均水深 45 米,最深处 90 余米。湖中有五个全岛、三个半岛和一个海堤连岛。湖中各岛亭亭玉立,形态各异,林木葱郁,翠绿如画,身临其间,水天一色,清澈如镜,藻花点缀其间,缓缓滑行于碧波之上的猪槽船和徐徐飘浮于水天之间的摩梭民歌,使其更增添几分古朴、几分宁静,是一个远离尘嚣,未被污染的处女湖。

Exercises

Make a simulated introduction of the Lugu Lake using the methods of introduction you have learnt. Pay attention to the body language and other tips of introduction.

Unit 11
Incidents while Escorting Tour Group (I)
带团事故(1)

PART I   *ABC for Tour Guides*

New Words and Expressions

inaccurate	/in'ækjurit/	*adj.*	错误的,不准确的
apology	/ə'pɔlədʒi/	*n.*	道歉
cordial	/'kɔːdiəl/	*adj.*	热忱的,诚恳的

Listening

Direction: Listen to the passages carefully and fill in the blanks with the missing information you have heard from the tapes.

1. **What is the incident that the guide is not present when tourists arrive? What might be some of the causes?**   什么叫漏接事故？造成"漏接事故"的原因是什么？

   (1) It means that there is no tour guide to meet the tourists upon their arrival.

   (2) The causes might include:

      (a) The sponsor travel agency fails to inform the (A) _____ travel agency of the arrival time;

      (b) The local travel agency gives the guide inaccurate information;

      (c) The guide remembers the wrong time and (B) _____ of arrival;

      (d) The guide is held up by a traffic accident.

2. **How can a guide avoid the incident that he is not present when tourists arrive? How could he handle the case?**   导游员应如何预防"漏接事故"？发生"漏接事故"后如何处理？

   (1) After accepting the assignment, the guide should check and (C) _____ check the date, time and place of the tourists' arrival.

   (2) On the day of their arrival, the guide should confirm the information and inform the driver of the time and location of the arrival. If necessary, the guide may contact the (D) _____ travel agency, the airport or railway station to confirm the exact time of their arrival.

(3) The guide should set aside enough time to make sure he arrives at the meeting place ahead of time.

If the incident happens, the guide should do the following;

(a) First, give an (E) _____ and make a sincere apology to the tourists and try to win their trust by offering them cordial and attentive service;

(b) The guide may not be responsible for the incident. However, since the tourists suffer from the (F) _____ because of the incident, the guide should do an apology on behalf of the travel agency.

New Words and Expressions

solution	/səˈljuːʃən/	*n.*	办法，决定
immediately	/iˈmiːdjətli/	*adv.*	立即，即刻

Readings

Direction: Read the following passage aloud and fill in the blanks with words or phrases you think appropriate.

apology	arrangements	picked	information	mistake
tourists	sponsor	hand	leader	claim

1. What is "an incident of taking tourists by mistake"? What might be some of the causes? 什么叫"错接事故"？产生"错接事故"的原因是什么？

   (1) The incident means that the guide has met tourists other than his own, while his own tourists are left at the airport or station or, have been (A) _____ up by some other tour guide.

   (2) The main cause is that the guide has not followed basic guiding procedures. He might have forgotten checking the name of the sponsor travel agency, the group number, the number of tourists and the name of the tour (B) _____, etc.

2. How could a guide prevent the occurrence of "an incident of taking tourists by mistake"? What is he supposed to do if the incident happens? 导游怎样防止出现"错接事故"？如果"错接事故"发生以后应当如何处理？

   (1) It is easy to avoid such a mistake of taking tourists by mistake if the guide checks the (C) _____ of the tour group carefully.

   (2) The solutions to solve the problems include: checking the name of the sponsor travel agency, the group number, the number of (D) _____ and the name of the tour leader.

   (3) If the guide mistakes the tour group of another travel agency for his own group, he should first report to his own travel agency and (E) _____ it over to the right travel agency. Meanwhile he should do an apology to the tourists.

(4) If his own tour group remains at the airport or station, the guide should report to the travel agency for making (F) _____ for picking them up immediately.

(5) If the group belongs to the same agency that he works for, but he is not supposed to be their guide, the guide may make the best of the (G) _____ and act as their guide, picking them up without telling them who is who.

Quickies

Role-play: Miss Shi Jian, a guide from Nanchang Peace Travel Service arrives at the airport to pick up the tour group from Ireland. He mistakes the American tourists for her own tour group. What would you do as her colleagues?

PART II *Situational Dialogue*

New Words and Expressions

ravine	/rɔ'viːn/	n.	沟壑,峡谷,溪谷
grotto	/'grɔtəu/	n.	洞穴,岩穴
deity	/'diːiti/	n.	神,神性
craggy	/'krægi/	adj.	多峭壁的,崎岖的
tier	/tiə/	n.	列,行,排,层
splash	/splæʃ/	v.	溅,泼

Proper Nouns

Mount Lushan	庐山	Hanyang Peak	汉阳峰
Immortal Cave	仙人洞	Islam	伊斯兰教(在中国旧称回
Christianity	基督教		教,清真教)
Wulao Feng	五老峰	Sandie Spring	三叠泉

Dialogue 1

Mount Lushan

Miss Shi Jian takes tourists around Mount Lushan, one of the most marvelous mountains in China. She asks them to keep pace so that they will not get lost in the mountain.

(A=Miss Shi Jian; B=Jackson)

A: Mount Lushan is one of the most famous mountains in China. The tallest peak is the Hanyang Peak which soars to a height of 1473 meters.

B: I've heard of this mountain. Although it is not very high the landscape is worth of a visit.

A: Yes, on Mount Lushan you can appreciate ravines, waterfalls, grottoes, rocks and little streams. There are 12 main scenic areas, together with 37 attractions, over 900 cliff inscriptions, and over 300 steles.

B: From your introduction I know we can watch not only the landscape but also historical interests. Just now, you mentioned there are a lot of cliff inscriptions and steles on Mount Lushan.

A: You're right. There goes a saying, "Mountain is famous not for its height, but for the immortals there." There is an Immortal Cave on Mount Lushan.

B: Do you mean there are some deities on the mountains?

A: Not exactly. I mean Mount Lushan is outstanding not only for the landscape, but also for the historical significance. Mount Lushan is also a religious center of ancient China.

B: A religious center? Do you mean different religions are practiced on Mount Lushan?

A: Yes, you can find five different religions on Lushan over the past 1,600 years. During the Ming and Qing dynasties, Islam and Christianity were already preached here.

B: I couldn't expect that Christianity spread on Mount Lushan as early as in the 16th century!

A: As we talk about Mount Lushan we've arrived at Wulao Feng. It is 1,436 meters above sea level. From here you can have a view of the distant mountains, trees and lakes.

B: What a wonderful view! I see an endless sky on the horizon.

A: The Sandie Spring just lies below Wulao Feng. It drops through three craggy tiers with a fall of 155 meters. It is considered to be the best of the Lushan waterfalls.

B: I see the upper part of the spring is like snow falling down to the pond; the middle part twists with splashing sprays in the air.

A: What about the lower part of the spring? It looks like a jade dragon running in the pond. Do you think so?

B: Exactly!

Exercises

Do the dialogue again and pay attention to your facial expressions and body language.

New Words and Expressions

gourd	/ɡuəd/	n.	葫芦
sailboat	/ˈseilbəʊt/	n.	帆船
billow	/ˈbiləu/	v.	翻腾
raft	/rɑːft/	n.	筏,救生艇,橡皮船

toss	/tɔs/	v.	投,掷
precisely	/prɪ'saɪsli/	adv.	正好
safari	/sə'fɑːri/	n.	旅行,狩猎远征

Proper Nouns

Poyang Lake	鄱阳湖	Dagu Hill	大孤山
Shoe Hill	鞋山	"food-begging birds"	"乞食鸟"

Dialogue 2

Poyang Lake

The tourists are cruising on the Poyang Lake, the largest fresh-water lake in China. Miss Shi Jian asks them to take care while introducing the waterscape with a loudspeaker

(A=Miss Shi Jian; B=Jackson)

A: Now we're traveling on the Poyang Lake. It is the largest fresh-water lake in China, like a huge gourd tied on the waist of the Yangtze River.

B: Vow, look out over the vastness of Poyang Lake, its blue waves stretch to the horizon. It looks like we were looking out over an ocean.

A: Your description of the waterscape is marvelous. Now the sun is rising and the water of the lake seems to meet on the horizon.

B: Sailboats on the lake are traveling back and forth at a high speed. They dart too high as if they want to fetch the billowing clouds.

A: Rafts float on the lake one after another like big moving dragons. Our travel boat is just one of the dragon boats among hundreds of the rafts.

B: What a fantastic cruise on the Poyang Lake! Such a travel experience is rare in my life. Look, something like a shoe is floating far ahead. What is that?

A: It is the Dagu Hill. Dagu Hill is an island in the Poyang Lake. When you see it from a distance, it looks like a large shoe floating in the blue water. It is also known as the Shoe Hill.

B: Shall we come close to have a look?

A: Sure. Look, Dagu Hill is only one peak with precipices on its three sides. The island rises steeply from the lake. When we get off the boat you can hike to the top of the hill and have a look at the vast Poyang Lake below.

B: What are those magic birds? All tourists are throwing food to them.

93

A: They're called "food-begging birds." The birds have strong wings and sharp eyes. No matter whether the food is tossed high in the air or dropped close to the surface of the lake, they catch it precisely.

B: Terrific! I'll try to toss the food to the birds. Got it, got it!

A: Birding safari is also a tour item on the Poyang Lake. I hope you'll enjoy it.

B: Thank you!

Cultural Notes

Mount Lushan 庐山：庐山位于江西省九江市,紧临鄱阳湖和长江,海拔 1474 米,以雄、奇、险、秀闻名于世。庐山富有独特的文化,具有重要的科学与美学价值,1996 年联合国批准庐山为"世界文化景观",列入《世界遗产名录》。庐山最高峰为大汉阳峰、五老峰、香炉峰等,山间经常云雾弥漫,所以人们常说"不识庐山真面目,只缘身在此山中"。庐山有独特的第四纪冰川遗迹,河流、湖泊、坡地、山峰等多种地貌类型,因此也有"地质公园"之说。

Poyang Lake 鄱阳湖：鄱阳湖是中国最大的淡水湖,位于长江中下游,江西省北部,总面积为 22,400 公顷,1988 年 5 月,经国务院批准为国家级自然保护区。世界自然基金会主席前来观赏考察后称这里是"鹤之王国""野生动物的""安全绿洲"。鄱阳湖有鸟类 310 种,其中国家一级保护鸟类 10 种,二级保护鸟类 44 种,仅白鹤就为 2,896 只,占全球白鹤总数的 98%。每年 11 月底至次年三月处,是观鸟的大好时机。

Exercises

Imagine that you are a local guide and your classmates are tourists. Make up a situational dialogue about Mount Lushan or the Poyang Lake.

PART III *Ethnic Culture*

New Words and Expressions

hospitable	/ˈhɔspitəbl/	adj.	好客的,招待周到的
yarn	/jɑːn/	n.	纱,纱线
velour	/vəˈluə/	n.	[纺]丝绒,天鹅绒
luster	/ˈlʌstə/	n.	光彩,光泽
durability	/ˌdjuərəˈbiliti/	n.	经久,耐久力
waistband	/ˈweistbænd/	n.	腰带,束腰带
sentimental	/ˌsentiˈmentl/	adj.	多情的
lyric	/ˈlirik/	n.	抒情诗,歌词
improvisational	/imˌprɔviːzɑːˈtɔːrei/	adj.	即兴的
humorous	/ˈhjuːmərəs/	adj.	幽默的,滑稽的

Proper Nouns

| Zhuang | 壮族 | Singing Festival | 歌圩 |
| Liu Sanjie | 刘三姐 | Valentine's Day | 情人节 |

Zhuang Culture

The Zhuang ethnic minority is the largest minority group in China with a long history and glorious culture. The Zhuang people are so hospitable that any guests are honored by the whole village. Wine is a must when treating the guests. Guests are shown a unique way of drinking each other's wine in the spoon by crossing each other's arms. Nobody eats before the elderly people begin, just to show respect to them.

Like some other ethnic group women, the Zhuang women are skilled at weaving and embroidering. These women have a great reputation for the distinctive designs of cotton woven yarn brocade they make in colorful velour. Zhuang brocade is renowned for its color, luster, durability and the wide range of use. Another skill such as dying with wax is also popular. You can appreciate the excellent skills used in handicraft carpets, aprons, bed covers, waistbands, tablecloth and curtains as a beautiful purchase for homes all over the world. Now, Zhuang brocade is not only a wonderful handicraft favored by the people in China but also has won international fame and enjoys a large market both at home and abroad.

The Singing Festival is a traditional occasion which was held before 1940 to visit graves of the ancestors. Now it has become a grand sentimental occasion using songs for their expression. On that day, after sacrificing Liu Sanjie (a Zhuang minority girl good at singing), the Zhuang people will sing to each other to challenge not only the song itself but also wit. Lyrics are usually improvisational and humorous that makes every one burst into laughter. It is also a perfect day for the young men to express their love to the girls by singing, so it is also reputed as the Valentine's Day of the Zhuang ethnic minority.

Questions

True or False:

(1) _____ Wine is a must when the Zhuang people treat the guests. Guests are invited to drink wine in the bowl by crossing each other's arms.

(2) _____ Zhuang brocade is well-known for its color, luster, durability and the wide range of use and enjoys the international reputation.

(3) _____ The Zhuang people compose songs at advance and sing to each other not only for challenging the song itself but also the wit.

PART IV *Practical Writing for Tourism*

A Letter of Complaints 投诉信

August 12, 2008

Jiujiang Overseas Travel Service, Ltd.
No. 17, 4th Block, 1st Ring Road,
Jiujiang, Jiangxi

Attn: Mr. Lin Yunzhi
Dear Mr. Lin,

We made a five-day trip around Jiujiang arranged by your travel service last month. We had a good time quite well for most of the time; however, we were dissatisfied with something unhappy which happened during our travel.

First, when we were in Jiujiang, the local guide took us to various curio and souvenir stores within our 2-day tour. It is true that we did want to buy some souvenirs to bring home; however, shopping for one or two times was enough because we came here for sightseeing after all. With too much time spent on shopping, our tour in the scenic spots was always in a hurry. It occurred often that we hardly arrived at the tourist sites when we had been asked to leave.

Second, according to the contract concluded between us we were to stay in a five-star hotel. However, we were transferred to a three-star hotel where the air-conditioner broke down during our stay. The heat of July in Jiujiang was nothing for the citizen there, but so unbearable for us that we couldn't fall asleep at night.

Therefore, we request you to give us an explanation and compensate us for 300 dollars per person due to your unreasonable arrangement.

We are looking forward to your prompt reply.

Sincerely yours,
Jane Moore

Exercises

Write a letter of complaints in which you lodge a claim on the travel agency for the poor guiding service.

Unit 12
Incidents while Escorting Tour Group (II)
带团事故(2)

PART I *ABC for Tour Guides*

New Words and Expressions

postponement	/pəust'pəunmənt/	*n.*	延期,延缓
cancellation	/ˌkænsə'leiʃən/	*n.*	取消
disrupt	/dis'rʌpt/	*v.*	使中断,使陷于混乱

Listening

Direction: Listen to the passages carefully and fill in the blanks with the missing information you have heard from the tapes.

1. **What is the incident that a guide fails to meet tourists at the airport or station? How should a guide handle it?** 什么叫"空接事故"？如何处理？

   (1) The incident means that the guide arrives on time at the airport or station but the tourists have not (A) _____ yet. The reasons for the delay could be: delayed departure from the airport, delay en route, or incomplete information of itinerary from the national guide.

   (2) In case of the incident, the guide should first report to his travel agency to confirm what has happened.

   (3) If tourists are expected to arrive within a short time, the guide should stay and wait. Otherwise, the guide should return to the travel agency and make (B) _____ arrangements including the postponement or cancellation of any meal or hotel reservations.

   (4) When tourists arrive, the guide should greet them cordially on behalf of the travel agency and let them feel at home.

2. **What is "an incident of missing the airplane"? What might be the consequences?** 什么叫"误机事故"？其后果如何？

   (1) "An incident of missing the airplane" means that the tour group does not arrive at the airport on time and fails to catch the (C) _____ flight, thus disrupting the travel schedule.

The incident might have serious consequences:

(a) The incident delays the tourist's departure from the present stop, and worse, may delay the time of (D) _____ to a foreign country.

(b) The travel agency may have to extend the tourists' stay at the present stop, cancel scheduled activities, or make additional payment for the alternative transportation.

(2) If the incident is not properly handled, tourists may feel dissatisfied and lodge a (E) _____, which will possibly affect the reputation of the travel agency.

New Words and Expressions

appease	/əˈpiːz/	v.	平息,安抚,缓和
endorsement	/inˈdɔːsmənt/	n.	批准,认可
resume	/riˈzjuːm/	v.	再继续,重新开始
modify	/ˈmɔdifai/	v.	更改,修改
penalize	/ˈpiːnəlaiz/	v.	处罚

Readings

Direction: Read the following passage aloud and fill in the blanks with words or phrases you think appropriate.

postpone	flight	appease	board	delay
accommodation	traffic	vehicle	penalized	notice

How should a guide handle "the incident of missing the airplane"? 发生"误机事故"后导游员应如何处理?

(1) First the guide should report to the travel agency, and try to (A) _____ the tourists.

(2) The guide should contact the airlines and arrange other modes of transportation for departure. Upon endorsement of the travel agency the guide may rent a (B) _____, an airplane, a coach or even a ship to send the tourists off so that they can resume their travel schedule.

(3) If tourists have to stay on, the manager or administration staff of the travel agency should do an apology to them, and arrange for the (C) _____ and provide necessary services during their stay. The guide should confirm the details of the next stop of the modified travel schedule and inform the related parties.

(4) The person who causes the incident should be (D) _____ and pay for the economic loss.

Quickies

98

Role-play: The Canadian tourists are held up by a serious traffic accident on the way to the railway station. They can not catch the train which is due to leave for Wuhan, the capital city of Hubei Province. Replay the scene and tell you classmates how to handle the case.

PART II *Method of Introduction*

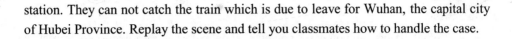

New Words and Expressions

arouse	/əˈrauz/	v.	唤醒,唤起
ultimate	/ˈʌltimeit/	adj.	最大的,最佳的
conservancy	/kənˌsəːvənsi/	n.	保护,管理
skip	/skip/	v.	跳过,忽略
omit	/əuˌmit/	v.	省略

Proper Nouns

Sand Flying Spillway	飞沙堰	Bottle-Neck Channel	宝瓶口
Temple of Two Kings	二王庙	Anlan Suspension Bridge	安澜索桥
Wolong Nature Reserve	卧龙自然保护区	Giant Panda	大熊猫
Gully of Hero	英雄沟	Valley of Silver Dragon	银龙峡谷
Dengsheng Virgin Forest	邓生原始森林		

The Method of Introduction with a Focus on Key Events
突出重点法

It is a method of introduction with which a guide introduces the striking characteristics of the tourist sites or scenery area that are different from others. By this way, the guide can not only arouse tourists' interest, but also impress tourists so as to achieve the ultimate effect of the introduction. An introduction of this kind can make tourists aware of the essentials of the tourist sites so that they can focus on the main events or major part of the place that they visit and remember what they have travel even after they come back to their residences or working places.

For instance, when a guide introduces the Dujiangyan Irrigation Project, he may focuses on the Fish Mouth, Sand Flying Spillway and Bottle-Neck Channel, which are regarded as the most important parts of the water conservancy project, while skip over the Temple of Two Kings and Anlan Suspension Bridge. We can also take the Wolong Nature Reserve for an example. A guide should lay his focus on introduction of the Giant Panda, the national treasure, as well as the marked achievements in protecting and breeding Giant Panda. The other tourist sites in Wolong, such as the Gully of Hero, the Valley of Silver Dragon and Dengsheng Virgin Forest, etc. are less important. The guide may omit them or just have a few words about them.

Quickies

1. What effects can you expect when a guide makes an introduction of tourist sites using the method of introduction with a focus on key events?
2. Which parts should be emphasized while other parts may be skipped over when you introduce the Dujiangyan Irrigation Project?

PART III Tourist Site

New Words and Expressions

pothouse	/'pɒthaʊs/	n.	酒馆
shabbily	/'ʃæbili/	adv.	破旧地
Taoist	/'tauist/	n.	道士,道教信徒
glaze	/gleiz/	v.	上釉
theme	/θiːm/	n.	题目,主题
porcelain	/'pɔːslin/	n.	瓷器
depict	/di'pikt/	v.	描述,描写
fabulous	/'fæbjuləs/	adj.	寓言般的,难以置信的
panoramic	/ˌpænə'ræmik/	adj.	全景的

Proper Nouns

Yellow Crane Tower	黄鹤楼	Snake Hill	蛇山
Wuhan	武汉	Old Xin	老辛(辛先生)

Yellow Crane Tower

Yellow Crane Tower is located on the Snake Hill in Wuhan, Hubei Province. According to legend, Yellow Crane Tower was built by the family of an old pothouse owner living in Wuhan City long ago, named Old Xin. One day, a shabbily dressed Taoist priest came to the pothouse and asked for some wine. Old Xin paid no attention to him, but his son was very kind and gave the Taoist some wine without asking for money. Then the Taoist priest drew a crane on the wall of the pothouse which would dance. When people in the city heard of this, they flocked to the pothouse to see the dancing crane. The Xin family soon became rich and they built the Yellow Crane Tower as a symbol of gratitude to the Taoist priest.

The Tower had different architectural features in different dynasties. However the tower which stands today is based on the one designed during the Qing Dynasty. It stands 51.4 meters high and has five floors. The appearance of the tower is the same regardless of the direction it is viewed from. The roof is covered by 100,000 yellow glazed tiles. With yellow upturned eaves, each floor seems to have been designed to resemble a yellow crane spreading its wings to fly.

Yellow Crane Tower offers visitors an abundance of things to see. The exhibit on each floor has a theme, for example, the theme of the first floor is about legends. On the wall, there is a nine-meter long and six-meter wide painted porcelain picture which depicts clouds, rivers and cranes to represent a romantic mood in the heaven. The third floor mainly shows poems written to praise the tower in different dynasties. On top of the tower, visitors are treated to a fabulous panoramic view of the Yangtze River, its bridge and the surrounding buildings in Wuhan City. Outside the tower, there are bronze yellow cranes, memorial gateways and pavilions.

Cultural Notes

Yellow Crane Tower 黄鹤楼：黄鹤楼位于湖北的武汉武昌蛇山上，与江西滕王阁、湖南岳阳楼齐名，并称为"江南三大名楼"，也是国家 5A 级景区、国家旅游胜地四十佳。黄鹤楼始建于三国吴黄武二年，孙权为实现"以武治国而昌"（"武昌"的名称由来于此），筑城为守，建楼瞭望。黄鹤楼几经战乱，毁于光绪十年（公元 1884 年），1985 年重建落成。新建黄鹤楼飞檐 5 层，攒尖楼顶，金色琉璃瓦屋面，通高 51.4 米，底层边宽 30 米，顶层边宽 18 米，全楼各层布置有大型壁画、楹联、文物等。楼外铸铜黄鹤造型、胜像宝塔、牌坊、轩廊、亭阁等一批辅助建筑，将主楼烘托得更加壮丽。登楼远眺，"极目楚天舒"，长江风光尽收眼底。

Quickies

1. True or False:

(1) _____ According to the record the Xin family built the Yellow Crane Tower as a symbol of gratitude to the Taoist priest.

(2) _____ With yellow upturned eaves, the top floor has been designed to resemble a yellow crane spreading its wings to fly.

(3) _____ The exhibit on each floor has a theme, for example, the second floor mainly shows poems written to praise the tower in different dynasties.

2. Read the passage aloud and introduce the Yellow Crane Tower using the methods of introduction you have learnt. The method of introduction with a focus on key events is one of the choices.

Tips

- Draft your own commentary before you make your presentation.
- Speak colloquial English and use simple and short sentences.

- Animate your introduction with facial expressions and body language.
- Apply at least one method of introduction. It is highly recommended that you use two or three methods of introduction.

PART IV *Simulated Introduction*

New Words and Expressions

crisscross	/'kriskrɔs/	*adj.*	十字形的
valuable	/'væljuəbl/	*n.*	贵重物品
orchid	/'ɔːkid/	*n.*	[植] 兰花
cherry	/'tʃeri/	*n.*	樱桃, 樱桃树
osmanthus	/ɔs'mænθəs/	*n.*	[植]桂花, 木樨属植物
plum	/plʌm/	*n.*	[植] 桃花
epigraph	/'epigrɑːf/	*n.*	铭文

Proper Nouns

East Lake	东湖
Chu culture	楚文化
West Lake	西湖
Hangzhou	杭州
Tingtao Xuan (The Listening-to-the-Waves Tower)	听涛轩
Mo Hill (Millstone Hill)	磨山
Xingyinge (the Poetry-reciting Pavilion)	行吟阁
Qu Yuan	屈原
Botanical Viewing Garden	植物观赏园
Cherry Blossom Garden	樱花园
Hirosaki	(日本)弘前市
Plum Blossom Garden	梅园
Zhu Bei Pavilion (Zhu De's Stele Pavilion)	朱碑亭

East Lake

Ladies and gentlemen, we'll cruise on the East Lake to enjoy the waterscape as well as the Chu culture. Some of you maybe heard of the West Lake in Hangzhou, but I think the East Lake is more worthy of a visit. East Lake is the biggest tourist attraction in Wuhan and also the largest lake within a city in China. It covers an area of 87 square kilometers that is five times greater than the area of the West Lake. Because of its winding banks and crisscrossing ponds and brooks, it is called "a lake with 99 bays." Among the six scenic areas of the East Lake, Tingtao Xuan (The Listening-to-the-Waves Tower) and Mo Hill (Millstone Hill) are the most famous and are open to tourists.

Now, our travel boat is passing by the Tingtao Scenic Area. Look ahead, the famous Tingtao Xuan stand elegant and delicate there. It is one of the famous buildings in this area. On the north, the center of this area, is the Xingyinge (the Poetry-reciting Pavilion). It was built for memori-zing works of Qu Yuan, the great patriotic poet of the State of Chu. Many exhibits about Qu Yuan are on display in this building, including his great literary masterpieces.

Ladies and Gentlemen, our travel boat is heading for the Mo Hill Scenic Area. This tourist resort has the beautiful landscape, abundant plants, and unique gardens. Many tourists travel here to view the East Lake and enjoy the customs of the state of Chu, from home and abroad. How time flies! and We've arrived at our destination. Please take your valuables and get off the boat one by one.

Here we come to the Botanical Viewing Garden. There are more than 360 kinds of plants in 13 special gardens. Flowers bloom all the year round—orchids and cherry blossoms in spring, lotus in summer, osmanthus in autumn, and plum blossoms in winter. Two of the gardens are most famous. The Cherry Blossom Garden is said to be one of the three cherry blossom capitals in the world. The other two are Hirosaki in Japan and Washington in America. The Plum Blossom Garden is listed as the top of the four plum gardens in China.

It's the time for free sightseeing. After twenty minutes we'll visit the Zhu Bei Pavilion (Zhu De's Stele Pavilion). It stands on the first peak of the Mo Hill. It is famous for a red stele on which the epigraph of Zhu De was inscribed. On the second floor of the pavilion you will have a panaramic view of the beautiful East Lake.

Have fun!

Cultural Notes

East Lake 东湖：武汉东湖生态风景旅游区位于"九省通衢"的武汉市东部，总面积82平方公里，其中水域面积33平方公里，是中国最大的城中湖。1982年被国务院列为首批国家重点风景名胜区，2000年被国家旅游局评定为首批4A级旅游风景区。目前已对外开放的有听涛、磨山、吹笛、落雁四大景区，景观景点100多处。东湖也是最大的楚文化游览中心，楚风浓郁，楚韵精妙，行吟阁名播遐迩，离骚碑誉为"三绝"，楚天台气势磅礴，楚才园名人荟萃，楚市、屈原塑像、屈原纪念馆，内涵丰富，美名远扬。

Exercises

Make a simulated introduction of the East Lake using the methods of introduction you have learnt. Pay attention to the body language and other tips of introduction.

Unit 13 *Documents and Luggage Lost*
遗失证件、行李

PART I *ABC for Tour Guides*

New Words and Expressions

identity	/aiˈdentiti/	*n.*	身份,特性
passport	/ˈpɑːspɔːt/	*n.*	护照
submit	/səbˈmit/	*v.*	提交,递交
testimonial	/ˌtestiˈməunjəl/	*n.*	证明书,推荐书
visa	/vizə/	*n.*	签证

Proper Nouns

Public Security Bureau 公安局   Consulate General 总领事馆

Listening

*Direction: **Listen to the passages carefully and fill in the blanks with the missing information you have heard from the tapes.***

1. **If a tourist loses his documents and belongings, how should a guide handle the case?** 游客遗失证件物品,导游员如何处理?

   (1) The guide should help the tourist recall whether he has left the documents with someone else or put it somewhere (A) _____ .

   (2) If the loss is confirmed, the guide should help search for it.

   (3) If the lost documents are not found, the guide should report to the travel agency and help the tourist apply for the new documents. The loss (B) _____ issued from the travel agency is a must.

2. **How does a foreign tourist apply for a new passport and visa if he loses them in China?** 外国游客在华丢失护照和签证,应如何申请补办?

   (1) The foreign tourist should report his loss to the local Public Security Bureau in China. He

should submit the written testimonial of the travel agency along with his (C) _____.

(2) With the testimonial issued by the Public Security Bureau, he should apply for a new passport in his own country's Embassy or Consulate (D) _____ in China.

(3) With the newly issued passport, he should apply for a new (E) _____ in the office of the entry and exit visas for foreigners under the Public Security Bureau in China.

New Words and Expressions

compatriot	/kəm'pætriət/	n.	同胞
valid	/'vælid/	adj.	[律]有效的
necessity	/ni'sesiti/	n.	必需品
reimbursement	/ˌriːim'bəːsment/	n.	付还,退还

Proper Nouns

laissez passer	通行证
Hong Kong	香港
Macao	澳门
China Travel Service	中国旅行社
Emigration Office for Overseas Chinese	侨办
luggage tag	行李签
lost-and-found office	失物招领处

Readings

Direction: Read the following passage aloud and fill in the blanks with words or phrases you think appropriate.

| register | package | agency | validity | tag |
| forget | exit | claim | repay | necessities |

1. **What should a citizen of Hong Kong, Macao or a compatriot of Taiwan do if he loses his travel certificate?** 港澳居民和台湾同胞丢失旅行证明,应该如何处理?

(1) If a tourist from Hong Kong or Macao loses his laissez-passer, he should report to the local Public Security Bureau with the testimonial made by the travel (A) _____. After the loss is confirmed, he may be given the exit pass of the People's Republic of China issued by the office in charge of entry and exit under the Public Security Bureau. The pass is valid for a one time use only.

(2) If a Taiwan compatriot loses his travel certificate, he should report to the local residence office, China Travel Service or the Emigration Office for Overseas Chinese. After the loss is confirmed, he will be issued an entry and (B) _____ pass valid for one time use.

2. **What should a guide do when a tourist finds his luggage missing when he arrives at the airport?** 游客到达机场后发现行李丢失,导游员如何处理?

(1) Although he is not responsible for the loss, the guide should help the tourist look for the luggage and (C) _____ the loss.

(2) The guide should take him to the lost-and-found office to register the lost property. With his ticket and luggage (D) _____ in hand, the tourist should specify the number of pieces and the exterior characteristics of the luggage, and leave a phone number for further contact.

(3) The guide should also write down the address and phone number of the airline office and of the lost-and-found office at the airport, as well as the name of the person in charge. In this way, he can keep contact with the people concerned during the travel. According to the regulations of the airline company, a passenger who loses the luggage may buy some daily (E) _____ and submit receipts for reimbursement.

(4) If he can not find luggage before he leaves the present stop, the guide should inform the airline company of the address and phone number of the next stop. Meanwhile, he may help the tourist lodge a (F) _____ against the airline company.

Quickies

1. **Fill in the blanks with the proper words or phrases given below:**

counter	leader	payment	written	tag
count	claim	inconvenience	agent	missing

The Lost Luggage

Luggage is most likely to get lost when it is delivered from the airport to the hotel. The following measures are to be taken to minimize and prevent the loss of luggage: 1. To minimize the loss of luggage, the guide should sort out and (A) _____ the luggage before handing it over to the porter. 2. Then, if the tourist cannot find the luggage after checking in at the hotel, it may have been (B) _____ on the way, or the porter has sent the luggage to the wrong rooms. The local guide, along with the national guide, or the porter of the hotel should help the tourist look for the luggage. 3. If the luggage is not found, the (C) _____ of the travel agency should give an explanation and do an apology to the tourist and help him lodge a claim regarding the lost luggage. 4. The guide should help him solve the problem of (D) _____ brought about by the loss of luggage. 5. The guide should submit a (E) _____ report to the travel agency.

2. **Role-play:** Jack has lost his passport on Mount Huangshan. Miss Yao Kailing tries to help him look for the passport but in vain. She helps Jack renew his passport and visa so that he can continue with his travel.

PART II *Situational Dialogue*

New Words and Expressions

pedestrian	/piˈdestriən/	*adj.*	步行的,徒步的
maroon	/məˈruːn/	*adj.*	栗色的
flagstone	/ˈflægstəʊn/	*n.*	石板
curio	/ˈkjuəriəu/	*n.*	古董,古玩
knick-knack	/næk/	*n.*	小装饰品;小摆设
flavor	/ˈfleivə/	*n.*	风情,风味
logo	/ˈləugəu/	*n.*	标志或商标

Proper Nouns

Tunxi Ancient Street	屯溪老街	Mount Huangshan	黄山
Pingyao Ancient City	平遥古城	Anhui style	徽记,安徽风格
Tunxi Museum	屯溪博物馆	four treasures of study	文房四宝
Wancuilou	万粹楼		

Dialogue 1

Tunxi Ancient Street

After they tour Mount Huangshan, Miss Yao Kailing takes tourists to go shopping in the Tunxi Ancient Street.

(A= Miss Yao Kailing; B=Hilton)

A: After we tour Mount Huangshan, we'd like to tour the Tunxi Ancient Street. It is situated in the old town of the Tunxi District.

B: I've been to some ancient streets, say the Ming and Qing Street in Pingyao Ancient City. What is their difference?

A: In the Tunxi Ancient Street shops stand on both sides of the street. They generally have two or three floors with the local Anhui style of stone base, brick construction and tile roof.

B: The folk houses are really unique. You see, the pedestrian street is also very special. It is paved with maroon flagstones. The color of the flagstones well matches the color of the buildings in the street.

A: Right. Well, I'd like to point out another difference compared with others. The layout of these buildings takes on the appearance of shops in front while houses and workshops are to the rear.

B: So I guess they can do business in the shops while they make their products in the rear houses.

A: Oh yeah, along the street there are many shops that have existed for over one hundred years. Curios and knick-knacks including ink slabs, brushes, and local teas are available for sale.

B: I'd like to buy some souvenirs for my friends. Miss Yao, I hope that you could recommend something that really has the flavor of Anhui culture.

A: I will. Here is the Tunxi Museum. The furniture from the Ming and Qing dynasties is on display on the first floor and an exhibition of calligraphy, paintings and china is upstairs.

B: But I'd like to buy the Chinese brushes or ink slabs. I especially love the traditional Chinese paintings.

A: Then, I'll take you to another shop which specializes in the Chinese four treasures of study: writing brushes, ink sticks, ink slabs and paper.

B: Ok. Where is the shop? Please take me to the shop right now!

A: The shop is Wancuilou, a four-storey structure not far from here. There you can find the biggest ink slab of more than 12,500 kilograms. Do you want to buy that one?

B: It is too big for me. It's better to keep it in the shop as a logo.

Exercises

Do the dialogue again and pay attention to your facial expressions and body language.

New Words and Expressions

enthusiastically	/inˈθjuːziæzəmˌtikə/	*adv.*	热心地,狂热地
clan	/klæn/	*n.*	部落,氏族,家族
observe	/əbˈzɜːv/	*n.*	遵守
ethics	/ˈeθiks/	*n.*	道德规范
loyalty	/ˈlɔiəlti/	*n.*	忠诚
chastity	/ˈtʃæstiti/	*n.*	贞节
charity	/ˈtʃæriti/	*n.*	仁慈
execute	/ˈeksikjuːt/	*v.*	处死
behead	/biˈhed/	*v.*	斩首,砍头

Proper Nouns

Tangyue Memorial Archways	棠樾牌坊群
Shexian County	歙县
Ci Xiao Li Archway (Filial Piety Archway)	"慈孝里"牌坊

Bao Sheyan	鲍佘岩
Bao Shousun	鲍寿逊
ancestral temple	祠堂

Dialogue 2

Tangyue Memorial Archways

Memorial archway is a special construction in China. Miss Yao enthusiastically introduces the archways, especially its historical significance.

(A= Miss Yao Kailing; B=Mr. Hilton)

A: Tangyue Memorial Archways is a complex of seven arches. It is located in the Tangyue village six kilometers west of the famous town of arches—Shexian County.

B: What is the memorial archway? Could you explain it with more details?

A: The memorial archway is set up by the family clan to honor those who observe the ethics of the family.

B: I see. Look over there! Are they the archways? They stand in the main street of the village. I think they have stood there for many years.

A: Yes, the seven archways stand in order of "loyalty, filial piety, chastity and charity." Three were constructed in the Ming Dynasty, and the other four in the Qing Dynasty.

B: So it has probably a history of 600 years, longer than the history of my country.

A: Oh, yeah. Behind every archway there is a touching story. The Ci Xiao Li Archway (Filial Piety Archway) was built in honor of Bao Sheyan, the father; and Bao Shousun, the son.

B: What is the story? I hope it is not an invented story.

A: It is a true story. According to historical records, the father and son were captured by a general. He decided to execute one of them. Bao Shousun wanted to save his father, and begged the general to behead him instead of his father.

B: He is a heroic son. I think the father must be proud of his son.

A: But the father was also a good father, and asked to be executed to save his son. Their action and love moved the general. He finally released both of them.

B: A touching story, an excellent archway. I think they match very well.

A: Later, the court knew the fact and approved to build the archway in praise of their filial piety and self-sacrificial spirit.

B: I think they are worthy of the memorial

archway, even a monument.

A: I agree. Not far away from the seven archways there are two ancestral temples of the Baos'.

B: What is the ancestral temple?

A: The ancestral temple was a place to worship the honorable men in the family. Do you want to have a look?

B: That's my pleasure.

Cultural Notes

Tunxi Ancient Street 屯溪老街：屯溪老街安徽黄山市，建筑古朴典雅，是一条具有明清建筑风格的步行商业街。老街起于宋代，明清时期发展成为徽州物资集散中心。老街店铺，密集紧凑，店面、作坊、住宅三位一体，保留古代商家"前店后坊"或"前铺后户"的经营格局和特色。建筑高仅两三层，多为木穿榫式结构，石础、砖砌、马头墙、小青瓦、徽派木雕、金字招牌、朱阁重檐、古朴典雅、华丽高洁，被誉为"活动着的清明上河图"。

Tangyue Memorial Archways 棠樾牌坊群：棠樾牌坊群位于安徽歙县歙城西的棠樾村。牌坊群由7座牌坊组成，以忠、孝、节、义的顺序相向排列，分别建于明代和清代，旌表棠樾人"忠孝节义"。歙县棠樾牌坊群一改以往木质结构为主的特点，几乎全部采用石料，且以质地优良的"歙县青"石料为主。这种青石牌坊坚实、高大挺拔、恢宏华丽、气宇轩昂。在牌坊群旁，还有男女二祠，建筑规模宏大，砖木石雕特别精致，近年已修复如旧。中国牌坊博物馆也在这里筹建。

Exercises

Imagine that you are a local guide and your classmates are tourists. Make up a situational dialogue about the Tunxi Ancient Street or the Tangyue Memorial Archways.

PART III *Ethnic Culture*

New Words and Expressions

costume	/ˈkɔstjuːm/	*n.*	装束，服装
appeal	/əˈpiːl/	*v.*	吸引
askew	/əsˈkjuː/	*adj.*	歪斜的
scarf	/skɑːf/	*n.*	围巾
jut	/dʒʌt/	*v.*	(使)突出，((使)伸出
lace	/leis/	*v.*	扎带子，饰以花边
hem	/hem/	*v.*	给……缝边
kerchief	/ˈkəːtʃif/	*n.*	方巾
cape	/keip/	*n.*	斗篷，披肩
tassel	/ˈtæsl/	*n.*	穗，络缨

pest	/pest/	n.	害虫,有害物
organ	/'ɔːgən/	n.	[乐]风琴,管风琴
antiphonal	/æn'tifənl/	adj.	交互轮唱

Proper Nouns

| Yi | 彝族 | "Ziti" | "兹提" |
| "Hero Knot" | "英雄结" | Torch Festival | 火把节 |

Yi Culture

The Yi ethnic minority is reputed as an ethnic group with a long history and splendid culture. Their costume is one of the important identities of the nation. The Yi costumes with unique designs appeal to the tourists from all over the world. Yi men wear black jackets with tight sleeves and right-side askew fronts and pleated wide-bottomed trousers. They usually keep a mass of hair three or four inches long on the head, and wear a scarf made of a long piece of bluish cloth. The end of the cloth is tied into the shape of a thin horn jutting out from the right side of the forehead, which is named "Ziti" in the Yi language, or "Hero Knot" in Chinese. In addition, they also wear on the left ear a big yellow and red pearl strung by red silk thread. Women often wear laced or embroidered jackets and pleated long skirts hemmed with colorful multi-layered laces. Some women wear black scarves, while middle-aged and young women prefer embroidered square kerchiefs with the front covering part of the forehead. They also wear earrings and like pinning silver flowers on their collars. When going outdoors, both men and women wear a kind of dark cape made of wool and hemmed with long tassels that reach the knees.

The Yi people have many traditional festivals, the most important of which is the Torch Festival. Usually, the Yi people have a three-day holiday when the Torch Festival starts from the twenty-fourth day of the sixth lunar month. Early in the morning, people put on their holiday best and then gather on the flat outside the village for celebration. During the daytime, some people participate in wrestling, bullfighting, archery contests and horseracing, and many others watch the games and drink wine during the celebration. At night, people light up thousands of torches. They walk around their houses and fields, and plant pine torches on field ridges in the hope of driving away pests. After making their rounds, the villagers will finally gather on the flat outside the village again, singing and dancing around bonfires. While girls perform the moon dance, boys play bamboo flutes, moon guitars (a four-stringed plucked instrument with a moon-shaped sound box) and mouth organs, dancing and drinking throughout the night to pray for a good harvest. Besides, the Torch Festival is also an occasion for young people to look for a life partner through their antiphonal singing. The joyous activities of celebration may go on until dawn. The fantastic dances, the exotic lifestyle and the primitive religion, attract a lot of tourists to come and visit this mysterious land.

Quickies

True or False:

(1) _____ The end of the cloth is tied into the shape of a bow jutting out from the right side of the forehead, which is named "Ziti" in the Yi language, or "Hero Knot" in Chinese.

(2) _____ When they go outdoors, both men and women wear a kind of dark cape made of wool and hemmed with long tassels that reach their feet.

(3) _____ Torch Festival is an occasion for young people to look for their sweet hearts through their antiphonal singing.

PART IV *Practical Writing for Tourism*

Laundry Registration 衣物清洗表

Huating Hotel   No.

Name:	
Signature:	
Date	Room No.

PLEASE TICK ONE
- [ ] REGULAR SERVCE—GARMENTS RECEIVED BEFORE 10:00 A.M. RETURNEN THE SAMEDAY
- [ ] EXPERSS SERVCE—GARMENTS RECEVED BEFORE 2:00 P.M RETURNEN THE SAMEDAY

SPECIAL SERVCE: □ REPAIRING □ BUTTONING □ STAIN-REMOVNG

GUEST COUNT	HOTEL COUNT	LADIES	UNIT PRICE	AMOUNT
		BLOUSE	¥4.00	
		BRASSIERE	2.00	
		DRESS	8.00	
		HANDKERCHIEF	1.00	
		EVENING DRESS	10.00	
		UNDERPANTS	2.00	
		PAJAMAS	4.00	
		SHORTS	4.00	
		SKIRT	6.00	
		PLEATED SKIRT	15.00	
		SLACKS	6.00	
		SOCKS	1.00	
		STOCKINGS	1.00	
		SUIT	15.00	
		SWEATER	9.00	
		T-SHIRT	3.00	
		UNDERSHIRT	2.00	

GUEST	HOTEL COUNT	GENTLEMEN	UNIT PRICE	AMOUNT
		BATHROBE	¥5.00	
		DRESS SHIRT	1.00	
		HANDKERCHIEF	4.00	
		PYJAMAS (SET)	4.00	
		NORMAL SHIRT	4.00	
		SHORTS	1.00	
		SOCK	5.00	
		SWEATER	3.00	
		SWIM SHORT	6.00	
		TROUSERS	3.00	
		T-SHIRT	2.00	
		UNDERPANTS	2.00	
		VEST	4.00	
		SPORTS SHIRT	10.00	
		WAFUKU	9.00	

1. GUEST IS REQUIRED TO COMPLETE LIST OTHERWISE HOTEL COUNT MUST BE ACCEPTED AS CORRECT.
2. THE HOTEL IS NOT RESPONSIBLE FOR VALUABLES IN POCKETS.
3. IN CASE OF LOSS OR DAMAGE THE HOTEL WILL BE LIABLE TO NOMORE THAN TEN TIMES THE REGULAR PROCESSING CHARGE OF THE ITEM.
4. ALL CLAIMS MUST BE MADE WITHIN 24 HOURS AFTER DELIVERY AND MUST BE ACCOMPANED BY THE ORIGINAL LIST.

SPECIAL INSTRUCTIONS BASIC CHARGE_____?
50% EXTRA CHARGE FOR EXPRESS _____?
10% SERVICE CHARGE _____?
GRAND TOTAL _____?
BILIED BY:

衣物清洗表

华亭饭店 姓名_____ 签名_____ 日期_____ 房间号_____	编号： 请选一项： □ 普通服务,上午10点前收洗衣物,当天送还。 □ 快洗衣服务,下午2点前收取洗衣物,当天送还。

特殊服务：□缝补　　　　　□钉纽扣　　　　　□清洁污渍

客人计数	酒店计数	女衣	单位价格	总计	客人计数	酒店计数	男衣	单位价格	总计
		恤衫	4.00				浴衣	5.00	
		胸罩	2.00				礼服	1.00	
		连衣裙	8.00				手帕	4.00	
		手巾	1.00				睡衣	4.00	
		晚礼服	10.00				恤衫	4.00	
		紧身短裤	2.00				短裤	1.00	
		睡衣	4.00				短袜	5.00	
		短裤	4.00				白毛衣	3.00	
		短裙	6.00				泳裤	6.00	
		褶裙	15.00				西裤	3.00	
		长裤	6.00				T恤	2.00	
		短袜	1.00				内裤	2.00	
		长袜	1.00				运动衣	4.00	
		西装	15.00				和服	10.00	
		白毛衣	9.00						
		T恤	3.00						
		内衣	2.00						

1. 客人应填写好此表，否则，以酒店计数为准。
2. 请勿将贵重物品放入衣袋内，否则，本酒店概不负责。
3. 如果衣服有损坏或丢失的话，酒店有责任赔。但赔偿费用不超过洗价费用的10倍。
4. 任何有关清洗服务的投诉，须拿原衣物清洗单据在收到衣服之后24小时之内进行。

特殊情况说明	
基本费用	¥
快衣服务加收50%	
服务费	
总计	¥
计帐员	

Exercises

Fill in the Laundry Registration and present it to the Housekeeping. Make a situational dialogue accordingly.

Unit 14 Tourists Missing

游客走失

PART I ABC for Tour Guides

New Words and Expressions

lag	/læg/	v.	缓缓而行,滞后
exterior	/eks'tiəriə/	adj.	外部的,外在的
brochure	/brəu'ʃjuə/	n.	小册子
emergency	/i'mə:dʒəns/	n.	紧急情况,突发事件

Proper Nouns

"bring up the rear"　　　　"断后"（走在游客后面）

Listening

Direction: Listen to the passages carefully and fill in the blanks with the missing information you have heard from the tapes.

What measures should a guide take to prevent tourists from getting lost? 导游应注意采取哪些措施以预防游客走失?

(1) Every morning, the guide should tell tourists about the itinerary (A) _____ of the day, including the places for sightseeing and meals, so that tourists can catch up with the group if he lags behind.

(2) On arrival at the tourist site, the guide should ask tourists to remember the number and the (B) _____ characteristics of the coach, the parking place and the time for departure. The guide may point out the travel route on the tourist map at the site.

(3) While traveling, the guide should count tourists from time to time. Generally speaking, the local guide introduces the scenery while the (C) _____ guide "brings up the rear" and reminds the tourists to keep up with the others.

(4) During the time for free sightseeing and (D) _____, the local guide should remind tourists not to go too far, not to return too late and not to go to places with poor security.

(5) When they go out alone, he should ask them to take with them the business card or (E) _____ of the hotel with the phone number and address on it. Since mobile phones are popular nowadays, he may keep the tourists' mobile numbers subject to their approval, in case of emergency.

New Words and Expressions

blame	/bleim/	v.	责备,谴责
criticize	/'kritisaiz/	v.	批评,责备
severely	/si'viəli/	adv.	严格地,激烈地

Readings

Direction: Read the following passage aloud and fill in the blanks with words or phrases you think appropriate.

| lost | reception | fall | another | behind |
| escort | where | worry | criticizing | report |

If a tourist is found missing during the sightseeing time, what should the guide do? 游客在游览活动中发生走失,导游员如何处理?

(1) The guide should first determine when and (A) _____ the tourist was seen last time and then arrange for people to look for him.

(2) If there are more than two guides, one guide should take care of the tour group while (B) _____ guide looks for the missing tourist along the route. In case that he fails to find the missing tourist, the guide should report to the local police station at the scenic area for help. He should also call the (C) _____ desk at the hotel to check whether the tourist has returned.

(3) If the tourist is still missing, the guide should ask the travel agency to send personnel to handle the matter while he continues to (D) _____ the tour group according to the itinerary, as planned.

(4) After getting the tourist back, the guide should apologize if he is to blame; if the tourist is to blame, the guide, instead of (E) _____ him severely, should remind him gently not to get away from the group again.

(5) If the tourist disappears and nothing is heard from him after the parties concerned try their best, the guide should hand in a written (F) _____ to the travel agency.

Quickies

116 **Role-play:** Act as a local guide and a national guide respectively. Look for Jack who is missing when he hikes on Mount Qingcheng in Sichuan Province.

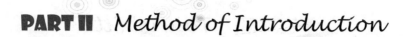

PART II *Method of Introduction*

New Words and Expressions

suspend	/səs'pend/	v.	中止,延缓
inspire	/in'spaiə/	v.	鼓舞,激发
stimulate	/'stimjuleit/	v.	刺激,激励

Proper Nouns

Wanjuan Tower of Chen Shou 陈寿万卷楼

The Method of Suspense-Creating Introduction
制造悬念法

This method tends to excite tourists' curiosity and desire for knowledge by suspending the introduction suddenly when a guide explains the key point of a tourist site. It turns out to be one of the most effective ways to catch tourists' attention, and inspire tourists to participate in seeking the truth. If they fail to come up with it, the guide then could help them find the way out and resolve the riddle. For example, before introducing the Wanjuan Tower of Chen Shou the guide may ask tourists why the Tower is built up at the mountaintop and how many steps leads to the top of the mountain. When tourists start to climb the mountain, he may ask them to count the number of steps which leads up to the tower instead of telling them directly the exact number. By this way the suspense is created, which arouses their interest as well as stimulates their enthusiasm. Tourists' attention is successfully oriented to ascending the steps and discovery of the riddle in the Tower. When they reach the Tower on the mountaintop the guide gives the answer and resolves the suspense.

Quickies

1. What effects could the guide achieve when he makes the suspense in his introduction?
2. How many ways could a guide use to create the suspense in his introduction?
3. Give an example to show you can create the suspense in your introduction.

PART III *Tourist Site*

New Words and Expressions

posthumous	/'pɔstjuməs/	*adj.*	死后的，身后的
regime	/rei'ʒiːm/	*n.*	政体，政权
apparent	/ə'pærənt/	*adj.*	显然的
defiance	/di'faiəns/	*n.*	蔑视，挑衅
overshadow	/ˌəuvə'ʃædəu/	*v.*	遮蔽，使……失色
erect	/i'rekt/	*v.*	树立，建立
homage	/'hɔmidʒ/	*n.*	敬意
genius	/'dʒiːnjəs/	*n.*	天才，天赋
accomplishment	/ə'kɔmpliʃmənt/	*n.*	成就，造诣
calligrapher	/kə'ligrəfə(r)/	*n.*	书法家
sculptor	/'skʌlptə(r)/	*n.*	雕刻家
load	/ləud/	*n.*	负荷，承重

Proper Nouns

Wu Yuanhen	武元衡	Pei Du	裴度
Liu Gongchuo	柳公绰	Lu Jian	鲁建
"Tablet of Three Wonders"	"三绝碑"		

Wuhou Temple

The present Wuhou Temple was reconstructed on its old site in 1672 during the Qing Dynasty. A horizontal board hangs on the entrance gate inscribed with four Chinese characters: 汉昭烈庙 (Zhaolie Temple of Han). "Zhaolie" is the official posthumous title of Liu Bei and "Han" is the name of Liu's regime. This suggests that the Temple was originally built in honor of Liu Bei, the king of the Shu Kingdom. But why do people call it "Wuhou Temple" in apparent defiance of the emperor's dignity? Because people believed that Zhuge Liang made remarkable contributions to the Shu Kingdom, and his fame overshadowed that of Liu Bei. Small wonder the Temple bears the name of the posthumous title of Zhuge Liang—Wuhou.

Along the lane to the main hall, six inscribed stone tablets are erected on both sides of the passageway from the front gate to the second gate. Four of them were constructed in the Qing Dynasty, one in the Ming Dynasty, and another, the most famous one, in the Tang Dynasty. The 3.67 meter high tablet of the Tang Dynasty catches tourist's eye with its three artistic achievements. It was constructed after Wu Yuanhen, the Commander-in-Chief and concurrent governor of West Sichuan, together with his 27 assistants, had paid homage to Zhuge Liang in the Temple during the Tang Dynasty. Pei Du, a literary genius and a prime minister for three emperors of the Tang Dynasty, composed the essay, in which Zhuge Liang's accomplishments for Shu Kingdom and his efforts to reunify the whole country were highly praised. Liu Gongchuo, a famed calligrapher, inscribed it in a beautiful handwriting style. Lu Jian, the well-known stone sculptor engraved the calligraphic work onto the tablet. The three celebrities joined their hands and united their talents to perfect the tablet. No wonder it enjoys the fame of being called "Tablet of Three Wonders" for its superb essay,

calligraphy and sculpture. Another tablet is a relic of the Ming Dynasty, recording the history of the Temple. The round base of the tablet is made of a whole stone, symbolizing one of the nine sons of the dragon, capable of bearing a heavy load.

Cultural Notes

Wuhou Templ 武侯祠:武侯祠又名"汉昭烈庙",是纪念三国时期蜀国皇帝刘备和丞相诸葛亮的君臣合庙祠堂,1961 年列为全国重点文物保护单位。唐代时,武侯祠与刘备墓和刘备庙毗邻。明代初年,武侯祠被并入刘备庙。明代末年,祠庙毁于战火,清代康熙十一年(1672 年)重建。今天的武侯祠占地 37000 平方米,主体建筑坐北面南,中轴线上依次是大门、二门、刘备殿、过厅、诸葛亮殿五重,西侧是刘备陵园及其建筑。二门至刘备殿与东西廊,过厅至诸葛殿东西两厢房,形成两组四合建筑结构,轴线建筑两侧配有园林景点和附属建筑。

Quickies

1. **True or False:**

   (1) _____ Wuhou Temple was built to commemorate Zhuge Liang because people believed that he made remarkable contributions to the Shu Kingdom.

   (2) _____ There are six inscribed stone tablets erected on both sides of the passageway, among which the Ming tablet is the most renowned.

   (3) _____ Tablet of Three Wonders is outstanding for three things: the superb essay, elegant calligraphy and marvelous sculpture.

2. Read the passage aloud and introduce the Wuhou Temple using the methods of introduction you have learnt. The method of suspense-creating introduction is one of the choices.

Tips

- Draft your own commentary before you make your presentation.
- Speak colloquial English and use simple and short sentences.
- Animate your introduction with facial expressions and body language.
- Apply at least one method of introduction. It is highly recommended that you use two or three methods of introduction.

PART IV *Simulated Introduction*

New Words and Expressions

artifacts	/ˈɑːtifækts/	*n.*	史前古器物
twig	/twig/	*n.*	树枝，末梢
triangular	/traiˈæŋgjulə/	*adj.*	三角形的
rotation	/rəuˈteiʃən/	*n.*	旋转
incarnation	/ˌinkɑːˈneiʃən/	*n.*	化身

Proper Nouns

Sanxingdui Museum	三星堆博物馆	Guanghan City	广汉市
Yan Daocheng	燕道诚	sacrificial pit	祭祀坑
Shang Dynasty	商朝	Venus n.	[罗神]维纳斯
yaoqian tree	摇钱树	Jade Mountain	玉山
King of Bianzhang	边璋之王		

Sanxingdui Museum

Good morning, ladies and gentlemen!

Welcome to the Sanxingdui Museum, the wonder of the Shu civilization!

Sanxingdui Museum is located about 8 kilometers to the west of Guanghan City and about 40 kilometers from Chengdu, the capital city of Sichuan Province. In the spring of 1929, a peasant named Yan Daocheng found a pit full of delicate jade and stone artifacts when he dug a ditch in front of his house. In July 1986, two large sacrificial pits full of many exquisite relics during the period of the Shang Dynasty were found. Sanxingdui became instantly famous throughout the world, and so the ancient Shu civilization.

Ladies and gentlemen, we are getting into the Sanxingdui Museum. Please do not use flashers when you take photos! The objects in the showcases are all national treasures. There are six exhibition halls in the Museum. We'll visit them one by one and meet at the sixth exhibition hall. There I'll ask you six whys. We'll discuss the six wonders about the Sanxingdui Ruins. So when I introduce the objects in the Museum please listen carefully. If you have any questions please do not hesitate to ask me!

At the entrance, we've already seen the enlarged holy tree in the lobby. In front of us is the original holy tree. It is emplaced in the 3rd exhibition hall. Please look at the top of the holy tree! Although its top is missing, it is still up to 3.95 meters. So this tree is undoubtedly the largest one of the eight holy trees unearthed from the No.2 pit. Look at the middle part of the tree carefully! The tree has three branches, and each of them has three twigs; on each of the twig there is a fruit. Please notice that one fruit upward and the other two fruits downward. So the three fruits are in a triangular arrangement. A bird stands on each of fruit and faces upwards.

Miss Brown, I'd like to ask you some questions: Why are there nine birds on the tree? Why are they birds, not any other animals?

We know, the rising of the sun from the east and setting in the west is related to the rotation of the earth, but in ancient times, people did not know the moving of the earth. They regarded the movement of the sun as the flying birds, and the bird is the incarnation of the sun. That's why you see birds perching on the holy trees. Look, nine birds are ready to fly into the sky.

My dear friends, please look at the bottom of this holy tree! Can you find something special? Right, there is a dragon with one head and two bodies. The face of this dragon looks like horse's, the body of the dragon like ropes which twist up around the entire holy tree. The dragon was regarded as a link between heaven and earth, but unfortunately, the tail of the dragon can not be found as well as the top of the tree. But it doesn't matter because it leaves us some space to imagine what the holy tree really looks like on earth, just like the Venus without arms. Do you think so, my friends?

Well, so much for my introduction of the holy tree! Before we leave the 3rd exhibition hall, We'll see something special here. In the corner of the hall, there is a "yaoqian" tree. There are more than 300 copper coins on the six-layer tree. If you shake this tree, and get the coins from the tree, you will be rich and lucky. Ok everybody! We'll go to the fourth exhibition hall. There you can see hundreds of jade articles, especially the "Jade Mountain" and the "King of Bianzhang."

This way please!

Cultural Notes

Sanxingdui Museum 三星堆博物馆：三星堆博物馆位于四川省广汉市三星堆遗址东北角，是我国一座现代化的专题性遗址博物馆。三星堆文物是宝贵的人类文化遗产，古蜀文化的杰出代表。在这些古蜀秘宝中，有光怪陆离奇异诡谲的青铜造型，有高 2.62 米的青铜大立人、有宽 1.38 米的青铜面具、更有高达 3.95 米的青铜神树等，均堪称独一无二的旷世神品。而以流光溢彩的金杖为代表的金器，以满饰图案的边璋为代表的玉石器，亦多属前所未见的稀世珍品。三星堆博物馆以其文物、建筑、陈列、园林为四大特色，是首批国家 4A 级旅游景区、享誉中外的文化旅游胜地。

Exercises

Make a simulated introduction of the Sanxingdui Museum using the methods of introduction you have learnt. Pay attention to the body language and other tips of introduction.

Unit 15 *Illness and Care*

生病与护理

PART I *ABC for Tour Guides*

New Words and Expressions

board	/bɔːd/	v.	上（船、飞机等）
prescribe	/prisˈkraib/	v.	下处方，开药
alimentary	/ˌæliˈmentəri/	adj.	食物的，营养的
toxicosis	/ˌtɔksiˈkəusis/	n.	[医]中毒
acute	/əˈkjuːt/	adj.	[医]急性的；剧烈的
onset	/ˈɔnset/	n.	[医]发作

Proper Nouns

carsickness	晕车	
alimentary toxicosis	食物中毒	

Listening

*Direction: **Listen to the passages carefully and fill in the blanks with the missing information you have heard from the tapes.***

1. **How should a guide help the tourist who suffers from carsickness?** 导游员应如何给晕车游客以必要的帮助？

   (1) The guide should remind him not to eat too much before (A) _____ the coach.

   (2) He can advise him to take the medicine prescribed for carsickness with him.

   (3) If possible, he may let him sit in a (B) _____ seat or a seat nearby the window so that he can have a smoother ride or take the fresh air.

2. **What is typical of alimentary toxicosis? How can it be avoided and treated?** 食物中毒的典型特征是什么？如何预防和处理？

   (1) The disease is (C) _____ with a short onset. If not treated in time, the patient may die.

(2) To avoid its occurrence, the guide should take the tourist only to have meals in the (D) _____ restaurants, and always remind them not to eat food sold by street vendors.

(3) If the tourist is poisoned, the guide should ask him to drink water to (E) _____ out the poison and send him to the hospital immediately.

New Words and Expressions

symptom	/'simptəm/	n.	[医]症状,征兆
dizziness	/'dizinis/	n.	头晕眼花
nausea	/'nɔːsjə/	n.	反胃,恶心,作呕
vomit	/'vɔmit/	v.	呕吐
coma	/'kəumə/	n.	昏迷
breezy	/'briːzi/	adj.	有微风的,通风好的
unfasten	/ˌʌn'fɑːsn/	v.	解开,放松
fluid	/'flu(ː)id/	n.	流质食物
alleviate	/ɔːl'evətrɔn/	v.	使(痛苦等)减轻
ambulance	/'æmbjuləns/	n.	救护车
sunstroke	/'sʌnstrəuk/		中暑
angina pectoris			心绞痛

Readings

Direction: Read the following passage aloud and fill in the blanks with words or phrases you think appropriate.

sunshine	prescribe	hot	vomit	fluids
toothache	salty	ambulance	up	cough

1. **What is typical of sunstroke? How should a guide treat the tourist if he has sunstroke?** 中暑有什么典型特征? 如果游客中暑如何处理?

   (1) The symptoms of sunstroke include excessive sweating, thirst, dizziness, ringing in the ears, and nausea.

   (2) The patient may also (A) _____ and develop a fever. In the case of a serious sunstroke, the patient may be delirious or in a coma.

   (3) If the tourist feels sick, the guide should help him rest in a cool and breezy place, unbutton his collar and unfasten his belt.

   (4) If possible, the guide should give the patient (B) _____ water to drink.

   (5) For the patient who develops a fever, the guide may bathe his body with cool water and help him to drink some (C) _____.

(6) When the patient feels better, the guide should let him have a rest. If the sunstroke is very serious, the guide should send the tourist to the hospital after the first aid.

2. **When a tourist suffers from an angina pectoris, and an elderly tourist nearby tells the guide he has brought with him medicine to alleviate the symptoms, what should the guide do under such a circumstance?** 游客突发心绞痛,旁边一位老年游客向导游表示,愿意捐出随身携带的治疗心绞痛的药物,导游员该怎么办?

(1) The guide should not offer the patient his own medicine, for he has no authority to (D) _____ for a patient. He should not take any medicine from the elderly tourist to offer the patient too if neither of them are the doctors.

(2) The guide should have the patient lie down with his head slightly held (E) _____. If the patient has his own medicine with him, the guide could help him take it.

(3) The guide should call for an (F) _____ to take the patient to a nearby hospital for the treatment if it is a serious case.

Quickies

Role-play: Mr. Brown suffers from an angina pectoris. An elderly tourist hands him medicine for the first aid. The local guide and other tourists take part in the first aid. Replay the scene while paying attention to the right procedures of the first aid.

PART II *Situational Dialogue*

New Words and Expressions

axis	/ˈæksis/	n.	轴
wing	/wiŋ/	n.	厢房,边房
interior	/inˈtiəriə/	adj.	内部的
cryptograph	/ˈkriptəuɡrɑːf/	n.	密文,密码
cipher	/ˌsaifə/	n.	密码
restrict	/risˌtrikt/	v.	限制,约束
draft	/drɑːft/	n.	汇票,汇款
watermark	/ˌwɔːtəmɑːk/	n.	水印
financial	/faiˌnænʃəl/	adj.	财政的,金融的

Proper Nouns

Rishengchang Exchange Shop	日升昌票号	Pingyao Ancient City	平遥古城
Xidajie Street	西大街	Morse	莫尔斯式电码

Dialogue 1

Rishengchang Exchange Shop

Mr. Wang Jun takes tourists around the Pingyao Ancient City. Today they will visit one of the earliest banks in China.

(A=Mr. Wang Jun; B=Alice)

A: Alice, I'd like to ask you some questions before we tour other sites in the Pingyao Ancient City. When did the earliest bank appear in China? What did it look like?

B: I've no idea.

A: You can find the answer when you enter the Rishengchang Exchange Shop at No. 105 Xidajie street in Pingyao.

B: Really? I'd like to look at what the earliest bank looks like in China. Where is the bank?

A: It was just the building complex in front of you. This Chinese bank was set up in about 1823. It had twenty-one buildings around three courtyards on a north-south central axis.

B: Is this a bank? It looks like a classic Chinese garden. Anyhow, where is the exchange center? How did they do the banking business?

A: The three rooms in the middle courtyard are the exchange center. The counters are arranged on either side of the front yard. Guest rooms are located in the wings beside the main hall. In the rear court there are five main halls.

B: Wow, it is a big complex. Mr. Wang, look over there! An inscribed board hangs on the wall just opposite the door. I think it matches well with the interior decoration of the house.

A: Yes, in fact, the board is inscribed with a few lines of poetry. They are some of the earliest cryptograph characters, like Morse code.

B: What a surprise! The banking cryptograph is just on the wall. Everybody can see it.

A: But you may not interpret it. The cipher was constantly changed so as to restrict its interpretation to just a few senior ones.

B: Did the bank issue the drafts?

A: Yes, for the safety, other security techniques, such as seals, watermarks, and handwriting of certain styles, were applied to the drafts issued by the bank.

B: I think this bank was one of the most advanced banks in Pingyao and had a strong influence on the local economics.

A: Certainly. Pingyao was the financial center in China at that time. There were twenty-two banks in Pingyao among the total of fifty-one banks in the country.

125

B: Thank you for your introduction. I come to know the Rishengchang Exchange Shop is not a shop, but the earliest bank in China.

Exercises

Do the dialogue again and pay attention to the facial expressions and body language.

New Words and Expressions

elaborate	/iˌlæbərət/	*adj.*	精心的,精巧的
cluster	/ˌklʌstə/	*n.*	串,丛,群
maze	/meiz/	*n.*	迷宫,迷津

Proper Nouns

Wang's Compound	王家大院	Lingshi County	灵石县
Qiao's Compound	乔家大院	East Courtyard	东院
Gaojiaya	高家崖	Hongmenbao (Red Gate Castle)	红门堡

Dialogue 2

Wang's Compound

After touring the Pingyao Ancient City they arrive at the Wang's Compound. It is typical of the compounds in Shanxi Province.

(A=Mr. Wang Jun; B=Alice)

A: Now, we've arrived at the Wang's Compound. It is located in Lingshi County, 35 kilometers from the Pingyao Ancient City.

B: What a beautiful compound! I think this compound is far more splendid than the Qiao's Compound.

A: Well, I'd like to say yes. Wang's Compound is a luxurious residence built during 1762—1811 by the descendants of the Wang Family. The family is one of the Four Families of the Qing Dynasty in Shanxi Province.

B: That's great. If Wang's Compound were not a typical example of residential architecture in Shanxi, you wouldn't have taken me here.

A: You're right. Wang's Compound is considered as the most elaborate example of the building art of the Ming and Qing dynasties. Here is the East Courtyard, also called Gaojiaya.

B: Mr. Wang, you walk too fast. I'm afraid I'll get lost. The alley is very long and there are so many yards here and there.

A: The Compound is a cluster of courtyards. Each yard has its own kitchen yard and private school yard. You won't get lost if you keep pace with me.

B: Well, how could we get out of here now? I'm afraid we're trapped in the maze.

A: Don't worry! At the four sides of the East Courtyard there are four gates: east gate, south gate, west gate and north gate. Follow me please! Now, we are getting out through the west gate.

B: At last, we're out of this big compound! Mr. Wang, what is the red gate opposite? It looks like a castle.

A: It is the West Courtyard, also called Hongmenbao. Hongmenbao means Red Gate Castle.

B: Judging from its appearance I believe it is also a big compound.

A: Right. Hongmenbao has 27 courtyards of different styles. All of the courtyards are splendid or delicate.

B: Shall we go in to have a look?

A: Of course.

Cultural Notes

Rishengchang Exchange Shop 日升昌票号：日升昌票号是中国第一家专营存款、放款、汇兑业务的私人金融机构，开中国银行业之先河。日升昌票号成立于清道光三年(1823 年)，由山西省平遥县西达蒲村富商李大金出资与雷履泰共同创办。总号设于山西省平遥县城内繁华街市的西大街路南，占地面积 1600 多平方米，分号达 35 处之多，遍布全国大中城市和商埠重镇。日升昌票号以汇通天下闻名于世，现已被辟为"中国票号博物馆"。

Wang's Compound 王家大院：王家大院位于山西省灵石县城东 12 公里处的静升镇，距世界文化遗产平遥古城 35 公里。 王家大院是清代民居建筑的集大成者，由历史上灵石县四大家族之一的太原王氏后裔——静升王家于清康熙、雍正、乾隆、嘉庆年间所建，总面积达 25 万平方米以上。现有高家崖、红门堡两大建筑群和王氏宗祠等，大小院落共 123 座，房屋 1118 间，面积 4.5 万平方米，有"中国民居艺术馆"、"中华王氏博物馆"之美誉。

Exercises

Imagine that you are a local guide and your classmates are tourists. Make up a situational dialogue about the Rishengchang Exchange Shop or the Wang's Compound.

PART III *Ethnic Culture*

New Words and Expressions

oracle	/'ɔrəkl/	n.	[宗]神谕,预言
quartz	/kwɔːts/	n.	石英
convention	/kən'venʃən/	n.	习俗,惯例
adolescence	/ˌædəʊ'lesəns/	n.	青春期
kneel	/niːl/	v.	跪下
kowtow	/ˌkəʊ'tau/	v.	叩头,磕头
amulet	/'æmjulit/	n.	护身符
ram	/ræm/	n.	公羊
revere	/ri'viə/	v.	尊敬,敬畏
sorcerer	/'sɔːsərə/	n.	男巫士,魔术师
unsophisticated	/ˌʌnsə'fistikeitid/	adj.	不懂世故的,单纯的
ribbon	/'ribən/	n.	缎带,丝带

Proper Nouns

Qiang	羌族	Yunyun shoes	云云鞋

Qiang Culture

The Qiang have a profound history of over 3,000 years as evidenced by inscriptions on oracle bones. The Qiang people believe that everything in nature has a spirit. They especially consider white quartz stone as the symbol of rightness having the power of gods, while the black quartz represents evil. Every third day of a New Year, the Qiang worship gods, such as the god of the mountain, the god of the stone king, the god of the ox king, etc.

It has long been the Qiang convention for a fifteen-year-old boy to hold an initiation (growing-up) ceremony, which signifies the transition from adolescence to adulthood in a person's life. At the ceremony, friends and relatives are invited to gather around the bonfire. After the boy kneels down and kowtows before the statue of the ancestor, he will be granted an amulet, which is composed of some colorful cloth strips fastened with thread made of ram wool. Then a revered old man of the clan will tell stories of their ancestors, and the sorcerer will pray and offer sacrifice to the family god and the sheep god.

Embroidery and weaving are Qiang's traditional handicrafts. Every Qiang woman is an expert embroiderer. The brightly colored, exquisitely patterned embroideries are quite attractive. Their traditional costumes are simple and unsophisticated. A man usually wears a long blue gown and a sheepskin jacket, with a black scarf wrapped round his head. A woman's clothes are somewhat brighter, as she wears a long blue or green skirt edged with colorful embroidered patterns. In addition, Qiang women usually wear an apron with embroidered patterns, a colored ribbon round the waist, and a black or white kerchief on their heads. On festive occasions, the Qiang women like to wear Yunyun shoes—interesting homemade cloth shoes, shaped like small boats. The toes of the shoes are slightly upturned and the sides are decorated with colorful embroidered patterns.

Quickies

True or False:

(1) _____ The Qiang people consider white quartz stone as the symbol of rightness having the power of gods, while the black quartz represents evil.

(2) _____ At age of 15, the Qiang girl will be granted an amulet, which is composed of some colorful cloth strips fastened with thread made of ram wool.

(3) _____ On festive occasions, the Qiang women wear the Yunyun shoes. The homemade cloth shoes take shape of small boats.

PART IV *Practical Writing for Tourism*

1. Visa Application Form 签证申请表

VISA APPLICATION FORM

THE PEPPLE'S REPUBLIC OF CHINA
VISA APPLICATION FORM

Stick Photo Here

1. Surname (Last name) _____ Given name _____
   In Chinese (if any) _____
2. Nationality _____ Date of Birth _____ Year _____
   Month _____ Day _____ Sex _____
3. Place of birth _____ Occupation _____
4. Passport type _____ No. _____ Valid until _____
   Year _____ Month _____ Day _____
5. Place of work _____ Tel. No. _____
6. Home address _____ Tel. No. _____
7. Purpose of Journey _____
   Host unit in China (for business only) _____
8. Date of departure from U.S.A. _____
   Intended date of entry _____

9. Duration of stay in China _____

   Places to visit in China _____

10. Relatives or friends in China, if any _____

   Name _____ Nationality _____

   _____

   Occupation and address _____

   _____

   Relationship to applicant _____

   _____

I guarantee that the statement given above is true and correct.

Applicant's signature _____ Date of application _____

Remarks _____

签证申请表

中华人民共和国签证申请表

1. 姓_____ 名_____ 中文姓名_____ 请贴照片

2. 国籍_____ 出生日期_____ 年_____ 月_____ 日

   性别_____

3. 出生地点_____ 职业_____

4. 护照种类_____ 号码_____ 有效期至_____ 年_____ 月_____ 日

5. 工作处所_____ 电话号码_____

6. 家庭住所_____ 电话号码_____

7. 来中国事由_____ 邀请单位_____

8. 离境日期_____ 拟入境日期_____

9. 拟在中国停留期限_____ 入境后前往地点_____

10. 在华亲友(此项只需探亲者填写)_____

   姓名　　　　　　国籍　　　　　　职业及住址　　　　　　与申请人关系

   _____　　_____　　_____　　_____

   _____　　_____　　_____　　_____

我保证以上填写的全部内容属实

申请人签字_____ 填写日期_____

备注_____

2. Arrival Card 入境登记卡

Arrival Card

Family Name		Given Name					
Nationality		Date of Birth	Day	Mon	Year	☐ Male	☐ Female
Passport No.		Occupation					
Chinese Visa No.		Place of Issue					
Accompanied by							
Address in China (Hotel)		Host Organization					
Date and Flight No.		Signature					

入境登记卡

姓		名					
国籍		出身日期	日	月	年	男 ☐	女 ☐
证件号码		职业					
中国签证号码		签发地点					
偕行人							
在华地点		接待单位					
日期和航班号		签名					

Exercises

Fill in the Visa Application Form and Arrival Card and present them to the immigrant officials in the airport. Make a dialogue between the tourist and immigrant officials.

Unit 16 First Aid

急 救

PART I ABC for Tour Guides

New Words and Expressions

cardiovascular	/ˌkɑːdiəu'væskjulə/	adj.	心脏血管的
fetch	/fetʃ/	v.	接来,取来
surgical	/'səːdʒikəl/	adj.	外科的
console	/kən'səul/	v.	安慰
preliminary	/pri'liminəri/	adj.	预备的,初步的
fracture	/'fræktʃə/	v.	破裂,骨折
dressing	/'dresiŋ/	n.	敷裹,敷料
bandage	/'bændidʒ/	n.	绷带
tourniquet	/'tuəniket/	n.	止血带
rinse	/rins/	v.	冲洗,漂净
splint	/splint/	n.	(外科用的)夹板
immobilize	/i'məubilaiz/	v.	固定

Proper Nouns

surgical operation	外科手术	blood vessel	血管

Listening

Direction: Listen to the passages carefully and fill in the blanks with the missing information you have heard from the tapes.

1. **If a tourist suddenly becomes seriously ill on journey, how should a guide handle the case?**
   旅游途中游客突发重病,导游员该如何处理?

   (1) When a tourist becomes seriously ill, the guide should not offer him medicine. Instead he should ask whether the tourist has brought medicine with him for the disease. People who suffer from (A) _____ diseases usually carry with them first-aid medicine. If the patient does have the medicine, the guide may assist him in taking it.

(2) If the patient's life is in danger, the guide should call the nearest first-aid station for fetching the patient, or hire a (B) _____ to take him to the nearest hospital. If necessary, the guide may suspend the travel for the time being, and take the patient to the nearest hospital by coach.

(3) While rescuing the patient or sending him to hospital, it would be better if the tour leader or national guide or the patient's relative were (C) _____. Any surgical operation should be approved in a written form by the tourist's relatives or the national guide or the tour leader. The local guide should keep the relevant files and records for further investigation.

(4) During the process of the rescue, the guide should report to the travel agency as soon as possible for instruction. If necessary, he may ask the travel agency to send personnel to handle the matter so he may (D) _____ his duties and continue to escort the tour group.

(5) If the patient must remain in the hospital, the guide or the staff of the travel agency should visit him from time to time and console him. If the patient's visa needs an (E) _____ _____, the guide should help him get an extension.

(6) The patient is responsible for the medical expenses and related charges in the hospital. The travel agency should (F) _____ the money for the remaining items of the tour that the patient has not yet taken according to the contract.

2. **What a preliminary treatment can a guide provide for the wounded tourist? What should he do if the tourist has suffered a fractured limb?** 游客受伤或发生骨折,导游员应做哪些初步处理?

(1) The guide should first attempt to stop the bleeding by:

    (a) Pressure: use fingers, palm or fist to press the blood (G) _____ above the wound;

    (b) Bandage: place thick dressing on the wound and bind it tightly with a bandage;

    (c) Tourniquet: wrap a tourniquet tightly above the (H) _____.

(2) The guide should bind up the wound of the tourist. Before binding, he should first rinse the wound and then wrap it up gently, tying the knot away from the wound.

(3) The guide should put a fractured limb in a (I) _____ made of any available material to immobilize the joint and avoid moving the fractured limb.

New Words and Expressions

scorpion	/'skɔːpiən/	n.	[动]蝎子,心黑的人
suck	/sʌk/	v.	吸,吮
ammonia	/'æməunjə/	n.	[化]氨,氨水
antidote	/'æntidəut/	n.	[医]解毒剂
circulation	/ˌsəːkju'leiʃən/	n.	循环,流通
vertical	/'vəːtikəl/	adj.	垂直的,直立的
incision	/in'siʒən/	n.	切开,切口

| topica | /'tɔpikə/ | n. | [医]局部药,外用药 |

Proper Nouns

| liquor potassii permanganatis | 高锰酸钾溶液 | normal saline | 生理盐水 |

Readings

Direction: Read the following passage aloud and fill in the blanks with words or phrases you think appropriate.

| fatal | poison | sting | unconscious | antidotes |
| horizontal | circulation | wrap | vertical | stretcher |

1. **How should a guide treat the tourist who has been stung by a bee or a scorpion?** 游客被蜂、蝎蜇伤后应如何处理?

   (1) The guide should try to pull out the sting and suck out the (A) _____ with his mouth or a straw.

   (2) After sucking out the poison he should rinse the wound with soapy water if available: 5% soda water, or 3% ammonia water.

   (3) The guide may ask the patient to take some (B) _____.

2. **How should a guide treat the tourist who has been bitten by a poisonous snake?** 游客被毒蛇咬伤,导游员应如何抢救?

   (1) If the bite is on the limb, the guide should wrap the limb 5 or 10 centimeters above the bite, but make sure not to stop the blood (C) _____.

   (2) The guide may also make a (D) _____ incision of 0.5 centimeter in length at the bite site, and suck out the poison.

   (3) Afterwards he should rinse the bite with water if the topica is available: liquor potassii permanganatis (1:5000) and 5%—10% of normal saline.

Quickies

1. **True or False:**

   (1) _____ When the foreign tourist dies on the journey the local guide should ask the national guide or the tour leader to inform the relatives of the dead. If the dead is a foreign tourist, the guide should report to the local Foreign Affairs Office, the officials of which will inform the deceased's Embassy or Consulate General in China.

   (2) _____ The guide should handle the remains of the deceased according to the wishes of his relatives or as instructed by the Embassy or Consulate in China; an oral statement is preferred.

(3) _____ The guide should handle all the relevant certificates such as: death certificate, first aid report, cremation certificate and the certificate for transporting the deceased's ashes out of China.

(4) _____ The guide should help the relatives sort out the articles left by the deceased. If no relatives of the deceased are present, the local guide should sort, identify and list all personal effects. He should put his signature on the list of the articles and keep a copy of the list.

(5) _____ The guide is supposed to help handle the compensation issue.

2. Role-play: Mary has a fractured limb and can not continue to walk. Miss Liu Deyun gives her preliminary treatment, and then sends her to the hospital nearby.

PART II *Method of Introduction*

New Words and Expressions

concise	/kən'sais/	adj.	简明的,简练的
highlight	/'hailait/	n.	精彩场面,最显著(重要)部分
essence	/'esns/	n.	[哲]本质,精华
fascinate	/'fæsineit/	v.	使着迷,使神魂颠倒
crucial	/'kruːʃəl/	adj.	至关紧要的
resemble	/ri'zembl/	v.	象,类似
tremendous	/tri'mendəs/	adj.	极大的,巨大的
interpretation	/in,təːpri'teiʃən/	n.	解释,阐明
posture	/'pɔstʃə/	n.	(身体的)姿势
recline	/ri'klain/	v.	斜倚;躺
bosom	/'buzəm/	n.	胸部,胸怀
enlighten	/in'laitn/	v.	启发,启蒙
convincing	/kən'viniŋ/	adj.	令人信服的

Proper Nouns

Reclining Buddha in Leshan	乐山睡佛	Leshan Giant Buddha	乐山大佛
Wuyou Hill	乌尤山	Lingyun Hill	凌云山
Guicheng Hill	龟城山		
"A Buddha extant in a Buddha"	"佛中有佛"		

The Method of Introduction of Giving a Crucial Touch to the Picture
画龙点睛法

This method can greatly impress tourists with the concise wording. A guide can sum up the highlights of a tourist site with a few words, and help tourists catch the essence of the place of interest. For example, while touring the Jiuzhaigou Valley tourists are fascinated by the beautiful alpine lakes and waterfalls, etc, but they may not grasp the essence of the tourist resort. So the guide can give a crucial touch to the landscape: Water is the soul of Jiuzhaigou Valley. "No one will watch the waterscape again after he travels back from the Jiuzhaigou." Here we take the Reclining Buddha in Leshan as one more example:

Leshan Giant Buddha is surrounded by several hills. The hills just look like a giant with its head, body and feet being made up of Wuyou Hill, Lingyun Hill and Guicheng Hill respectively. The rocks, bamboo trees, pavilions and temples on Wuyou Hill look like its hair bun, eyebrows, nose, lips and chin; the nine mounds on Lingyun Hill resemble its tremendous chest, waist and legs; in turn Guicheng Hill stretches out just like its feet. A guide may ask what the figure looks like before he tells the truth. Of course, tourists may have different interpretations about it. When they argue, the guide may depict the posture of a reclining figure and give a crucial touch to the scenery: The three hills make up a reclining Giant Buddha while the statue of Leshan Giant Buddha itself is situated in its bosom. This scene presents a miracle of "A Buddha extant in a Buddha." This kind of introduction can greatly enlighten and impress tourists, and it proves to be very convincing and appealing.

Questions

1. Why does the guide use the method of giving a crucial touch to the picture?
2. What do you think is the crucial touch when you introduce the Jiuzhaigou Valley?
3. Please point out the highlights of the Reclining Buddha in Leshan.

PART III Tourist Site

New Words and Expressions

confluence	/'kɔnfluəns/	n.	汇合处
contrast	/'kɔntræst/	v.	和……形成对照
vermilion	/və'miljən/	adj.	朱红色的
adorn	/ə'dɔːn/	v.	装饰
authentic	/ɔː'θentik/	adj.	真实的,可信的
atelier	/'ætəliə/	n.	工作室,画室

| spoil | /spɔil/ | v. | 宠坏,溺爱 |
| duration | /djuə'reiʃən/ | n. | 持续时间 |

Proper Nouns

| Ciqikou | 磁器口 | Jialing River | 嘉陵江 |
| Chongqing Municipality | 重庆市 | | |

Ciqikou

Situated on the bank of the Jialing River, not far from its confluence with the mighty Yangtze is the ancient village of Ciqikou. Covering an area of some 1.2 square kilometres (291.6 acres) it is 14 kilometres to the west of Chongqing Municipality.

The majority of the houses date from the Ming and Qing dynasties, periods during which many masterpieces of Chinese architecture were created. Much of the two and three storey construction is of bamboo and timber. Blue bricks and pillars set off the snow-white walls that contrast in turn with vermilion doors and lattice windows. Black tablets and lanterns adorn the gates to complete the authentic and traditional appearance of the properties.

The three notable attractions of the village are the tea bars, the artists' studios and the Shu Embroidery workshops. Surprisingly, there are more than a hundred tea bars each with their own particular characteristics. Here friends enjoy a chat or meet to discuss business. So the tea bars offer the opportunity for you to meet the locals and also become acquainted with the unique folk opera.

The ateliers, where you may see the work of the local artists will be of great interest. It has been said that the more beautiful a place may be, the more artists it will attract. You are sure to be amazed by the quality of the work on show and in progress as the many artists record the local scenes with skill and dedication. With so many artists working in Ciqikou, you will be spoiled for choice when seeking a souvenir of your visit.

It is often said that a visit to China is a cultural experience. This is never more true than when you visit a place such as Ciqikou where you will find the local residents dedicated to their traditional way of life, unaffected by modern influences to be found in the larger towns and cities. Above all, you will find a friendly welcome awaits you as the people of Ciqikou share their special way of life with you for the duration of your visit.

Cultural Notes

Ciqikou 磁器口:古镇磁器口位于重庆市区近郊,东临嘉陵江,南接沙坪坝,西界童家桥,北

靠石井坡,面积 1.18 平方公里,以明清时盛产及转运瓷器得名。镇上建筑极具川东民居特色,石板路与沿街民居相依和谐,房屋结构多为竹木结构,穿斗夹壁或穿半木板墙。沿街铺面多为一进三间,长进深户型,铺面后房一般为四合院,为商贾大户居所。雕梁画栋,窗花户棂图案精美,做工精巧。1998 年被国务院确定为重庆市重点保护历史街区,沙坪坝区人民政府已规划磁器口为巴渝文化特色旅游新区。

Quickies

1. True or False:

(1) _____ The three notable attractions of the village are the tea bars, the artists' studios and the Shu Embroidery workshops.

(2) _____ There are many artists working in Ciqikou, so tourists are likely to buy some fake souvenirs.

(3) _____ Ciqikou is a place where you will find the local residents dedicated to their traditional way of life, which is to some extant affected by the lifestyle of modern artists living there.

2. Read the passage aloud and introduce Ciqikou using the method of introduction you have learnt. The method of introduction of giving a crucial touch to the picture is one of the choices.

Tips

- Draft your own commentary before you make your presentation.
- Speak colloquial English and use simple and short sentences.
- Animate your introduction with facial expressions and body language.
- Apply at least one method of introduction. It is highly recommended that you use two or three methods of introduction.

PART IV Simulated Introduction

New Words and Expressions

gorge	/gɔːdʒ/	n.	山峡,峡谷
evaporation	/iˌvæpəˈreiʃən/	n.	蒸汽,蒸发(作用)
ascend	/əˈsənd/	v.	攀登,上升
entrust	/inˈtrʌst/	v.	委托
anticipate	/ænˈtisipeit/	v.	预期,期望
conquer	/ˈkɔŋkə/	v.	征服,占领
retreat	/riˈtriːt/	v.	撤退,退却
reluctantly	/riˈlʌktəntli/	adv.	不情愿地

stalactite	/'stæləktait/	n.	[地]钟乳石

Proper Nouns

Baidicheng (White Emperor City)	白帝城	Kuimen	夔门
Gongsun Shu	公孙述	Ziyang	子阳城
Mingliang Palace	明良殿	Observing Star Pavilion	观星亭
Zhang Xianzhong	张献忠	Stealing Water Holes	偷水洞
Pass-locking Iron Chains	铁锁关		
Phoenix Drinking Spring Water	凤凰泉		
White-painted Wall	粉壁石刻 (粉壁堂)		
Three Gorges	三峡		

Baidicheng (White Emperor City)

Look! My friends, the marvelous gorge is just ahead. This is the first gorge of the Yangtze River called the Qutang. The old construction complex on the mountain on our left ahead is the historical site of the Baidicheng, which means White Emperor City in English. Baidicheng has a history of more than 1900 years. It is surrounded by water on three sides and mountains on one side. The magnificent Kuimen is just located here.

Can anyone know why is the city called "Baidicheng" or "White Emperor City"? Nobody knows? Ok, let me tell you about it. According to historical records, Gongsun Shu occupied the land of Sichuan area in the West Han Dynasty. He built a city here called "Ziyang." There was a well in the city and white evaporation often rose up from the well like a flying white dragon. Gongsun Shu believed this was a good omen for him to ascend the throne in the future. So he called himself "White Emperor" and renamed "Ziyang" as "White Emperor City."

Ladies and gentlemen, we'll not get up to the Baidicheng because of the limited time. However, I'd like to tell you more about the city on the travel boat. Baidicheng is where Liu Bei entrusted his son to his Prime Minister Zhuge Liang on dying bed. Inside the City there is a palace called Mingliang Palace. In the temple the huge colored statues of Liu Bei, Zhang Fei, Guan Yu and Zhuge Liang are enshrined and worshiped. In the Tuogu Hall the colored statues of 21 figures in the period of the Three Kingdoms are on display. If you went there you could see an Observing Star Pavilion where Zhuge Liang observed the positions and movements of stars. He anticipated what would happen in the future from the moving stars.

Look ahead! You'll enjoy the beauty to your heart's content because the scenic spots are numerous here. There is a row of holes in the cliff of Baidi Mountain. It's said that the leader of the peasant army Zhang Xianzhong conquered Baidicheng during the Ming Dynasty, and guarded the mountains and all passes. The enemy blocked the river and cut off the water passage. Zhang Xianzhong ordered his soldiers to fetch water through holes dug in the cliff. The enemy found that their tricks failed and retreated reluctantly. The later generations call these holes "Stealing Water Holes." The two iron bars on the rock in front of "Stealing Water Holes" are the relics of "Pass-locking Iron Chains." In the past, iron chains could block the Yangtze River.

Ladies and gentlemen, please look to the right side of the gorge. You can see a stalactite about 20 metres tall and 6 metres round. It is in the shape of a phoenix raising its neck. A stream of spring water is flowing down slowly along the neck. So people call it "Phoenix Drinking Spring Water." On the cliff near "Phoenix" is the "White-painted Wall." There are many inscriptions, and there you can see the development of Chinese culture in the past.

So much for my introduction of Baidicheng! You may have a short rest while watching the marvelous landscape along the Three Gorges.

Cultural Notes

Baidicheng (White Emperor City) 白帝城位于瞿塘峡口的长江北岸,东依夔门,西傍八阵图,三面环水,雄踞水陆要津,距重庆市区 451 公里。西汉末年,公孙述割据四川,自称蜀王,因见此地一口井中常有白色烟雾升腾,形似白龙,故自称白帝,遂于此建都,并将子阳城名改为白帝城。现存白帝城乃明、清两代修复遗址。白帝城是观"夔门天下雄"的最佳地点。历代著名诗人李白、杜甫、白居易、刘禹锡、苏轼、黄庭坚、范成大、陆游等都曾登白帝,游夔门,留下大量诗篇。故白帝城又有"诗城"之美誉。

Exercises

Make a simulated introduction of the Baidicheng (White Emperor City) using the method of introduction you have learnt. Pay attention to the body language and other tips of introduction.

Unit 17 Traffic Accidents

交通事故

PART I ABC for Tour Guides

New Words and Expressions

precaution	/pri'kɔːʃən/	n.	预防,防范
casualty	/'kæʒuəlti/	n.	伤亡
bankruptcy	/'bæŋkrəp(t)si/	n.	破产
quit	/kwit/	v.	离开,放弃
vehicular	/vi'ikjulə/	adj.	车辆的,用车辆运载的
exhausted	/ig'zɔːstid/	adj.	耗尽的,疲惫的
fatal	/'feitl/	adj.	致命的,重大的

Proper Nouns

traffic accident	交通事故	packaged holiday	包价度假旅游
fatal accident	恶性交通事故		

Listening

Direction: Listen to the passages carefully and fill in the blanks with the missing information you have heard from the tapes.

1. **What are the possible consequences of a traffic accident on journey? What precautions can be done to minimize its occurrence?** 旅游交通事故会造成什么后果? 如何预防?

   (1) Accidents may cause (A) _____ and endanger the life and property of the tourists.

   (2) Accidents may cause great damage to the reputation of a travel agency and may cause (B) _____ hardship and even bankruptcy to small and medium sized travel services.

   (3) Accidents may affect the reputation of the tourist destination. Some tourists may quit the tour; fewer tourists will travel in the area where accidents happen, and travel agency may have more difficulty in (C) _____ packaged holidays.

   (4) Vehicular accidents are the most common form of the accident. Travel agency should keep coaches in good (D) _____. Drivers are not allowed to drive when they are tired

or exhausted.

(5) The guide should not chat with the driver who is driving; always remind the driver to drive (E) _____ , and not to drive while drunken.

2. How should a guide handle a fatal traffic accident? 发生恶性交通事故后导游员应如何处理?

(1) The guide should immediately organize a rescue for the injured. First of all, he should keep calm and remove the tourists to a safe (F) _____ from the accident. Then he should help stop bleeding of the injured tourists, bandage up the wounded and send the badly wounded to the nearest hospital.

(2) The guide should report to the traffic police and the travel agency as soon as possible. A serious accident may result in heavy casualties, even fatalities, so the guide must report immediately to the traffic (G) _____ and the local government for help and rescue.

(3) The guide is supposed to protect the accident site for the police (H)_____.

(4) He should submit to the travel agency a written report which has a detailed account of the accident, including: the cause of accident, the sequence of events, the process of (I) _____ the accident, the tourists' feedback and the account of those responsible for the accident.

New Words and Expressions

cancel	/'kænsəl/	v.	取消,删去
replace	/ri(ː)'pleis/	v.	取代,替换

Readings

Direction: Read the following passage aloud and fill in the blanks with words or phrases you think appropriate.

block	earthquake	instruction	slide	safety
replace	injure	dissatisfaction	ambulance	casualties

On the way to a tourist site, the guide is informed that the site is closed because of a traffic accident. What is the guide expected to do in such a case? 导游率团前往某景点途中,突然得知该景点因交通事故而封闭,导游该怎么办?

(1) The guide must first contact the sponsor travel agency for (A) _____.

(2) The guide may either cancel the planned visit or (B) _____ it with another tourist site, according to the instruction from the travel agency.

(3) The guide should make an interesting introduction of the alternative tourist site and let them enjoy the new site; minimize their possible (C) _____ because of the accident.

Quickies

Role-play: Mr. Jiang Xiangeng is taking tourists to the scenery when an accident happened. Some tourists are injured while others are terrified. How could he handle the accident?

PART II *Situational Dialogue*

New Words and Expressions

lap	/læp/	*v.*	泼溅,拍打
furthermost	/'fɜːðəməʊst/	*adj.*	最远方的,最远的
elope	/i'ləup/	*v.*	私奔;潜逃;出走
suicide	/'sjuisaid/	*n.*	自杀,自毁
eternal	/i(ː)'təːnl/	*adj.*	永恒的,永远的

Proper Nouns

Tianya Haijiao	天涯海角	Hainan	海南省
Romeo	罗密欧	Juliet	朱丽叶
Sanya City	三亚市		

Dialogue 1

The Tianya Haijiao

Tourists arrive at the Tianya Haijiao, a romantic sea resort in Hainan. The guide is introducing the beautiful scenic view while telling them a Chinese story of Romeo and Juliet.

(A=Mr. Jiang Xiangeng; B=Jack)

A: Here is the Tianya Haijiao, a romantic and beautiful tourist resort in the west of Sanya City. Many tourists come here from all over the world every year since its open in 1988.

B: The beach here is marvelous. The crystal clear blue sea stretches to the edge of the sky while the waves lap the soft white sand.

A: When you walk along the seashore you'll see more beautiful sights that will certainly surprise you.

B: Oh, yeah, I saw two big rocks over there. They are huge rocks I have never seen before in the ocean.

A: They are Tianya Haijiao. One stone is carved with Chinese characters of Tianya and another stone carved with the characters of Haijiao.

B: Tianya and Haijiao… Can you interpret them in English?

A: Tianya Haijiao means "the furthermost part of the sky and the sea." Hainan, the southernmost part of China, is believed to be the location of Tianya Haijiao.

B: Oh, I see. We've arrived at the southernmost part of China. I believe here is definitely a furthermost part of the sky and the earth.

A: Here is an ideal place for wedding ceremonies in China. Every year thousands of young lovers hold their wedding ceremonies.

B: Why do they come here to enjoy their honeymoon?

A: There is a romantic Chinese story of Romeo and Juliet about the two stones. In ancient times, two young lovers eloped here because their parents disapproved of their marriage.

B: How could they survive here? The sun, sand and sea are good for tourists, but could not help the young lovers.

A: So they jumped into the sea and committed suicide. Suddenly, they were hit by lightning and changed into two stones. People regard these two stones as symbols of eternal and faithful love.

B: No wonder so many young lovers choose Tianya Haijiao for their wedding ceremony. What a pity! I've already got married.

Exercises

Do the dialogue again and pay attention to the facial expressions and body language.

New Words and Expressions

gulf	/gʌlf/	n.	海湾
pristine	/'pristain/	adj.	质朴的
coral	/'kɔrəl/	n.	珊瑚
reef	/riːʃ/	n.	暗礁

Proper Nouns

Yalong Bay (the Asian Dragon Bay)	亚龙湾
Hawaii	夏威夷
Kylin	麒麟
Luban Prize	鲁班奖

Dialogue 2

Yalong Bay (the Asian Dragon Bay)

After touring the Tianya Haijiao the tourists come to Yalong Bay (the Asian Dragon Bay), one of the most beaches in the world.

(A=Mr. Jiang Xiangeng; B=Jack)

A: Now, here is the place you have been longing for—Yalong Bay (the Asian Dragon Bay). It is a 7.5-kilometer long, crescent-shaped bay, one of the famous tourist sites in Hainan Province.

B: Wow, what a fantastic beach! The scenery is amazing: endless rolling hills, serene gulfs, clear blue sea and silvery sand beaches.

A: It is one of the most beautiful beaches in the world—three times as long as any beaches in Hawaii.

B: I've been to Hawaii. Hawaii is nothing to compare with Yalong Bay in terms of the natural settings. Look, the golden sands, crystal sea water, endless seashore, unspoiled hills and pristine vegetation, all are marvelous!

A: Thank you for your praise. Here you can dive to watch the well-preserved coral reefs, especially the tropical fish of different kinds, colors and shapes.

B: I'd like to dive to see the underground world of the sea. Is it safe for diving? Are there any sharks?

A: Don't worry, the ocean here is crystal clear and also very safe. You can watch underwater sights up to 10 meters deep from the surface.

B: Terrific. After the sunbath I'll dive to take some coral reefs as souvenirs if the rule permits. Look, what is the building over there? It looks very high.

A: It is a Totem Pole in the Yalong Bay Square. The pole is 27 meters high. On the pole the God of Sun, and Gods of Wind, Rain, and Thunder are engraved.

B: I also see some legendary animals on the pole, such as Dragon, Phoenix, Kylin and Fish. The sculpture is really marvelous.

A: Yes, the design of this pole has won Luban Prize—award of the top level design of architecture in China. Come on, let's get ready to have the sunbath now.

B: Ok.

Cultural Notes

Tianya Haijiao 天涯海角，位于三亚市西郊23千米处。天涯海角风景区总体规划陆地面积 10.4平方公里，海域面积6平方公里，背负马岭山，面向茫茫大海。这里海水澄碧，烟波浩瀚，

帆影点点,椰林婆娑,奇石林立水天一色。海湾沙滩上大小百块岩石耸立,"天涯"、"海角"和"南天一柱"巨石突兀其间,昂首天外,峥嵘壮观。史载"天涯"两字为清雍正年间崖州知州程哲所题,刻在一块高约 10 米的巨石上。"海角"两字刻在"天涯"右侧一块尖石的顶端,据说是清末文人题写。这两块巨石合称"天涯海角"。

Yalong Bay 亚龙湾,位于三亚市东南 28 千米处,是海南最南端的一个半月形海湾,全长约 7.5 千米,是海南名景之一。亚龙湾沙滩绵延 7 千米且平缓宽阔,浅海区宽达 50—60 米。沙粒洁白细软,海水清澈澄莹,能见度 7—9 米。海底世界资源丰富,有珊瑚礁、多种热带鱼、名贵贝类等。亚龙湾集中了现代旅游五大要素海洋、沙滩、阳光、绿色、新鲜空气于一体,呈现明显的热带海洋性气候,年平均气温 25.5℃,海水温度 22—25.1℃,终年可游泳,被誉为"天下第一湾"。

Exercises

Imagine that you are a local guide and your classmates are tourists. Make up a situational dialogue about the Tianya Haijiao or the Yalong Bay.

PART III *Ethnic Culture*

New Words and Expressions

hairpin	/'hɛəpin/	n.	发夹,束发夹,夹发针
prevail	/pri'veil/	v.	流行,盛行
picnic	/'piknik/	n.	野餐
precede	/pri(ː)'siːd/	v.	领先(于),在……之前
gorgeous	/'gɔːdʒəs/	adj.	华丽的,灿烂的
dainty	/'deinti/	adj.	秀丽的,优美的
indispensable	/ˌindis'pensəbl/	adj.	不可缺少的,绝对必要的
pestle	/'pestl/	v.	用槌磨,用杵捣

Proper Nouns

Li	黎族	bamboo pole rice	竹筒饭
Sanyuesan	"三月三"	Bamboo Pole Dance	竹竿舞

Li Culture

The Li ethnic minority lives mainly in Hainan Province. The Li women comb their hair into a bun with metal or bone hairpins. During festivals, they wear bracelets, ear rings, necklaces, and foot rings. The practice of tattooing girls which prevailed in ancient times is now mostly discontinued. When children grow into their teens, they are expected to move from their parents' house. Boys build their own houses, and girls will be under the authority of their parents. Usually these rooms are smaller than the ones they lived before. This is also the place where the youth find their love.

The staple food of the Li is rice, corn and sweet potatoes, and sometimes they enjoy the fruit of hunting. One of distinctive meals is the Bamboo Pole Rice that is similar to the Dai's and is wonderful for picnics. It has been said that all the families nearby can smell the fragrance from the bamboo pole rice cooked in one house.

Embroidery skills are the Li people's pride. As early as in the Tang and Song dynasties, their skill has preceded the Han people's. After the processes of spinning, dying, broidering and weaving, silk comes out to be gorgeous and delicate. Besides that, the Li have a tradition of dainty and delicate wood-craft. In both styles of a traditional Li house, one in the shape of a ship, the other of a pyramid; the weaving of bamboo vines is an indispensable adornment.

Sanyuesan, in Chinese, refers to the third day of the third month when this is celebrated. The elders are honored and visited by other people with yellow wine, cured vegetables and cakes; young people go out hunting and fishing and in the evening, they sing face to face, in traditional flowery clothes, and worship ancestors. This is also a wonderful time to express love to those persons who are dear to one's heart.

The Li people, like other ethnic minorities are good at singing and dancing. Their dances arise mainly from their work in the field, pestling the rice, worshiping ancestors, and so on. Among these, the Bamboo Pole Dance is probably the most attractive.

Quickies

True or False:

(1) _____ The practice of tattooing girls which prevailed in ancient times has been handed down from generation to generation.

(2) _____ As early as in the Tang and Song dynasties, the skill of Li's embroidery has preceded the Han people's.

(3) _____ The style of a traditional Li house is built in the shape of a ship, or in the shape of a tower.

PART IV *Practical Writing for Tourism*

1. Passengers' Health Declaration 旅客健康申报卡

PASSENGERS' HEALTH DECLARATION

Name in full _____ Sex _____ Age _____

Nationality _____ Occupation _____

Date of entry _____ Flight No. _____

1. Date & origination place of departure _____

2. Please Mark "√" before the symptom if any now.

☐ Fever ☐ Rash ☐ Cough ☐ Sore throat Bleeding

☐ Vomiting ☐ Diarrhoea ☐ Jaundice ☐ Lymph-gland Swelling

3. Any illness now: Psychosis, Leprosy, AIDS (Inc. AIDS virus carrier), venereal diseases, active pulmonary tuberculosis and other diseases

4. Please mark "√" in the items of the following articles, if you bring any of them with yourself.

Biologicals _____ Blood products _____ Second-hand clothes _____

5. Name of travel group _____

6. Contact address and host organization in China _____

旅客健康申请卡

姓名 _____ 性别 _____ 年龄 _____

国籍 _____ 职业 _____

入境日期 _____ 乘机航班号 _____

1. 这次旅行来自何地及出发日期 _____

2. 现如有以下症状,请在症状前划"√":

☐ 发烧 ☐ 皮疹 ☐ 咳嗽 ☐ 咽喉痛 ☐ 出血

☐ 呕吐 ☐ 腹泻 ☐ 黄疸 ☐ 淋巴腺肿

3. 现在是否患有:精神病、麻风病、艾滋病(包括艾滋病毒带毒者)、性病、开放性肺结核和其他疾病?

4. 如随身携带下列物品,请在下列项目内划"√":

生物制品 _____ 血制品 _____ 旧衣服 _____

5. 旅游团名称 _____

6. 在华住址和接待单位 _____

2. Baggage Declaration Form 海关申报表

Baggage Declaration Form

NAME _____

NATIONALITY _____ PASSPORT NO. _____

FROM /TO _____

NUMBER OF ACCOMPANYING CHILDREN UNDER 16 _____

HAND BAGGAGE _____ Pcs. CHECKED BAGGAGE _____ Pcs.

ITEM	ENTRY		EXIT	
CHINESE & FOREIGN CURRENCIES	Description & Amount			
GOLD & SILVER ORNAMENTS				
TRIP NECESSITIES	BRAND	PIECE	BRAND	PIECE
CAMERA				
TAPE RECORDER				
VIDEO & MOVIE CAMERA				
OTHER ARTICLES DUE TO CUSTOM PROCEDURES				
GOODS & SAMPLES	Yes / No ☐		Yes / No ☐	
RECORDED VIDEO TAPE	Yes / No ☐		Yes / No ☐	
PRINTED MATTER	Yes / No ☐		Yes / No ☐	
ANTIQUES	Yes / No ☐		Yes / No ☐	
DURABLE CONSUMER GOODS (PRICE $\geq$ RMB 50.00) AND GIFTS (TOTAL PRICE $\geq$ RMB 50.00)				
DESCRIPTION	BRAND	PIECE	Customer Remark	

IN ADDITION _____ PIECES OF UNACCOMPANIED BAGGAGE ARE TO BE IMPORTED THROUGH _____ WITHIN 3 MONTHS

SIGNTURE: _____ DATE: _____

CUSTOMS REMARKS: _____

海关申报表

姓名：_____

国籍：_____ 护照号码：_____

来自、前往 _____

同行未满16周岁子女人数 _____

手提行李 _____ 件；托运行李 _____ 件。

项目	携带进境		携带出境	
中国和外国货币 （大写）	币名和数量		币名和数量	
金银及金银制品				
旅行自用物品	牌名、型号	数量	牌名、型号	数量
照相机				
录音机				
摄影、摄像机				
其他应办理进出境海 关手续的物品				
货币及货样	有□	无□	有□	无□
录有内容的录像带	有□	无□	有□	无□
印刷品	有□	无□	有□	无□
文物	有□	无□	有□	无□
申请进口的耐用消费品(单价超过人民币50元) 和馈赠礼品(总价超过人民币50元)				
品名	牌名及型号		数量	海关批注

另有分离运输行李 ＿＿＿＿＿＿＿ 件, 将于三个月内从 ＿＿＿＿＿＿＿ 口岸运进。

旅客签字: ＿＿＿＿＿＿＿＿＿＿＿＿ 日期: ＿＿＿＿＿＿＿＿＿＿＿＿＿

海关记事: ＿＿＿＿＿＿＿＿＿＿＿＿＿＿＿＿＿＿＿＿＿＿＿＿

海关签章: ＿＿＿＿＿＿

Exercises

Fill in the Passengers' Health Declaration and Baggage Declaration Form and present them to the Customs officials. Make a dialogue between the tourist and the Customs officials.

Unit 18
Breach of Security and Fire Disaster
治安事故与火灾
PART I ABC for Tour Guides

New Words and Expressions

breach	/briːtʃ/	n.	违反,破坏
fraud	/frɔːd/	n.	欺骗,欺诈行为
indecency	/in'diːsnsi/	n.	下流,猥亵
evacuate	/i'vækjueit/	v.	疏散,撤出
crawl	/krɔːl/	v.	爬行,徐徐行进
sprinkle	/'spriŋkl/	v.	洒,喷洒
verbal	/'vɜːbəl/	adj.	口头的

Proper Nouns

emergency exit	紧急出品	power failure	停电

Listening

Direction: Listen to the passages carefully and fill in the blanks with the missing information you have heard from the tapes.

1. **What is a breach of security related to tourism and travel? How should a guide handle the incident? 什么叫旅游治安事故? 如何处理?**

   (1) A breach of security means that the tourist has suffered: theft, robbery, fraud, indecency or (A) _____ and their life or property has been endangered during the trip.

   (2) The guide should do his best to protect the safety and property of tourists and take them to safe places only. If tourists are injured the guide should (B) _____ them.

   (3) The guide should immediately report to the police for investigation when there is a breach of security.

   (4) When casualties or loss of property occur, the guide should ask the travel agency to give him instructions or request the (C) _____ of the travel agency to handle the incident.

(5) The guide should console tourists. He should continue with the scheduled travel if possible.

(6) The guide is supposed to submit a written report to the travel agency and help handle the issues (D) _____.

2. **In case of a fire accident, what steps should a guide take to safely evacuate the site?** 发生火灾事故后导游员应如何率领游客逃生?

(1) The guide should report the fire accident immediately to the police.

(2) The guide should tell tourists about the accident immediately and take them to a safe place through an (E) _____ exit. He should warn tourists not to take the elevator, for they may get trapped in the (F) _____ due to power failure caused by the fire.

(3) If they are surrounded by a big fire or dense smoke, tourists should take the following measures:

    (a) cover their mouth and (G) _____ and crawl out of the room with their face close to the floor;

    (b) If the door is blocked by fire, tourists should seal the (H) _____ with wet clothing and sprinkle water over the door to keep it cool and wet while waiting for the rescue;

    (c) Tourists should also wave colorful clothing out the window to signal for (I) _____.

(4) If tourists are injured in the fire the guide should send them to the hospital; if someone has died, he should handle the matter according to the relevant regulations.

(5) The guide should console tourists and encourage them to continue with their (J) _____ _____ if possible.

(6) He should make a verbal report to the travel agency and submit a written report after the trip is over.

New Words and Expressions

revise	/ri'vaiz/	v.	修订,校订
realistic	/riə'listik/	adj.	现实(主义)的

Readings

Direction: Read the following passage aloud and fill in the blanks with words or phrases you think appropriate.

arrangements	compensation	cooperation	revised	replace
adjustments	minimize	emergency	reserved	foresee

What should a guide do when the travel is interrupted for unforeseen reasons? 旅游途中因不可预见的原因致使旅游团队不能继续旅行,导游员该如何处理?

(1) The guide should first analyze the consequence of the interruption and propose an alternative (A) _____ program to the travel agency.

(2) The guide should then explain the situation to the tourists and ask for their support and cooperation. If necessary, the mental and physical (B) _____ will be taken into account for the tourists.

(3) The guide should finally make appropriate (C) _____ to the itinerary according to the alternative emergency program by (a) extending the travel time in a certain scenic area; (b) shortening the travel time; or (c) changing the itinerary.

(a) Extension of the travel time—If the guide has to extend the travel time in the scenic area, he should contact the travel agency, which should make the appropriate (D) _____ for meals, accommodation and modes of transportation and notify the travel agency at the next stop to make adjustments according to the (E) _____ itinerary. The guide may extend the time for sightseeing and add some entertainment programs.

(b) Shortening of the travel time—If the guide has to shorten the visit, he should contact the travel agency to cancel the (F) _____ meals, rooms, transportation and entertainment. If appropriate, the guide should do his best to complete the sightseeing schedule. If it is not possible, the guide may take tourists to visit the main tourist sites so as to (G) _____ their disappointment.

(c) Change of part of the program—If he has to cancel part or all of a planned visit or (H) _____ it with another site, as instructed by the sponsor travel agency, the guide should make a realistic but interesting introduction of the alternative tourist site so as to arouse their interest and hopefully get their understanding and (I) _____.

Quickies

Role-play: The Japanese tourists are sleeping soundly after touring Mount Taishan when the hotel catches the fire. Miss Zhang Yunfang, the local guide tries her best to take the tourists out of the hotel. Act as Miss Zhang and the Japanese tourists. Try your best to evacuate from the hotel on fire.

PART II *Method of Introduction*

Method of Introduction			
rough	/rʌf/	adj.	粗略的,大致的
dinosaur	/'dainəsɔ:/	n.	恐龙
excavation	/ˌəkskə'veiʃən/	n.	挖掘,发掘

fossil	/ˈfɔsl/	n.	化石
floorage	/ˈflɔːridʒ/	n.	地面面积
electronic	/iləkˈtrɔnik/	adj.	电子的
distribution	/ˌdistriˈbjuːʃən/	n.	分布,分类
thrive	/θraiv/	v.	繁荣,茁壮成长
precious	/ˈprəʃəs/	adj.	宝贵的,珍爱的
biological	/baiəˈlɔdʒikəl/	adj.	生物学的

Proper Nouns

Zigong Dinosaur Museum	自贡恐龙博物馆
Dashanpu	大山铺
Introduction Hall	序厅
Jurassic Fauna & Flora Hall	侏罗纪动植物厅
Specimen Hall	标本陈列厅
Dinosaur Fossil Cemetery	恐龙埋藏厅
bar chart	柱形或条形统计图表

The Method of Section-by-Section Introduction
分段讲解法

This method requires that the whole scenic area be divided into different sections in series so that a guide could introduce them one by one. First of all, the guide can give tourists a very brief account of the place they visit so that they can have a rough idea of the place before they visit the place of interests, including its history, location, aesthetical value and the names of its main tourist sites, through which tourists could have a preliminary impression on the scenic area they will visit. However, the guide should not introduce too much about the next scenic spot when he introduces the present one. Towards the end of his introduction, it is appropriate for the guide to briefly introduce the next scenic spot so as to arouse tourists' interest for the coming scene. This kind of introduction is especially useful when introducing a museum or a large project. Now, we take Zigong National Dinosaur Museum as an example:

Zigong Dinosaur Museum was built up at Dashanpu, the world-famous excavation site of dinosaur fossils, 11 kilometers away from the downtown of Zigong City. It is the largest museum in southwest China, one of the most specialized museums in the world with dinosaur fossils in great quantity and variety. The Museum was built and opened to public in 1986, the first one that was built right at the excavation site in China. It occupies an area of about 25,000 square meters, with a floorage of 6,000 square meters, and comprises Introduction Hall, Jurassic Fauna & Flora Hall, Specimen Hall, and Dinosaur Fossil Cemetery.

Now we come to the Introduction Hall—the world of dinosaurs. Visitors will first see the electronic distribution map of world dinosaur fossils, showing the locations of the dinosaur fossils on the earth as well as the periods in which the dinosaurs were living. Then they will see a bar chart that provides all the details about the dinosaur fossils unearthed in Zigong since 1915.

Here is the Jurassic Fauna & Flora Hall. It displays a collection of the animals and plants thriving during the dinosaur age. These fossils are precious because they serve as important evidence in the study of dinosaurs and the biological evolution process. The next hall is the Specimen Hall. It is the world-renowned "dinosaur cemetery" at Dashanpu, and provides an abundance of dinosaur fossils rich in varieties.

Questions:

1. Under what a circumstance does a guide use the method of section-by-section introduction?
2. What tips should a guide acquire when he uses the method of section-by-section introduction?
3. How many exhibition halls are there in the Zigong Dinosaur Museum?

PART III Tourist Site

New Words and Expressions

epitomize	/i'pitəmaiz/	v.	概括,成为……缩影
ascent	/ə'sent/	n.	攀登,上坡路
renovation	/ˌrenəu'veiʃən/	n.	翻新,革新
equip	/i'kwip/	v.	装备,配备
ropeway	/'rəupwei/	n.	索道,空中缆索
rugged	/'rʌgid/	adj.	高低不平的,崎岖的
adventure	/əd'ventʃə/	n.	冒险,冒险的经历

Proper Nouns

Mount Taishan	泰山	Five Sacred Mountains	"五岳"
East Route	东线	Imperial Route	帝王线
Dai Temple	岱庙	West Route	西线
Heaven and Earth Square	天地广场	Mid-heaven Gate	中天门
Jade Emperor Summit	玉皇顶	Peach Blossom Valley Route	桃花峪旅游线
Tianzhu Peak Route	天烛峰旅游线	Houshiwu	后石坞

Mount Taishan

The leader of the Five Sacred Mountains, Mount Taishan is located in the center of Shandong Province. It epitomizes splendid Chinese culture and was listed in the World Natural and Cultural Heritage List of UNESCO in 1987.

In ancient times, the first thing for an emperor to do on ascending to the throne was to climb Mount Taishan and pray to heaven and earth or their ancestors. It was said that 72 emperors of different dynasties made pilgrimages to this mountain. These special ceremonies and sacrifices earned the mountain widespread fame.

There are four ascents of the mountain.

East Route

This route is considered to be the Imperial Route because the emperors all took this way to make sacrifices. With elegant natural scenery, palaces, stone inscriptions are also scattered along the winding path. Dai Temple is the place where emperors stayed and offered their sacrifices. The temple was built in the Han Dynasty and expanded in the Tang and Song dynasties. After several renovations, it has become the biggest and most complete temple on the mountain.

West Route

The west route is made up of two parts. The first part is the highroad from the Heaven and Earth Square to the Mid-heaven Gate. The other part is the cable way from the Mid-heaven Gate to the top of the mountain. This route is well equipped with modern facilities and is the most fashionable way to reach the Jade Emperor Summit.

Peach Blossom Valley Route

This route is the most convenient way to climb the mountain, especially for tourists who drive or take a bus from northern places. Peach Blossom Valley can be accessed by taking the No. 104 national highway, then setting off from the big parking lot by bus to the cable-car stop. From there you reach the top in a few minutes. The ropeway is designed for sightseeing from the air giving a clear view.

Tianzhu Peak Route

Just as its name implies, Tianzhu Peak was named because it is shaped like a candle, with a pine tree standing on top like a flame. This route is the most rugged one and is suitable for the adventures. It is also a better way to appreciate the pine trees in the Houshiwu (a spot where most of the old pine trees are growing).

Cultural Notes

Mount Taishan 泰山：泰山古称岱山，又称岱宗。位于山东省中部，为中国五岳(泰山、华山、衡山、嵩山、恒山)之一。因地处东部，故称东岳。山势雄伟壮丽，气势磅礴，名胜古迹众多，有"五岳独尊"之誉。泰山主峰海拔 1,545 米，由于其特殊地位，受到历代帝王的尊崇，在此封禅祭祀，把它当作江山永固的象征。泰山丰富的历史文化价值，风格独特的美学价值和世界意义的地质科学价值使其成为世界著名的旅游胜地。1987 年被联合国教科文组织列为世界自然文化双遗产。

Quickies

1. **True or False:**

    (1) _____ In ancient times, the first thing for an emperor to do was to climb Mount Taishan and watch the sunrise after he ascends to the throne.

    (2) _____ Dai Temple is the place the biggest and most complete temple complex on the mountain where emperors offered their sacrifices.

    (3) _____ Tianzhu Peak Route is the most rugged one and is suitable for taking adventures and watching the peach trees.

2. Read the passage aloud and introduce Mount Taishan using the method of introduction you have learnt. The method of section-by-section introduction is one of the choices.

Tips

- Draft your own commentary before you make your presentation.
- Speak colloquial English and use simple and short sentences.
- Animate your introduction with facial expressions and body language.
- Apply at least one method of introduction. It is highly recommended that you use two or three methods of introduction

PART IV   *Simulated Introduction*

Simulated Introduction

moat	/məut/	*n.*	护城河,城壕
vigorous	/ˈvigərəs/	*adj.*	有力的,健壮的
refute	/riˈfjuːt/	*v.*	驳倒,反驳
profundity	/prəˈfʌnditi/	*n.*	深奥,深刻

Proper Nouns

Qufu	曲阜	Confucius	孔子
Temple of Confucius	孔庙	Graveyard of Kong Family	孔林
"Three Kongs"	"三孔",即孔庙、孔府、孔林		
Kong Family Mansion	孔府	Holy City of the East	"东方圣城"
10,000 Ren Palace Wall	"万仞宫墙"	Emperor Qianlong	乾隆皇帝
Zi Gong	子贡		

Qufu

My dear friends:

First of all, welcome to Qufu, the hometown of Confucius. Confucius had a famous remark: "Isn't it a pleasure to have friends from afar?" Today I am very glad to have an opportunity of making new friends and to be at your service as a tour guide. I'll be much obliged to you for your cooperation, and I am ready to take your timely advice on my service.

Before we start visiting the major tourist sites in Qufu, I'd like to give you a brief introduction of Qufu and tell you something about Confucius.

Look at the inscribed stone tablet erected on the southern bank of the moat outside the southern gate of the old city. Inscribed on the tablet was "one of China's top historical and cultural cities." In the middle you will see "Qufu." These two characters were written by the late great leader Mao Zedong. His calligraphy is bold and vigorous, as we can see from here. Mao visited Qufu two times in his lifetime. The first visit was in March 1919 when he left Beijing for Shanghai. The second was on Oct. 28, 1952. During that tour, Mao visited the Temple of Confucius, Graveyard of Kong Family and some other cultural relics.

Qufu lies in southwest of Shandong Province. It has a total population of 630,000, including 100,000 urban residents. It covers an area of 896 km^2. Although it is small, Qufu is an old cultural city with a history of 5000-year civilization. In 1982 Qufu was listed by the State Council as one of the first 24 famous historical and cultural cities. In 1994 the "Three Kongs" (i. e., the Temple of Confucius, the Graveyard of Kong Family and Kong Family Mansion) were officially inscribed on the World Heritage List by UNESCO. Thanks to its great contributions to the oriental culture, Qufu is regarded as one of the three sacred cities in the world—known as the "Holy City of the East."

Ladies and gentlemen, this is the southern gate of Qufu City. It was built in the Ming Dynasty. On the city gate hangs an inscribed

159

board of four characters "10,000 Ren Palace Wall." They were Emperor Qianlong's handwriting. The words came from Confucius's student Zi Gong. When someone argued that Zi Gong's knowledge was extensive and profound, and could match that of Confucius's Zi Gong refuted immediately, "How dare I compare with my teacher Confucius? The knowledge of my teacher is like a wall. Mine is only I ren (1 ren = 2.6 metres) high and can be seen through at first sight; the knowledge of my teacher is several rens high and you can not measure its profundity without entering into it." In order to describe the profundity of Confucius's learning, later generations inscribed these four characters onto the gate tower.

Now, we're going to get into the city gate. Follow me please!

Cultural Notes

Qufu 曲阜：曲阜是中国古代伟大的思想家、教育家孔子的故乡。据《史记》记载，这里曾是神农故都、黄帝故里、商殷故国、周汉鲁都。曲阜不仅以悠久的历史著称于世，而且以丰富的历史文物蜚声中外，成为中国历史文化名城。曲阜也是大汶口文化、龙山文化主要地区，有重点文物保护单位 112 处，其中国家重点文物保护单位 4 处，省级 12 处，1994 年孔庙、孔府及孔林被联合国教科文组织列入《世界文化遗产名录》。

Exercises

Make a simulated introduction of Qufu using the method of introduction you have learnt. Pay attention to the body language and other tips of introduction.

Unit 19 Religion and Regulations
宗教与法规

PART I *ABC for Tour Guides*

New Words and Expressions

refrain	/ri'frein/	v.	节制,避免
amicable	/'æmikəbl/	adj.	友善的,和平的
restraint	/ris'treint/	n.	抑制,克制
prostitute	/'prɔstitjuːt/	n.	妓女
smuggle	/'smʌgl/	v.	走私

Listening

Direction: Listen to the passages carefully and fill in the blanks with the missing information you have heard from the tapes.

1. **If foreign tourists speak ill of the present policies and leaders of China, what should a guide do?** 如果有外国游客攻击我国现行方针政策,诬蔑我国领导人时,导游员如何处理?

   (1) Handle the matter factually: The guide should tell them the facts so that they can have a better understanding of Chinese current (A) _____.

   (2) Handle the matter cautiously: The guide may simply express his own idea. It is recommended that the guide would refrain from (B) _____ with tourists so as to maintain an amicable atmosphere on the journey.

   (3) Handle the matter with restraint: The guide may graciously (C) _____ the tourists who intentionally speak ill of China while he should continue to provide warm service to all the tourists.

2. **When he finds that some tourists seek for prostitutes or smuggle antiques, what is the guide supposed to do?** 导游发现某些游客嫖娼并走私文物,应该如何处理?

   (1) The guide should tell them that it is illegal to seek for prostitutes and smuggle (D) _____ according to the policies and regulations of China.

(2) He should report to the police for (E) _____ .

New Words and Expressions

pious	/'paiəs/	*adj.*	虔诚的
Catholic	/'kæθəlik/	*adj.*	天主教的
preach	/priːtʃ/	*v.*	鼓吹,传教

Readings

Direction: Read the following passage aloud and fill in the blanks with words or phrases you think appropriate.

pray	murmur	religious	preach	sacrifice
incense	regulations	sanctuary	police	probe

When a pious Catholic tourist hands out copies of the *Bible* and other religious souvenirs to the local people, should the guide stop him from doing so? Why? 一位虔诚信奉天主教的游客向当地群众散发《圣经》和其它宗教纪念品。请问:导游员是否应该出面制止? 为什么?

(1) According to Chinese policies and regulations, all foreign tourists are forbidden to (A) _____ , preside over any religious service or hand out religious materials to the public without permission from the relevant authorities.

(2) The guide should tell them about Chinese policies and (B) _____ and ask them to stop doing so.

(3) If he persists the guide should report to the local (C) _____ and ask them to solve the problem.

Quickies

Role-play: A group of Irish tourists are traveling in Xi'an. When they walk on the city wall Mr. Smith, a pious Christian begins to hand over *Bibles* to some Chinese tourists. Miss Xiao Ming, the local guide argues with him, but in vain. As her colleague what do you say to Miss Xiao and how could you help solve the problem?

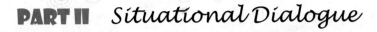

PART II *Situational Dialogue*

New Words and Expressions

abbot	/'Abət/	n.	(修道院、寺庙等)主持
cradle	/'kreidl/	n.	摇篮,发源地
sutra	/'suːtrə/	n.	佛经,经典
hierarch	/'haiərɑːk/	n.	教主,高僧
Sanskrit	/'sænskrit/	n.	梵语
talisman	/'tælizmən/	n.	辟邪物,护身符
landmark	/'lændmɑːk/	n.	标志,里程碑

Proper Nouns

Da Ci'en Temple	大慈恩寺	Xuanzang	玄奘
Chang'an	长安	Marco Polo	马可波罗
Bell Tower	钟楼	Drum Tower	鼓楼
Big Wild Goose Pagoda	大雁塔		

Dialogue 1

Da Ci' en Temple

(A=Miss Xiao Ming; B=Tourists)

A: Now, we've arrived at the Da Ci'en Temple or the Temple of Great Mercy and Kindness. In front of us is the statue of Xuanzang.

B: Who is Xuangzang?

A: Xuanzang is the abbot of the Da Ci'en Temple in the Tang Dynasty. He started off from Chang'an (the ancient Xi'an) along the Silk Road and through deserts, finally arrived in India.

B: Why did he travel all the way from China to India?

A: You know, India is the cradle of Buddhism. In order to learn Buddhism and get Buddhist sutra he traveled across 100 countries in 17 years.

B: That's a great journey. I believe he is the great Marco Polo in China.

A: Yes. After he came back from India he took with him 657 kinds of sutras, and several Buddha relics. As the first abbot of the Da Ci'en Temple, he asked 50 hierarchs to trans-

163

late sutras from Sanskrit into Chinese.

B: I think Xuanzang did a good job. No wonder I saw his statue at the entrance of the Temple.

A: Follow me please! We'll walk across a small bridge and get into the Temple.

B: Miss Xiao, I see a pair of lion stones standing in front of the temple gate. Why are there always stone lions in front of the temple gate?

A: A good question! They are guarding lions of the Temple. The Temple looks grand and sacred because lions are believed to function as talismans.

B: I see. Shall we get into the Temple now?

A: Ok. After you enter the Temple the first two buildings you see are: Bell Tower in the east and Drum Tower in the west. Along the central axis you'll visit many famous buildings. One of the most remarkable buildings is the Big Wild Goose Pagoda.

B: Big Wild Goose Pagoda! I know it is the landmark of Xi'an city.

A: Let's go.

(to be continued)

Exercises

Do the dialogue again and pay attention to your facial expressions and body language.

New Words and Expressions

merciful	/'mə:siful/	*adj.*	仁慈的,慈悲的
disciple	/di'saipl/	*n.*	弟子,门徒
panorama	/ˌpænə'rɑːmə/	*n.*	全景
acoustic	/ə'kuːstik/	*adj.*	声学的

Proper Nouns

Emperor Gaozong	(唐)高宗皇帝	Bodhisattva	菩萨
North Square	北广场		

Dialogue 2

Big Wild Goose Pagoda

(A=Miss Xiao Ming; B=Jack)

A: In front of us is the world famous pagoda, the Big Wild Goose Pagoda. It was originally built in 652 during the reign of Emperor Gaozong of the Tang Dynasty.

B: What a magnificent pagoda! Who could construct such a marvelous pagoda at that time!

A: It was Xuangzang who supervised the building of the pagoda. He built this pagoda to collect Buddhist materials he took from India.

B: Why is it called Big Wild Goose Pagoda?

A: There is a legend about it. One day a group of big wild geese flied by, a monk said to himself: "Today we have no meat. I hope the merciful Bodhisattva will give us some."

B: Monks dared want to eat the wild geese! Unbelievable!

A: At that very moment, the leading wild goose broke its wings and fell to the ground. All the monks were surprised and moved. They built a pagoda where the wild goose fell and stopped eating meat. The Pagoda was named "Big Wild Goose Pagoda."

B: I think the monks were inspired by such a miracle. Monks should show their mercy; do not eat or kill any animals.

A: Right, please look up! The Pagoda was first built to a height of 60 meters with five stories. Now it is about 65 meters high with an additional two stories.

B: So there are seven stories. Though it is not very high the Pagoda looks elegant and beautiful.

A: Jack, the figure seven has special meaning. There goes a saying, "Saving a life exceeds building a seven-storied pagoda." Buddhist disciples attached importance to the value of life.

B: I see. Shall we go upstairs to have a look?

A: Of course, inside the Pagoda, stairs twist up so that visitors can climb up. You can overlook the panorama of Xi'an City from the arch-shaped doors on four sides of each storey.

B: When we reach the top would you please introduce more about the Pagoda?

A: Sure. I'll also give you an introduction about the North Square below. It holds many records: in Asia, it is the biggest Tang-culture square, the biggest fountain and waterscape square. In the world, it has the most benches, the longest light-belt and the largest-scale acoustic complex.

B: Thank you, Miss Xiao.

(the end)

Cultural Notes

Da Ci'en Temple 大慈恩寺:大慈恩寺坐落于陕西省西安市南部,是唐贞观二十二年(公元648年)太子李治为纪念亡母文德皇后以报答养育之恩而修建,故名"慈恩寺"。当时共有13处院落,房屋达1987间,并请赴印度取经回国的高僧玄奘主持寺务,著名的画家阎立本、吴道子都在此绘制过壁画。寺门内,钟、鼓楼东西对峙。钟、鼓是寺院的号令,俗有"晨钟暮鼓"之说。唐代学子考中进士后到慈恩塔下题名,谓之"雁塔题名",后沿袭成习。

Big Wild Goose Pagoda 大雁塔:大雁塔坐落于西安市的大慈恩寺内,是全国著名的古代建筑,被视为古都西安的象征。大雁塔全称"慈恩寺大雁塔",始建于公元652年,通高64米,塔体各层以青砖模仿我国唐代建筑砌檐柱、斗拱、栏额、檀枋、檐椽、飞椽等仿木结构,磨砖对缝砌成。每层四面均有券门,底层南门洞两侧镶嵌着唐太宗御撰的《圣教碑》和高宗李治所撰

165

《述圣记》两通珍贵石碑,具有很高艺术价值,人称"二圣三绝碑"。大雁塔1961年被国务院颁布为第一批全国重点文物保护单位。

Exercises

Imagine that you are a local guide and your classmates are tourists. Make up a situational dialogue about the Da Ci'en Temple or the Big Wild Goose Pagoda.

PART III *Ethnic Culture*

New Words and Expressions

Arab	/'ærəb/	adj.	阿拉伯的
mosque	/mɔsk/	n.	清真寺
funeral	/'fjuːnərəl/	n.	葬礼,出殡
convert	/kən'vəːt/	v.	皈依,使……改变信仰
permanently	/'pɜːmənəntli/	adv.	永存地,不变地
puritanical	/ˌpjuəri'tænikəl/	adj.	清教徒的,严格的
frown	/fraun/	v.	皱眉,不赞成
predict	/pri'dikt/	v.	预知,预言
pigeon	/'pidʒin/	n.	鸽子
divine	/di'vain/	adj.	神圣的,非凡的
tonic	/'tɔnik/	n.	滋补剂,滋补品
mule	/mjuːl/	n.	骡,倔强之人
infuse	/in'fjuːz/	v.	沏或泡(茶、药等)

Proper Nouns

Hui	回族	fortune teller	算命先生
Mohammed	穆罕默德	imam	[伊斯兰]阿訇,教长

Hui Culture

The Hui ethnic minority is descended from the Arab and Persian merchants who came to China during the 7th century. There are Hui living in almost all the provinces and cities of China. Most of the Hui people are Muslim and there is typically a mosque in each community. Islam has played a vital role in the development of the Hui ethnic minority. In fact, the religious thought has influenced them in all walks of life, ranging from etiquettes of living, dining, and marriage to funeral customs.

The living customs of Hui differ from the other ethnic groups. For example, marriage outside the Hui group is not encouraged. In the event a Hui wants to marry a non-Hui, the non-Hui youth must understand and respect the Hui culture as well as convert to Islam, or the marriage will be denied. For the marriage feast, there are usually 8 to 12 dishes. The even number of dishes is important as it symbolizes that the new couple will be a pair permanently.

The Hui live a puritanical life. They do not like to joke nor do they describe things with food. Smoking, drinking and gambling are frowned upon and young people are not permitted to sit with the elder members of the group. Use of a fortune teller to predict the future is prohibited. The Hui also obey many rituals. For example, before meals, they must wash their hands with fluid water. Also, they avoid sitting or stepping on any threshold, for it is said Mohammed used the threshold as his pillow.

Pigeons are considered a "divine bird" that may be eaten only under certain circumstances. For example, a pigeon are fed to the sick as a tonic, but only after it is approved by the Imam. Hui are generally forbidden to eat the meat of pigs, dogs, horses, donkeys, mules as well as the blood of animals. Moreover, if people of other nationalities use a pot or dish to hold pork, then Hui people will not use or touch the dish.

Visiting guests receive infused tea and are served fruits or home-made cakes. All the family members will come to greet their guests, and, if he is from afar, the guest will be seen off even out of the Hui people's village.

Questions

True or False:

(1) _____ If a Hui wants to marry a non-Hui, the non-Hui youth must understand and respect the Hui culture, then they can get married.

(2) _____ The Hui also obey many rituals. For example, before they pray or have meals, they must wash their hands with fluid water.

(3) _____ Pigeons are considered a "divine bird" that is not permitted to be eaten or used as a tonic for the sick.

PART IV *Practical Writing for Tourism*

Questionnaire 征求意见表

Thank You for Your Opinions

Thank you for taking time to complete this card

Date_____ time_____A.M/P.M

How many in your party? _____

```
Server's Name_____
                    HOSPITALITY
Were you greeted as you entered          ☐ YES  ☐ NO
Did the hostess/host seat you?           ☐ YES  ☐ NO
Did server introduce her/himself by name? ☐ YES  ☐ NO
                 FOOD AND SERVICE
Was food served promptly?                ☐ YES  ☐ NO
Was your order correct?                  ☐ YES  ☐ NO
Was food properly prepared?              ☐ YES  ☐ NO
Did you receive smiling service?         ☐ YES  ☐ NO
                  ENVIRONMENT
Did our staff have a neat, clean appearance? ☐ YES  ☐ NO
Were your dining area and dining utensils clean? ☐ YES  ☐ NO
Was the restaurant clean overall?        ☐ YES  ☐ NO
```

征求意见表

```
                     谢谢您填写此表

日期_____时间_____        你们一行几人?_____
服务员姓名_____
                       接  待
您进来时受到欢迎吗?                    ☐ 是    ☐ 否
服务员请您入座吗?                      ☐ 是    ☐ 否
服务员作自我介绍吗?                     ☐ 是    ☐ 否
服务员向您道谢请您再来吗?                ☐ 是    ☐ 否
                     食品及服务
上酒菜快吗?                           ☐ 是    ☐ 否
上的酒菜对吗?                         ☐ 是    ☐ 否
酒菜合胃口吗?                         ☐ 是    ☐ 否
您受到友好礼貌的服务吗?                  ☐ 是    ☐ 否
                       环  境
本店工作人员仪表整洁吗?                  ☐ 是    ☐ 否
进餐地方及餐具清洁吗?                    ☐ 是    ☐ 否
总的说来餐厅清洁吗?                     ☐ 是    ☐ 否
```

Exercises

Role-play: Ask tourists fill in the questionnaires before they leave the hotel. Discuss it with your colleagues to see what else the hotel may improve.

Unit 20

Quitting Tour and Extending Travel Time

退团与延期

PART I ABC for Tour Guides

New Words and Expressions

partial	/'pɑːʃəl/	*adj.*	部分的，局部的
dissuade	/di'sweid/	*v.*	劝阻

Proper Nouns

quit the tour	退团	visa extension	签证延期

Listening

Direction: Listen to the passages carefully and fill in the blanks with the missing information you have heard from the tapes.

1. **What might be some of the reasons for quitting the tour midway? How does a guide handle this?** 引起游客中途退团的常见原因有哪些？如何处理？

   (1) Usually the tourist quits the tour midway because of illness or an urgent business at home, but some quit because they are not satisfied with the (A) _____ guiding service.

   (2) Those who quit the tour midway for personal reasons may receive (B) _____ reimbursement for the service items that they have not enjoyed subject to the approval of both the local travel service and sponsor travel service.

   (3) For those who quit because they are not satisfied with the service, the guide should attempt to dissuade the tourists from quitting the tour. If the tourists insist on quitting, the guide should tell them that they are unable to obtain a (C) _____ for the items they have not yet enjoyed.

2. **If a foreign tourist must quit the tour midway due to an urgent business at home, how does a guide handle the related fares?** 外国游客因家中急事要求中途退团，有关费用怎么处理？

   After obtaining the approval of both the local and sponsor services, the guide may (D) _____ the tourist for some of the service items according to the contract.

Readings

Direction: Read the following passage aloud and fill in the blanks with words or phrases you think appropriate.

> injure   accident   illness   fractured   danger
> contract   adventure   expire   extension   disappointing

Can a guide agree when a tourist requests to extend his travel time? 游客要求延长旅游期,导游员能否同意?

(1) If a tourist wants to extend his tour, whether due to (A) _____ or personal interest, the guide is expected to help make the arrangements.

(2) If the tourist wants to join another tour group of the same travel agency, he should sign a new (B) _____.

(3) If a foreign tourist wants to extend his travel time, and his visa permits, the guide should assist him in making arrangements. Provided that the tourist is ill or injured, the guide should help him acquire a visa (C) _____.

Quickies

Role-play: Imagine that you are a guide from the local travel service and your deskmate from the sponsor travel service. Handle the case that some of your tourists insist on quitting the tour midway.

PART II *Method of Introduction*

New Words and Expressions

concrete	/'kɔnkriːt/	adj.	具体的,有形的
reveal	/ri'viːl/	v.	展现,显示
ignore	/ig'nɔː/	v.	忽视,不理睬
cascade	/kæs'keid/	v.	成瀑布落下
reverberate	/ri'vəːbəreit/	v.	反响
drooping	/'druːpiŋ/	adj.	下垂的,无力的
radiant	/'reidjənt/	adj.	发光的,容光焕发的
dazzling	/'dæzliŋ/	adj.	眼花缭乱的,耀眼的
glacial	/'gleisjəl/	adj.	冰状的,冰河的
bunch	/bʌntʃ/	n.	串,束
icicle	/'aisikl/	n.	垂冰,冰柱

Proper Nouns

Nuorilang Waterfall   诺日朗瀑布   Rizegou Gully   日则沟

The Method of Descriptive Introduction
描绘法

This method is used to describe a tourist site with concrete, vivid and elaborate words, just to reveal to tourists the characteristics of the scenic area that tourists may ignore. Not every tourist, in some cases, could appreciate the beauty of the landscape or the cultural values of the historical interests, and become inspired aesthetically without tour guide's descriptions. Tourists may better appreciate the places of interest after listening to the introduction made by the tour guide using the method of descriptive introduction. For example, the guide may describe the scenery of Nuorilang Waterfall in details with vivid words so that the tourists are inspired by the beauty of landscape:

Rushing over the cliff overgrown with willows, the massive water currents from Rizegou Gully drop some 30 meters down and make up a chain of spectacular waterfalls of diverse shapes and sizes in a stair-like style. During the rainy seasons, the cascading waterfall produces a tremendous noise reverberating unceasingly in the gully. When the sun rises, the gorgeous rainbows hang over the water fall. In the dry season of autumn, however, the waterfall presents another wonder. The gurgling streams of the fall seem like sheets of colorful silk cloth drooping over the cliff, setting off the multi-hued bushes around to add radiant beauty to each other. In winter, it becomes a dazzling glacial cascade hanging over the precipice. At its bottom, you can see bunches of icicles, some of which extend more than 2 meters long, suggestive of swords or spears.

Questions

1. Do you think the details of the description will help introduce the landscape?
2. What literary methods can a guide use to give a descriptive account of the landscape?
3. What do you think of the Nuorilang Waterfall after you listen to the introduction using the method of descriptive introduction?

PART III   *Tourist Site*

New Words and Expressions

immense	/i'mens/	*adj.*	极广大的,无边的
plateau	/'plætəu/	*n.*	高地,高原
soar	/sɔː/	*v.*	高飞,高翔
herald	/'herəld/	*v.*	宣布,传达,欢呼

| intact | /in'tækt/ | adj. | 完整的,尚未被人碰过的 |

Proper Nouns

Lhasa	拉萨
Shangri-La	香格里拉
Land of Snows	雪域高原
"the Rooftop of the World"	"世界屋脊"
Tibet Autonomous Region	西藏自治区
Potala Palace	布达拉宫
Barhkor Street	八角街

Lhasa

Referred to as "Shangri-La," "the Land of Snows," and "the Rooftop of the World," Tibet has long exercised a unique hold on the imagination of the West. Made up of an immense plateau, over 4000 meters above sea level, Tibet is mysterious in a way few other places are. In Tibet, the golden rooftops of the many Buddhist temples shine everywhere. Each year Tibet attracts millions of tourists from many different countries all over the world.   When you enter Lhasa you will be impressed by the deep notes of the Tibetan long horns, the remote sounds of the temple bells, the insistent drumbeats, and the distinctive chant of Buddhist scriptures.

At an elevation of 3,650 metres,   Lhasa is the capital of Tibet Autonomous Region and a famous cultural city with a 1,300-year history. Bathed in sunshine for more than 3,000 hours a year, it is also a "Sunshine City." Lhasa is the heart and soul of Tibet, and a place many tourists intend

to visit. The first sight of the Potala Palace, soaring over one of the world's highest cities, has heralded the marvels of this holy area to travelers for three centuries. The Palace dominates the Lhasa skyline. Lhasa' original look and old lifestyle are largely intact at the Barhkor Street in the old part of Lhasa, where all sorts of arts and crafts are on sale. You can go hunting for some souvenirs when you travel there.

Cultural Notes

Lhasa 拉萨:拉萨是西藏自治区的首府,西藏政治、经济、文化的中心,是一座具有1300多年历史的高原古城。拉萨海拔3650米左右,全年无雾,光照充足,有"日光城"之美誉。拉萨名胜古迹众多,布达拉宫、大昭寺、哲蚌寺、色拉寺和甘丹寺等驰名中外,是西藏重要的历史建筑和旅游胜地。1982年拉萨市被国务院公布为国家历史文化名城。

Questions

1. True or False:

(1) _____ Tibet is referred to as "Shangri-La," "the Land of Snows," "Sunshine City" and "the Rooftop of the World."

(2) _____ At an elevation of 3,650 meters, Lhasa is the capital of Tibet Autonomous Region and a famous cultural city with a 1,200-year history.

(3) _____ Lhasa is bathed in sunshine for more than 3,000 hours a year and it is called "Sunshine City".

2. Read the passage aloud and introduce Lhasa using the methods of introduction you have learnt. The method of descriptive introduction is one of the choices.

Tips

- Draft your own commentary before you make your presentation.
- Speak colloquial English and use simple and short sentences.
- Animate your introduction with facial expressions and body language.
- Apply at least one method of introduction. It is highly recommended that you use two or three methods of introduction.

PART IV *Ethnic Culture*

New Words and Expressions

dairy	/ˈdɛəri/	n.	奶制品
yak	/jæk/	n.	牦牛
festive	/ˈfestiv/	adj.	喜庆的,节庆的
melody	/ˈmelədi/	n.	悦耳的音调
nomad	/ˈnɔməd/	n.	游牧民
roam	/rəum/	v.	漫游,徜徉
pasture	/ˈpɑːstʃə/	n.	牧地,草原,牧场
altar	/ˈɔːltə/	n.	祭坛,圣坛
pilgrim	/ˈpilgrim/	n.	香客,朝圣

Proper Nouns

barley flour	青稞面	buckwheat flour	荞麦面
tsamba	糌粑	buttered tea	酥油茶
toast song	祝酒歌	Songpan	松潘县
Tibetan New Year	藏历新年	Zhuanshuanhui Festival	转山会
Huanglong Temple Fair	黄龙会	Huanglong Temple	黄龙寺
Mount Minshan	岷山		

173

Tibetan Culture

The Tibetan nationality is one of the Chinese ethnic groups with a long history and brilliant culture. The staple diet of Tibetans includes barley flour, buckwheat flour, mutton, beef and dairy products. Their favorite food is tsamba, roasted barley flour. Tibetan people take tsamba with them when they go to work, herd their yaks or go on a trip. They put tsamba in a bowl and mix it with buttered tea before eating it. Tibetans like to drink wine made from highland barley and barley wine has become an absolute daily necessity for them. It is used either on festive occasions or for treating guests. According to Tibetan customs, the hospitable host will offer three bowls of barley wine to treat his guest. For the first two bowls, the guest can drink as much as he likes, at least a little bit of it, but he must drink up the entire third bowl to show his respect to the host. After that, the guest and host may drink to their heart's content. When inviting the guest to drink, Tibetans often sing toast songs with touching melodies.

The Tibetan dwelling-places differ in pastoral and agricultural areas. Nomads have no fixed houses. They keep roaming on fine pastures with all their belongings—their tents and livestock. In the middle of the tent, there is a stove right in front of the fuel store, which divides the tent into two sections. On the right side of the stove are seats for men or guests while on the left are seats for women. The altar with sculptures of Buddha is often set on a wooden case behind the stove or to the left side of the men's seats. In the agricultural areas, Tibetans generally live in storied buildings of over 10 meters high. The buildings differ in architectural structure from place to place. For instance, Tibetans in Songpan live mainly in three-storied wooden houses. The ground floor shelters livestock and stores the fuel, and the second floor houses the family. The third floor is usually a storeroom for odds and ends as well as fodder; sometimes a sutra hall or a small bedroom is also on this floor. In front of the house, there is a yard enclosed with a mud wall.

The Tibetan New Year is one of the most important festivals, which is celebrated from December 29th to January 15th of the Tibetan calendar. Tibetans celebrate their own New Year shortly after the Han people celebrate their Spring Festival. In almost every place, April 8th of the lunar year is the day when the Zhuanshanhui Festival (a ceremony of walking around the mountain in tribute to Buddha) is held to celebrate Buddha's birth. Dressed in their holiday best, local Tibetans go camping and have picnics. They participate in a lot of recreational activities, singing folk songs and performing traditional dances. The Huanglong Temple Fair is held in front of Huanglong Temple, which is located at the southern foot of Mount Minshan in Songpan County. Annually, from June 10th of the Chinese lunar calendar, pilgrims, merchants and visitors from different places come to participate in the fair. In the course of the fair, people come to appreciate the grandeur of Huanglong Temple and enjoy Tibetan opera and the antiphonal singing. Young people are engaged in wrestling, archery competition, and other activities.

Questions

True or False:

(1) _____ For the first bowl, the guest can drink as much as he likes, but he must drink up the third bowl to show his respect to the host.

(2) _____ The ground floor shelters livestock and stores the fuel, and the second floor is where the Tibetans live.

(3) _____ On April 8th of the lunar year the Tibetans walk around the mountain in tribute to Buddha.

PART V *Simulated Introduction*

New Words and Expressions

clockwise	/'klɔkwaiz/	*adv.*	顺时针方向地
doorsill	/'dɔːsil/	*n.*	门槛
auspicious	/ɔːs'piʃəs/	*n.*	吉祥的,幸运的
balcony	/'bælkəni/	*n.*	阳台;包厢
stateliness		*n.*	威严,庄严
stupa	/'stuːpə/	*n.*	佛塔
foil	/fɔil/	*n.*	箔,金属薄片
amber	/'æmbə/	*n.*	琥珀
agate	/'æɡət/	*n.*	玛瑙
devotion	/di'vəuʃən/	*n.*	热爱;投入
genuine	/'dʒenjuin/	*adj.*	真实的,真正的,诚恳的
murmur	/'məːmə/	*v.*	发低沉连续的声音,咕哝

Proper Nouns

White Palace	白宫	Great East Hall	东大殿(措钦夏)
East Chamber of Sunshine	东日光殿	West Chamber of Sunshine	西日光殿
Red Palace	红宫	Great West Hall	西大殿
Bodhisattva	菩萨	Stupa Chapel	佛殿
stupa-tombs	灵塔	Three-world Hall	殊胜三界殿

Potala Palace

Ladies and gentlemen! Welcome to Lhasa! Welcome to the magnificent Potala Palace!

Before you get into the Palace, I'd like to have a few words about the regulations you have to follow. Here is the holy place for Tibetans. According to the local customs, you have to tour clockwise around; don't step on the doorsill; don't smoke in the halls; don't take photos without permission! Are you clear? Ok, let's get into the Palace.

Here is the White Palace. It is a seven-floor building built in 1645. The wall of the palace was painted to white to convey peace and quiet. The Great East Hall on the fourth floor is the largest hall in the Palace. It was also the site for holding religious meetings. The top floor consists of the East Chamber of Sunshine and the West Chamber of Sunshine. Because of the sunshine in the chambers all year round, the East and West Chambers are sunbathed in the auspicious atmo-sphere. When you stand on the spacious balcony of the chambers, you can look down at the beautiful Lhasa.

Ladies and Gentlemen, we've visited the magnificent White Palace. Let's go to another important building in the potala Palace. Look at this red building! The wall of the palace was painted to red, and represents stateliness and power. I think everybody knows it is the Red Palace. The Red Palace is famous for its religious status, gorgeous stupas and precious cultural relics. Here is the Great West Hall. It is the largest hall of Potala Palace and covers an area of 725 sq meters. Beautiful murals painted on inner walls described the glory and power of the lamasery, and the corridor upstairs is also painted with many religious murals such as the figures of Buddha, Bodhisattvas and other human figures.

Here we come to the Stupa Chapel. The stupa-tombs of many Lamas are placed here. Please look at this stupa-tomb. It is 14.85 meters high, covered by more than 3,000 kilograms gold foil and decorated with thousands of pearls, gems, corals, ambers and agates. Please look at the highest and the most luxury one! It is dedicated to a venerated Lama. Now we've come to the Three-world Hall, the holy shrine of Chinese emperors. This hall is located on the highest point of the Potala Palace. The venerated Lamas would come here to show their respect to the central government every year.

Ladies and Gentlemen! There are also many other buildings in the Potala Palace: gardens, courtyards, printing house and so on. Everything in the Potala Palace is in an air of devotion and trust. Here you can listen to the six-character genuine words murmured by the worshippers. You can watch hundreds of yak butter lamps, walk along the deep and serene corridors, view the murals and statues one after another. I think it is a unique travel experience in Lhasa, isn't it?

So much for my introduction! I hope you'll enjoy a wonderful trip in Lhasa City.

Cultural Notes

Potala Palace 布达拉宫：布达拉宫海拔 3700 多米，占地总面积 36 万余平方米，是世界上海拔最高，集宫殿、城堡和寺院于一体的宏伟建筑。布达拉宫依山而筑，宫宇叠砌，巍峨耸峙，气势磅礴，其建筑艺术体现了藏族传统的石木结构碉楼形式和汉族传统的梁架、金顶、藻井的特点，在空间组合上，院落重叠，回廊曲槛，既突出了主体建筑，又协调了附属的各组建筑，上下错落，前后参差，形成较多空间层次，富有节奏美感，是世界建筑史上的奇迹。1994 年布达拉宫被列入《世界文化遗产名录》。

Exercises

Make a simulated introduction of the Potala Palace using the methods of introduction you have learnt. Pay attention to the body language and other tips of introduction.

Unit 21 Complaints
投 诉

PART I *ABC for Tour Guides*

New Words and Expressions

accumulate	/ə'kju:mjuleit/	v.	积聚, 堆积
perfect	/'pə:fikt/	v.	使完美, 使熟练
cultivate	/'kʌltiveit/	v.	培养
criterion	/krai'tiəriən/	n.	标准, 规范
obnoxious	/əb'nɔkʃəs/	adj.	不愉快的, 讨厌的

Listening

Direction: Listen to the passages carefully and fill in the blanks with the missing information you have heard from the tapes.

1. **How can a guide avoid the complaints?** 导游人员应怎样避免旅游投诉的发生？

   (1) The guide should try to improve his own skill, (A) _____ working experience and perfect his own service.

   (2) The guide should cultivate his own occupational ethics and act according to the criterion of guiding service.

   (3) After he receives assignment of escorting a tour group, the guide should focus on the (B) _____ of the sites to be visited, keep in mind the ABC about the group members, and prepare mentally and emotionally for escorting tourists.

   (4) The guide should serve every tourist according to the basic service procedures, but also take into account (C) _____ differences, while providing exceptional service.

2. **How does a guide handle the tourist's complaints?** 导游员应如何处理游客的投诉？

   (1) However rude or obnoxious the tourist might be, the guide should remain calm and treat him patiently and (D) _____.

   (2) The guide should explain where possible, and apologize when necessary, and promise to do his best to improve his (E) _____.

(3) In case of a serious complaint, the guide should report to the travel agency for help in order to solve the problem to the (F) _____ satisfaction.

New Words and Expressions

remedy	/'remidi/	n.	补救,赔偿

Readings

Direction: Read the following passage aloud and fill in the blanks with words or phrases you think appropriate.

blame	blunder	troublesome	apology	careless
irritate	responsibility	picky	remedy	tolerant

How does a guide make an apology to tourists? 导游如何向游客道歉？

(1) The guide should smile graciously when making an (A) _____ to the tourist.

(2) The guide should be sincere to take his (B) _____ responsibility.

(3) The guide should do an apology and make a (C) _____ remedy on time.

Quickies

Role-play: After he checks in the Hangzhou Crown Hotel Mr. Brown has a bath, but he finds the water tap is out of service. He loses his temper and asks for a suite instead. Miss Wang Li explains patiently, but Mr. Brown refuses to listen. Replay the scene and tell her how to handle the complaint amicably.

PART II *Situational Dialogue*

New Words and Expressions

ordinance	/'ɔːdinəns/	n.	法令,训令
authority	/ɔː'θɔriti/	n.	权威,威信
tide	/taid/	n.	潮汐,潮流
octagonal	/ɔk'tægənl/	adj.	八边形的,八角形的

Proper Nouns

Liuhe Pagoda (Six Harmonies Pagoda) 六和塔

Qiantangjiang River	钱塘江
Wuyue State	吴越国

Dialogue 1

Liuhe Pagoda (Six Harmonies Pagoda)

The tourists are standing on the bank of Qiantangjiang River. They are watching the Liuhe Pagoda (Six Harmonies Pagoda).

(A=Mr. Wang Li; B=Stone)

A: The pagoda in front of us is one of the famous tourist sites in Hangzhou. It is the Liuhe Pagoda (Six Harmonies Pagoda).

B: "Six harmonies"? Can you interpret it?

A: All right. The name "six harmonies" comes from the six Buddhist ordinances: harmonies of the heaven, earth, north, south, east, and west.

B: I see, but why was this Pagoda built on the north bank of the Qiantangjiang River?

A: A good question! The Pagoda was first built in 970 AD by the king of Wuyue State. He wanted to demonstrate his authority by conquering the evil of the river tide of the Qiantangjiang River.

B: I don't believe it. The tide rises and falls according to the rotation of the moon.

A: Right. Please look at the Pagoda! It presents a quiet image of age-old majesty. Do you know how many stories the Pagoda have?

B: Let me see. er... I think there are 13 stories.

A: The Pagoda is an octagonal structure 200 feet tall. When you look from the outside, it looks like a 13-story building; in fact, there are only seven stories.

B: Really? Do you think the Pagoda could make up a miracle, and change a 13-story building into a 7-story building?

A: If you don't believe you may try to look at the Pagoda from different angle.

B: Could we climb up the Pagoda? We'd like to have a bird's eye-view of the surging Qiantangjiang River?

A: Why not? When you walk up the Pagoda you may be shocked and entertained by the arts of Chinese calligraphy and seal-cutting both inside and out of the Pagoda.

B: Thank you!

Exercises

Do the dialogue again and pay attention to your facial expressions and body language.

New Words and Expressions

seep	/siːp/	v.	渗出,渗漏
vein	/vein/	n.	纹理,矿脉
mineralize	/ˈminərəlaiz/	v.	无机物浸渍
ingredient	/inˈgriːdiənt/	n.	成分,因素
radon	/ˈreidɔn/	n.	[化]氡
beverage	/ˈbevəridʒ/	n.	饮料
brew	/bruː/	v.	泡,煮

Proper Nouns

Hupao Spring (Tiger Running Spring)	虎跑泉
Longjing Tea (Dragon Well Tea)	龙井茶
Daci Hill	大慈山
"two wonders of the West Lake"	"西湖二绝"

Dialogue 2

Hupao Spring (Tiger Running Spring)

After watching the tide of the Qiantangjiang, the tourists come to drink the Longjing Tea (Dragon Well Tea) at the Hupao Spring (Tiger Running Spring).

(A=Mr. Wang Li; B=Stone)

A: The Hupao Spring, also named Tiger Running Spring, is located at the foot of the Daci Hill, five kilometers away from Hangzhou City.

B: Why is called "Tiger Running Spring"? Do the tigers often come to drink the spring?

A: Don't worry, there are no tigers here. Legend has it that in the Tang Dynasty two tigers dug a hole here and spring gushed immediately to rescue the monk in the Daci Temple. So the spring was named Hupao Spring (Tiger Running Spring).

B: An interesting story, but why is this spring so popular in China? I heard that Longjing Tea and Hupao Spring are considered as "two wonders of the West Lake."

A: Actually, Hupao Spring is popular not because of the tigers running here. The spring is famous because the underground water seeps through veins and cracks within quartz sandstone.

B: May I drink the water?

A: Of course, it tastes pure, sweet and cold.

B: Wonderful! I'd like to have one more bowl.

A: Attention, please! Now I put a coin into the bowl. Look, the spring water rises three millimeters above a bowl edge, but no water overflows.

B: A miracle! Why does no water overflow the bowl?

A: Because the spring has low contents of mineralized ingredients and has high percentage of radon. And it doesn't overflow the edge of the bowl because of the high surface tension of the spring water.

B: Oh, that is it. It is really an ideal beverage for good health.

A: So when you come to Hangzhou there is a must you have to do: drink Longjing tea brewed with Hupao Spring.

B: I couldn't agree with you more. I have had two bowls of Hupao Spring. I'd like to enjoy the Longjing tea.

A: You will. Mrs. Brown, do you think it is a great pleasure to listen to the spring, watch the spring, taste the spring, feel the spring, and even dream the spring here?

B: Oh, yeah. I'll do as you do. I'd like to take some Hapao Spring to brew the Longjing tea.

A: Sure.

Cultural Notes

Liuhe Pagoda (Six Harmonies Pagoda) 六和塔：六和塔位于西湖之南，钱塘江畔月轮山上。北宋开宝三年(公元 970 年)，僧人智元禅师为镇江潮而创建，取佛教"六和敬"之义，命名为六和塔。原建塔身九级，顶上装灯，为江船导航。现存六和塔外观八面十三层，内分七级，高 59.89 米，占地 888 平方米。从塔内拾级而上，面面壶门通外廊，各层均可依栏远眺，壮观的大桥，飞驶的风帆，苍郁的群山，令人赏心悦目。六和塔为古建筑艺术之杰作，1961 年被国务院公布为全国重点文物保护单位。

Hupao Spring (Tiger Running Spring) 虎跑泉：虎跑泉在浙江杭州市西南大慈山白鹤峰下慧禅寺(俗称虎跑寺)侧院内，距市区约 5 公里。虎跑泉水从石英砂岩中渗过流出，清澈可见，泉水中含氡、钠离子，并含有微量有机氧化物和较多的游离二氧化碳。经化验分析，水质无菌，饮后对人体有保健作用。杭州有句俗话："龙井茶叶虎跑水"，用这里的泉水泡出的龙井茶，其茶味更觉清香。虎跑泉水晶莹甘冽，居西湖诸泉之首，被誉为"天下第三泉"。

Exercises

Imagine that you are a local guide and your classmates are tourists. Make up a situational dialogue about the Liuhe Pagoda or the Hupao Spring.

PART III *Ethnic Culture*

New Words and Expressions

cherish	/'tʃeriʃ/	v.	珍爱,怀抱(希望等)
inhabitant	/in'hæbitənt/	n.	居民,居住者
rite	/rait/	n.	仪式,典礼,习俗
contentment	/kən'tentmənt/	n.	满意,知己
bridal	/'braidl/	adj.	新娘的,新婚的
assimilate	/ə'simileit/	v.	同化,吸收
rectangular	/rek'tæŋgjulə/	adj.	矩形的
drain	/drein/	v.	排出沟外,排水
bucket	/'bʌkit/	n.	桶
firecracker	/'faɪəkrækə(r)/	n.	爆竹,鞭炮
celery	/'seləri/	n.	[植]芹菜
onion	/'ʌnjən/	n.	洋葱
garlic	/'gɑːlik/	n.	[植]大蒜
homonymous	/hɔ'mɔnɪməs/	adj.	双关的

Proper Nouns

Hakka	客家,客家人	"longevity grass"	"长生草"

The Hakka Culture

The Hakkas used to be the northern Hans living in Shanxi, Henan and Hebei. The Hakkas who immigrated to the south China cherish their own traditions. They retain their own language, culture, rites and customs. They don't have much contact with local inhabitants. As a result, they have their own unique customs.

The Hakkas, who were forced to leave home and wandered about, adopt various ways to express their desire of living and working in peace and contentment. When a couple is married, people will find a bunch of grass tied with a red string in a basket and hung at the head of the bed in the bridal chamber. The grass, called "longevity grass," is brought by the bride and must be planted in the vegetable garden of her husband's family on the wedding day, symbolizing that she will take root there and will not move in her later life.

The houses of the Hakkas show that they abide by their old tradition and refuse to be assimilated. A house usually holds several dozen to a hundred families. In square, rectangular, semicircular and round shapes, the surrounding houses or buildings often have two or three storeys with windows facing outside and the door facing inside. The rooms upstairs and downstairs serve as bedrooms, kitchens, storage places and livestock sheds. Between the buildings are courtyards where residents dry things on sunny days, drain water on rainy days, or hold outdoor actvities. In case of fire, the lanes and the courtyards help to prevent the fire from spreading. There is a pond in front of each house for collecting water drained from the courtyard. People raise fish and wash clothes and vegetables in the pond and water the vegetable garden with the water from the pond. If there is a fire, the water from the pond is used to put it out.

When sons grow up, the family holding will be shared among them. First of all, the father and sons discuss how to divide houses and property. When a man sets up his own household, his father-in-law will come with rice, wood and buckets in the morning amidst firecrackers. The buckets hold pots, bowls, ladles, cakes, onions, garlic and celery. They bring these in order to help their daughters and sons-in-law establish their own homes and also to express their wish that they will work hard and earn their income themselves (celery, onion, garlic and wood being homonymous with the words for diligence, clever, calculation and wealth in Chinese).

Questions

True or False:

(1) _____ When a couple is married, people will find a bunch of grass tied with a red string in a basket and hung on the wall in the bridal chamber.

(2) _____ In case of fire, the lanes and the courtyards help to prevent the fire from spreading.

(3) _____ The father-in-law brings celery, onion, garlic, wood and so on in order to help the young couple establish their own homes, and also express a good wish.

PART IV *Practical Writing for Tourism*

A Letter of Handling Complaints 投诉信回函

Ms. Jane Moore
Foxboro Company
150 Kenwood Parkway
New York
Dear Ms. Moore,

Thank you for your letter of August 12, promptly notifying us of your complaint on our service.

We've looked into these two matters concerning frequent shopping and poor room facility. As for the frequent shopping, there are only two shops designated by Hangzhou Tourism Bureau. The local guide had added extra shopping activity and extended the shopping time without permission. She had received a corresponding penalty for her misbehavior. Second, the change of accommodation is because the person on duty failed to provide the hotel with prompt information about the coming tour group. Consequently, room of the four-star hotel specified in the tour agreement was not available during that peak season, so the guide made a change. We shall make a refund of US$200 for the price difference and for the poor hotel facilities I suppose you will find the settlement acceptable.

Please accept our apology for all the inconvenience and discomfort that you have suffered from during the travel.

Yours truly

Ma Yuanliang
Manager

Exercises

Reply to a letter of complaints concerning the poor service of a tour guide who works in your travel agency.

Unit 22
Sending Tourists Off
送客离站

PART I *ABC for Tour Guides*

New Words and Expressions

guarantee	/ˌgærən'tiː/	v.	保证,担保
reschedule	/riːˈʃedjuːl/	v.	重新计划,重订……的时间表

Proper Nouns

return ticket	回程机票	wake-up call	叫醒服务
international flight	国际航班	domestic flight	国内航班

Listening

Direction: Listen to the passages carefully and fill in the blanks with the missing information you have heard from the tapes.

1. **What preparations does a guide make before the departure of the group?** 在送行前,导游员应提前落实哪些事宜?

    (1) Check the names, numbers of tourists and the return tickets. If the group is leaving by plane, the local guide should help (A) _____ the air tickets.

    (2) Confirm the time for the delivery of luggage;

    (3) Confirm the time and place for (B) _____;

    (4) Confirm the time for wake-up call and dinner;

    (5) Remind the tourists to pay their (C) _____ before they leave the hotel;

    (6) Return the tourists' identity cards or passports.

2. What is the difference between an OK ticket and an OPEN ticket? If a tourist who has an OK ticket does not depart within 72 hours, what procedures does he need to follow?
OK 票和 OPEN 票有何区别? 持 OK 票的游客如果停留超过 72 小时,应该办理什么手续?

(1) An OK ticket refers to the ticket with a (D) _____ seat.

(2) An OPEN ticket refers to the ticket with an unfixed return date and the tourist needs to confirm an available seat (E) _____.

(3) If a tourist who has an OK ticket does not depart within 72 hours, whether because of the delay or rescheduling, he must (F) _____ the seat of his next flight in advance, otherwise the airline company will not guarantee the seat.

New Words and Expressions

sort	/sɔːt/	v.	分类,拣选
questionnaire	/ˌkwestiəˈnɛə/	n.	调查表,问卷

Readings

Direction: Read the following passage aloud and fill in the blanks with words or phrases you think appropriate.

punctual	documents	postpone	domestic	bills
report	international	summary	train	catch

1. When should a local guide take the tour group to arrive at the airport or railway station for departure? 地陪带团到达机场或车站的时间应该是多少?

(1) Two hours in advance for (A) _____ flights.

(2) One hour and a half in advance for (B) _____ flights.

(3) One hour in advance for the (C) _____.

2. What else should a guide do after the group has departed? 客人离境后,地陪还有哪些后续工作应该处理?

(1) The guide should sort out the travel (D) _____ and handle unfinished business according to the requirements of the relevant regulations.

(2) He should submit the (E) _____ to the accounting department and settle the account within the given time.

(3) He should write a brief (F) _____ of the tour and review the tourists' opinions and suggestions from the questionnaires so as to improve his work in the future.

(4) If a serious accident occurred during the tour, the guide must submit a written (G) _____ to the travel agency.

Quickies

1. True or False:

(1) _____ A local guide should remind tourists to pay their bills before they leave the hotel.

(2) _____ The outbound tour group should arrive at the airport one hour and a half before departure.

(3) _____ Tourists can leave the country with the open tickets whenever they want to.

(4) _____ After he sends the tourists off the local guide should have a good rest because he is tired out.

2. Role-play: Miss Ye Xiaohua is sorting out the documents that she will take with her for sending the tour group off. As a senior guide reminds her of the preparations she should make before departure.

PART II *Farewell Speech*

New Words and Expressions

attentive	/ə'tentiv/	*adj.*	注意的,专心的
recite	/ri'sait/	*v.*	背诵,朗读
evaluation	/iˌvælju'eiʃən/	*n.*	估价,评价
recognition	/ˌrekəg'niʃən/	*n.*	识别,认出

Proper Nouns

Chengdu	成都
Chengdu Shuangliu International Airport	成都双流国际机场
boarding pass	登机牌
Couplet of Psychological Attack	"攻心联"
Jinsha Ruins	金沙遗址
postage paid	邮资已付

In a farewell speech, it is necessary for you to look back on the sightseeing activities and extend your compliments to tourists for their understanding and cooperation. You may ask them for the advices and suggestions on your service you rendered them on the trip so as to better your future work. You may tell tourists that you treasure the cordial friendship with them and that you hope to meet them again in the future. Finally, you wish tourists a pleasant journey back home or a good trip to the next stop or the following place of interest they are to visit. In a farewell speech there are three essential parts: the salutation, the body of speech and the concluding remarks.

A Farewell Speech

Good afternoon, ladies and gentlemen.

Time goes so quickly and your visit to Chengdu is drawing to a close. Tomorrow morning you will be leaving Chengdu for Guangzhou by plane. When you arrive at the Chengdu Shuangliu International Airport, I shall be very busy with handling the boarding pass and taking care of your luggage. I could hardly have time to say good-bye to everyone. So, let me take this opportunity to say something about our wonderful trip.

First of all, I wish to thank you all for the understanding and cooperation you have given us in the past two and a half days. You have been very punctual on all occasions, which made things a lot easier for our work. You have been very attentive when we had anything to tell you. Also, you have been kind enough to offer us suggestions on how to improve our guiding service. I'd like to add that you are the best group we've ever been with.

During your stay in Chengdu, you have visited the major tourist sites in Chengdu. Some of you are impressed by the "Couplet of Psychological Attack" in the Wuhou Temple; some appreciate the poems written by Du Fu, and even could recite some poems in the Thatched Cottage of Du Fu; some are fascinated by the great discovery of the Jinsha Ruins while others enjoy the Sichuan food and even take some snacks with them on your trip home.

Two days ago, we met as strangers; today, we bid farewell to each other as friends. As a Chinese saying goes, "A good friend from afar brings a distant land closer." I hope you'll take back happy memories of your travel in Chengdu.

By the way, please do me a small favor! Would you please leave your comments with us, as well as your friendship? Just fill the evaluation forms with postage-paid, and drop them in the mailbox before you board the plane.

Parting is such a sweet sorrow. It is happy to meet, sorry to depart, and happy to meet again. As you have probably observed, Chengdu is developing very quickly. When and if you come back in the future, the city may have changed beyond recognition. But I hope to see you again in the future and to be your guide again.

Once again, thank you for your cooperation and support!

Bon voyage!

Exercises

1. On behalf of a travel service which you work for, make a farewell speech to tourists who are leaving for England.

2. On behalf of China International Travel Service, make a farewell speech to tourists who will leave for the next tourist resort in China.

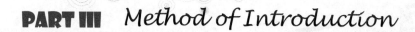

PART III *Method of Introduction*

New Words and Expressions

vision	/'viʒən/	n.	视野,想象力
association	/ə,səusi'eiʃən/	n.	联想
vista	/'vistə/	n.	展望,景象
tortuous	/'tɔːtjuəs/	adj.	曲折的,转弯抹角的
ambush	/'æmbuʃ/	n.	埋伏,伏兵
intruder	/in'truːdə/	n.	入侵者
dash	/dæʃ/	v.	猛冲,乱撞

Proper Nouns

Taoping Qiang Stockaded Village   桃坪羌寨

The Method of Introduction of Leading Someone to a Fascinating Vista
引人入胜法

It is a method of introduction with which a guide creates an aesthetic vision to help tourists better enjoy the real beauty of a tourist site or scenery area.   This kind of introduction can arouse tourists' interest and stimulate their imagination, and lead their associations to a fascinating vista. Just take the Taoping Qiang Stockaded Village as an example.

Entering the village lanes, you may think that each house is separated, but when stepping onto the flat roof you will discover that all the houses are connected by the roof.   With such an effective defense system the villagers could help each other in a moment of trouble. Furthermore, the shadowy lanes are winding and tortuous.   The whole village looks like a maze, in which the villagers might set up ambushes and the intruders were likely to lose their way and therefore dared not dash about.   Below this "mysterious ancient castle in the Orient," what is more, is a great hidden water network.   Making good use of the slope of the mountains, the Qiang people have dug an underground ditch that leads to every household. The ditch is lined and covered with greenish stones slabs.   Spring water flows through the ditch from the mountaintop to every household in the village so that the people can fetch water indoors. In danger of war they were not afraid of being surrounded by enemy forces, as the water supply system might help them hold fast to their post over a long period of time. Besides, this water network serves as a perfect fire-fighting facility and a safe underground passageway.

1. What effects can a guide achieve when he uses the method of introduction of leading someone to a fascinating vista?

2. What impress you most when you listen to the introduction using such a method?

PART IV Tourist Site

New Words and Expressions

unfathomable	/ʌnˈfæðəməbl/	*adj.*	深不可测的
ripple	/ˈripl/	*n.*	波纹
twinkle	/ˈtwiŋkl/	*v.*	闪烁,闪耀
myriad	/ˈmiriəd/	*n.*	无数,无数的人或物
fanciful	/ˈfænsiful/	*adj.*	奇怪的,稀奇的
dissipate	/ˈdisipeit/	*v.*	驱散,(云、雾、疑虑等)消散
azure	/ˈæʒə/	*adj.*	蔚蓝的
dusk	/dʌsk/	*n.*	黄昏
vanish	/ˈvæniʃ/	*v.*	消失,突然不见
mantle	/ˈmæntl/	*v.*	披风,覆盖
spellbind	/ˈspelbaind/	*v.*	迷惑,迷住
crimson	/ˈkrimzn/	*adj.*	深红色的
serried	/ˈserid/	*adj.*	密集的,重叠罗列的
lade	/leid/	*v.*	装载

Proper Nouns

Mugecuo	木格措	Dahaizi	大海子

Mugecuo

Mugecuo is also called Dahaizi, the biggest alpine lake in northwest Sichuan. Mugecuo has a depth of 70m and is surrounded on all sides by mountains, forests and grasslands. The weather changes constantly each day, and the scenery varies accordingly. At dawn, fogs hover over the lake surface, which appear to be a vast expanse of misty, rolling water, mysterious and unfathomable. At sunrise the blue ripples glitter and twinkle, rays of sunlight dye the clouds and fogs in a myriad of hues, creating a dreamy and fanciful sight. As the mist dissipates from bright sun and gentle wind we can clearly see the azure sky, and the white clouds, mountains, forests and flowers, insects, birds and animals reflected in the mirror-like surface of the lake. At dusk, the vanishing rays of the setting sun dance and sparkle on the lake, adding splendor to everything within sight. Surrounded by serene mountains and forests, tourists feel as if they were traveling in a dreamland.

As each season take its turn, the mountains and rocks, waterfalls and springs, mists and clouds become mantled with a unique look and form spellbinding spectacles. In summer time, tourists can enjoy a sunbath on the lakeside. In late autumn, mountains around the Mugecuo are crimson, covered with the serried and deep dyed woods, and the branches of trees are laden with tasty wild fruits. In the depth of winter, everything is clad with white snow. The endless lake surface is frozen into thick ice, on which tourists can go skating and play to their hearts' content.

Cultural Notes

Mugecuo 木格措:木格措,又叫野人海,有小九寨之称,距四川省甘孜州康定城郊 20 公里,海拔 2900—3800 米,也是贡嘎山风景名胜区的组成部分。景区内绮丽多彩的自然风光,充满神话色彩的民间传说,浓郁的民俗风情以及对人体康复有益的温泉是其特色,集雪山草原、温泉湖泊、叠瀑飞泉、杜鹃花山、奇峰异石和科属繁多的原始植被、珍禽异兽为一体,景点配置巧夺天工,是一处游览、娱乐、观赏、休息、疗养、健身、避暑、科考的理想胜地。景区内的主要景观有:七色海、药池沸泉、杜鹃峡、大海子等。

Quickies

1. **True or False:**

   (1) _____ Mugecuo is also called Savage Lake or Dahaizi. It is the biggest alpine lake in northwest Sichuan.

   (2) _____ At sunrise the blue ripples glitter and twinkle, rays of sunlight change the clouds and fogs in a myriad of hues, making up a dreamy and fanciful sight.

   (3) _____ In late autumn, the lake surface is frozen into thick ice, on which tourists can go skating and play to their hearts' content.

2. Read the passage aloud and introduce the Mugecuo using the method of introduction you have learnt. The method of introduction of leading someone to a fascinating vista is one of the choices.

Tips
   - Draft your own commentary before you make your presentation.
   - Speak colloquial English and use simple and short sentences.
   - Animate your introduction with facial expressions and body language.

- Apply at least one method of introduction. It is highly recommended that you use two or three methods of introduction.

PART V *Simulated Introduction*

New Words and Expressions

tease	/tiːz/	v.	取笑,逗恼
cub	/kʌb/	n.	幼兽;不懂规矩的年轻人
patch	/pætʃ/	n.	眼罩;斑纹
muzzle	/'mʌzl/	n.	动物之鼻口
camouflage	/'kæmuflɑːʒ/	n.	伪装
swing	/swiŋ/	v.	摇摆,摆动
naughty	/'nɔːti/	adj.	顽皮的,淘气的
court	/kɔːt/	v.	向……献殷勤,求爱
chunky	/'tʃʌŋki/	adj.	矮矮胖胖的
lumber	/'lʌmbə/	v.	笨拙地,动作迟缓地走
cane	/kein/	n.	甘蔗
prey	/prei/	v.	捕食,掠夺
carnivore	/'kɑːnivɔː/	n.	食肉动物
hug	/hʌg/	v.	拥抱

Proper Nouns

Wolong Nature Reserve	卧龙自然保护区
Baby Panda Garden	小熊猫苑
Giant Panda Garden	大熊猫苑
China Wolong Panda Museum	中国卧龙熊猫博物馆
Wuyipeng Observation Station	五一棚观测站
Giant Panda drunken with water	"熊猫醉水"

Wolong Nature Reserve

Ladies and Gentlemen! Welcome to the Wolong Nature Reserve!

Today we'll visit the Baby Panda Garden and Giant Panda Garden, the unique world-class China Wolong Panda Museum as well as Wuyipeng Observation Station. Before we travel to the first site I'd like to tell you some tips you have to observe: First, don't give any food to Giant Panda. Second, don't use the flash lamp when you take photos. Last but not the least, don't smoke and keep quiet. Remember to be friendly to Giant Panda; otherwise you'll be attacked when they're teased and angry!

Are you ready? Let's go! The first place we're going to visit today is the Baby Panda Garden. Dose a little panda look like his Mom or Dad when he was born? Just have a guess! Mary, you said "Mom," and Tom you said "Dad." As there goes a saying, "to see is to believe." You'll find what they really look like with your own eyes when you visit the Giant Panda Garden. Oh, look there, the little

cubs! You can get closer to have a look. In fact, newborn pandas are neither like Mom or Dad. They have a poor image: eyes closed, furless pink skin, long tail and unable to stand. On average they have a weight of 100 grams, which is only 0.1% that of their mother. What a little thing! Usually Giant Panda produces only one baby, and rarely have two. When the twins are born, the mother can raise only one; the other is left to die. You can imagine how hard it is for the mother to raise the weak cubs.

Now, let's go to another site! This way leads to the Giant Panda Garden. After about one month, the little cubs will grow and look like their handsome father and pretty mother. What do they look like? Yeah, all of you know their physical characteristics: black fur on their ears, on their eye patches, as well as on their muzzle, legs and shoulders while the rest of their coat is white. Can anybody tell me why their fur is black and white? Jack, you've got the answer. The black and white colors of Giant Panda provide effective camouflage blending in with the snowy and rocky surroundings for its safety.

Ladies and gentlemen, we've arrived at the Giant Panda Garden. Here are more than 60 Giant Pandas of various ages. Hey, look over there! Two pandas are climbing trees; others are swinging here and there. You know, Giant Pandas are naughty by nature. When they are young, Giant Pandas climb trees just for fun. When they grow older, they climb trees for enjoying the sunshine, or avoiding attacks of other animals and sometimes even making love in the trees. Well, what a pity! It's winter now. If you come back in spring, you can hear the Giant Pandas crying for love. You may watch their love affairs in the trees. Sometimes, several males fight for the right of courting with one female, but shortly after they make love, they'll live alone. Oh, My God! Look over there, the chunky, lumbering little panda is falling down from the swing!

Attention please, a "gentleman" is walking towards us! Please watch his lovely walking behavior. The little panda walks in a noble manner, looking around for the bamboo leaves. After he finds his food he adjusts himself to the most comfortable sitting position, bends over the bamboo from both hands, like a kid eating a sugar cane. How fantastic! Although he lives on a diet of 99% bamboo, occasionally, Giant Panda also eats the new leaves and fruits of other plants, such as carrots, apples, sweet potatoes, sugar cane. When he is very hungry he even preys on little animals such as bamboo rats. Keep in the mind that Giant Panda is the member of the carnivore order. Please do not make him angry, otherwise you'll be attacked and hurt.

Ha-Ha, look ahead! Several Giant Pandas are swimming in the brook, while others are drinking water. It's amazing, isn't it? Yes, Giant Panda loves drinking water and always chooses to live near springs or rivers. In winter, he breaks the ice with its paws for water. In summer, he goes down the deep valleys to look for water. Sometimes he drinks so much water that he can hardly move; then it simply lies down by the stream like a drunken man. The local villagers in Wolong call this lovely posture "Giant Panda drunken with water." The reason why Giant Panda loves water is that the bamboo contains so little water that he has to drink a lot of water that his body needs.

Now, it's time for free sightseeing. You can take pictures here and even hug the pandas if you adopt one of them. We'll meet here at 11'o clock.

Have fun!

Cultural Notes

Wolong Nature Reserve 卧龙自然保护区：四川卧龙国家级自然保护区创建于 1963 年,是我国建立最早、栖息地面积最大、以保护大熊猫及高山森林生态系统为主的综合性自然保护区。卧龙自然保护区地理条件独特、地貌类型复杂,风景秀丽、景型多样、气候宜人,集山、水、林、洞、险、峻、奇、秀于一体,浓郁的藏、羌民族文化是卧龙人文资源重要的组成部分。卧龙是"熊猫的故乡"、"生物基因库"和"天然动植物园",世界自然遗产大熊猫栖息地的核心保护区,1980 年被联合国教科文组织纳入世界"人与生物保护圈"。

Exercises

Make a simulated introduction of the Wolong Nature Reserve using the method of introduction you have learnt. Pay attention to the body language and other tips of introduction.

PART VI *Practical Writing for Tourism and Travel*

A Letter of Thanks

Dear Wendy,

Thank you so much for providing what we believe to be the world's most high quality, value for money, culinary and cultural tour of China. The accommodation, shows and food you included with our tour were amazing. We have so many happy memories and photos. It was truly a most enjoyable experience and we were also impressed with the friendliness of the Chinese people in general. You all made us feel so welcome.

Our 10 day tour of China was very well done by your travel service. Our guides were waiting at the airport when we arrived at each destination and our drivers were very good also. Our guides were very knowledgeable about their areas and we were able to learn a great deal from them. We really appreciated the cold water they kept in the vans since it was extremely hot and humid there. The case of keeping cold water for the Yangtze River Cruise was very much appreciated also. Our guides were very flexible and when we wanted to change our itinerary or cancel one of our sightseeing destinations each guide was very understanding and had wonderful suggestions for us. We can't give enough compliments and "thank you" to our guides.

Our guide in Beijing was absolutely delightful and so much fun to be with. His memory in regard to his historical knowledge is amazing as is his pride in his country and people. We hope that one day Li Yun will be able to come to visit our family in Australia and we have invited him to stay at our home. We have sons the same age as Li Yun also. All your drivers were absolutely professional in every way, although Mr. Lou, our driver in Beijing has earned a very special place in our hearts. We wish him much happiness and good health. Nothing was ever any trouble to him and we always felt that we were in good safe hands at all times. We hope you will pass our special kind wishes to him on our behalf.

We ate at wonderful restaurants that were included in the tour but it was too much. I think one of the meals (maybe lunch) should be very light with just lots of liquids for the heat. We would like to have had more time for shopping as we wanted to bring back something nice from our tour but we had too many things we wanted to see also. I would suggest that any stores that the guides may take us to be listed before we arrive so that we know we are going. And personally we like to see items when we first arrive so that we have a day or two to decide what we may want before departing. We especially liked the Bazaars since that is something we don't usually see. More store stop would be good.

We really enjoyed our tour and our guides. We certainly would travel with your travel service when we return to China.

Kathy Traina

Exercises

Reply to Kathy Traina and invite her to visit China again. You should thank her and other tourists for their kind cooperation and understanding.

Reference Keys

参考答案

Unit 1

Part I

Listening
(A) sightseeing　(B) entertainment　(C) lives
(D) feedback　(E) outbound　(F) liaison
(G) shopping

Readings
(A) accommodation　(B) conflict　(C) public
(D) courtesy　(E) sympathy　(F) reputation

Quickies
1) True　2) True　3) False　4) False

Unit 2

Part I

Listening
(A) arrangements　(B) situation　(C) differences
(D) satisfaction

Readings
(A) specified　(B) adjustments　(C) expenses
(D) transportation

Part III
1) True　2) False　3) False

Unit 3

Part I

Listening
(A) decently　(B) tattoos　(C) sleeveless
(D) complaints　(E) certificate　(F) formalities
(G) loudspeaker

Readings
(A) luggage　(B) banner　(C) positive
(D) telephone　(E) occupation　(F) banquets
(G) departure　(H) arrival　(I) claim
(J) porter　(K) parking

Part III
1. True　2. False　3. False

Unit 4

Part I

Listening
(A) local　(B) meeting　(C) services　(D) luggage

Readings
(A) instructions　(B) terms　(C) requirements

Part III
1) False　2) False　3) True

Unit 5

Part I

Listening
(A) standard　(B) three　(C) prepared　(D) expense
(E) health　(F) extra　(G) special

Readings
(A) discord　(B) vendors　(C) restaurant

Part III
1. False　2. False　True

Unit 6

Part I

Listening
(A) relatives　(B) permission
(C) pay　(D) reporter

Readings
(A) post　(B) commission　(C) contraband
(D) poor　(E) lifesaving　(F) objective
(G) troublesome

Quickies
(1) inspection　(2) deliver　(3) refuse
(4) approval　(5) recipient　(6) presence
(7) receipt

Part III
(1) False　(2) True　(3) False

Unit 7

Part I

Listening
(A) features　(B) tempo　(C) uninterrupted　(D) angle

Readings
(A) itinerary　(B) destination　(C) superstitious
(D) delay　(E) sightseeing　(F) insight

Quickies
1) False　2) True　3) False　4) True

196

Part III

1. False 2. True 3. False

Unit 8

Part I

Listening

1. (A) security (B) curious (C) undisciplined
   (D) vivid

Readings

(A) expectations (B) roundabout (C) entertainments

(D) explore (E) shopping

Quickies

1) False 2) True 3) False 4) False

Part III

(1) False (2) False (3) False

Unit 9

Part I

Listening

(A) refund (B) entertainment (C) tickets (D) cost

Readings

(A) recommend (B) departure

Part III

1. False 2 True 3. False

Unit 10

Part I

Listening

(A) extra (B) receipts

(C) peddlers (D) reliable

(E) traditional (F) tiger

Readings

(A) antique (B) authenticity (C) rake-off

(D) designated (E) quality

Quickies

1) True 2) False 3) False

Part III

1) False 2) False 3) False

Unit 11

Part I

Listening

(A) local (B) place (C) double

(D) sponsor

(E) explanation (F) inconvenience

Readings

(A) picked (B) leader (C) information

(D) tourists (E) hand (F) arrangements

(G) mistake

Part III

1. False 2. True 3. False

Unit 12

Part I

Listening

(A) arrived (B) alternative (C) reserved

(D) departure (E) claim

Readings

(A) appease (B) vehicle (C) accommodation

(D) penalized

Part III

1) False 2) True 3) False

Unit 13

Part I

Listening

(A) clsc (B) testimonial (C) photos

(D) General (E) visa

Readings

(A) agency (B) exit (C) register

(D) tag (E) necessities (F) claim

Readings

(A) count (B) missing (C) leader

(D) inconvenience (E) written

Part III

1. False 2. False 3. True

Unit 14

Part I

Listening

(A) details (B) exterior (C) national

(D) shopping (E) brochure

Readings

(A) where (B) another (C) reception

(D) escort (E) criticizing (F) report

Part III

1) False 2) False 3) True

Unit 15

Part I

Listening

(A) boarding (B) front (C) acute

(D) designated (E) flush

Readings

(A) vomit (B) salty (C) fluids

(D) prescribe   (E) up   (F) ambulance

Part III

1. True   2. False   3. True

Unit 16

Part I

Listening

(A) cardiovascular   (B) vehicle   (C) present

(D) resume   (E) extension   (F) refund

(G) vessel   (H) wound   (I) splint

Readings

(A) poison   (B) antidotes

(C) circulation   (D) vertical

Quickies

1) True   2) False   3) True   4) False   5) True

Part III

(1) True   (2) False   (3) False

Unit 17

Part I

Listening

(A) casualties   (B) financial   (C) promoting

(D) condition   (E) safely   (F) distance

(G) police   (H) investigation (I) handling

Readings

(A) instruction   (B) replace

(C) dissatisfaction

Part III

1. False   2. True   3. False

Unit 18

Part I

Listening

(A) murder   (B) rescue   (C) personnel

(D)concerned   (E) emergency   (F) elevator

(G) nose   (H) doorframe   (I) help

(J) trip

Readings

(A) emergency   (B)compensation (C) adjustments

(D) arrangements (E) revised   (F) reserved

(G) minimize   (H) replace   (I) cooperation

Part III

Quickies

(1) False   (2) True   (3) False

Unit 19

Part I

Listening

(A) policy   (B) arguing   (C) refute

(D) antiques   (E) investigation

Readings

(A) preach   (B) regulations   (C) police

Part III

1. False   2. True   3. False

Unit 20

Part I

Listening

(A) poor   (B) partial   (C) refund   (D) reimburse

Readings

(A) illness   (B) contract   (C) extension

Part III

1) False   2) False   3) True

Part IV

1. False   2. True   3. True

Unit 21

Part I

Listening

(A) accumulate   (B) details   (C) individual   (D)

respectfully   (F) service   (G) mutual

Readings

(A) apology   (B) responsibility   (C) remedy

Part III

1. False   2. False   3. True

Unit 22

Part I

Listening

(A) confirm   (B) departure   (C) bills

(D) confirmed   (F) beforehand   (G) reconfirm

Readings

(A) international (B) domestic   (C) train

(D) documents   (E) bills   (F) summary

(G) report

Quickies

1) True   2) False   3) False   4) False

Part IV

(1) True   (2) True   (3) False

Bibliography

参考书目

1. 朱歧新,张秀桂:《英语导游翻译必读》。 北京:中国旅游出版社,1999。
2. 朱华:《英语导游听说教程》。北京:北京大学出版社,2006。
3. 朱华:《四川英语导游景点讲解》。 北京:中国旅游出版社,2004。
4. 吴云:《旅游实践英语》。北京:广东旅游出版社,2007。
5. 周玮:《旅游英语应用文》。广州:广东旅游出版社,2000。
6. 程庆勋:《英语应用文写作大全》。北京:社会科学文献出版社,2003。
7. Wang Jun, Liu Lingyan. *Touring China*. Beijing: China Travel & Tourism Press, 2000.
8. Gwenda Syratt. *Manual of Travel Agency Practice*. UK, 1995.
9. Alan A. Lew (Editor), Lawrence Yu. *Tourism in China: Geographic, Political, and Economic Perspectives*. U.S.A., 1995.
10. www.chinapeacetour.com
11. www.chinavista.com
12. www.tourunion.com
13. lyw.sh.gov.cn/en
14. www.cangdian.com
15. www.travelchinaguide.com

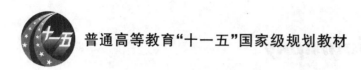

普通高等教育"十一五"国家级规划教材

《英语导游实务教程》（第二版）

尊敬的老师：

　　您好！

　　为了方便您更好地使用本教材，获得最佳教学效果，我们特向使用该书作为教材的教师赠送本教材配套听力资料。如有需要，请完整填写"教师联系表"并加盖所在单位系（院）公章，免费向出版社索取。

北京大学出版社

教 师 联 系 表

教材名称	英语导游实务教程（第二版）		
姓名：	性别：	职务：	职称：
E-mail：	联系电话：	邮政编码：	
供职学校：	所在院系：		（章）
学校地址：			
教学科目与年级：	班级人数：		
通信地址：			

　　填写完毕后，请将此表邮寄给我们，我们将为您免费寄送本教材配套听力资料，谢谢！

北京市海淀区成府路 205 号
北京大学出版社外语编辑部　李颖
邮政编码：100871
电子邮箱：evalee1770@sina.com

邮 购 部 电 话：010-62534449
市场营销部电话：010-62750672
外语编辑部电话：010-62767315